W9-BHG-158

Advance praise for
INVESTING IN SMALL-CAP STOCKS
REVISED EDITION
by Christopher Graja and Elizabeth Ungar, Ph.D.

A MAIN SELECTION OF THE MONEY BOOK CLUB

"THE FIRST EDITION OF THIS BOOK WAS THE BEST BOOK
I'VE READ ON SMALL-CAP STOCK INVESTING. THAT IS,
UNTIL NOW. A lot of thought and labor has gone into making this bigger, better, and even more necessary for the
smart investor."

> THOMAS J. DORSEY
> Author of *Thriving as a Broker in the 21st Century*
> President, Dorsey, Wright & Associates, Inc.

"THIS IS THE SINGLE, BEST GUIDE FOR MAKING MONEY IN
SMALL-CAP STOCKS. *Investing in Small-Cap Stocks* offers a
great combination of historical facts and practical advice.
EVERY SMALL-CAP INVESTOR NEEDS TO READ THIS BOOK."

> JAMES W. OBERWEIS
> Portfolio Manager,
> Oberweis Asset Management, Inc.
> Specialists in Extraordinarily Rapidly Growing
> Companies

"LOADED WITH USEFUL TIPS, THIS UP-TO-DATE MANUAL
ON INVESTING IN SMALL-CAP STOCKS IS A MUST FOR ANY
INTERESTED INVESTOR. Chris Graja and Elizabeth Ungar
continue to be the leaders in demystifying this often misunderstood and important investment category."

> ROB SHENK
> Group Director
> AOL Financial Services

Investing In
Small-Cap
Stocks

REVISED EDITION

Also available from
BLOOMBERG PRESS

Investing in REITs:
Real Estate Investment Trusts
by Ralph L. Block

Investing With Your Values:
Making Money and Making a Difference
by Hal Brill, Jack A. Brill, and Cliff Feigenbaum

Mastering Microcaps:
Strategies, Trends, and Stock Selection
by Daniel P. Coker

The Winning Portfolio:
Choosing Your 10 Best Mutual Funds
by Paul B. Farrell, Ph.D., J.D.

Investing in Latin America:
Best Stocks, Best Funds
by Michael Molinski

Investing in Hedge Funds:
Strategies for the New Marketplace
by Joseph G. Nicholas

The New Commonsense Guide to Mutual Funds
by Mary Rowland

Investing in IPOs:
New Paths to Profit with Initial Public Offerings
by Tom Taulli

BLOOMBERG PERSONAL BOOKSHELF

Investing In Small-Cap Stocks

REVISED EDITION

CHRISTOPHER GRAJA AND
ELIZABETH UNGAR, Ph.D.

BLOOMBERG PRESS
PRINCETON

Permissions credits appear on page 233.

Revised second edition published 1999
1 3 5 7 9 10 8 6 4 2

Graja, Christopher, 1966–
    Investing in small-cap stocks / Christopher Graja and Elizabeth Ungar.
        p.   cm. – (Bloomberg personal bookshelf)
    Includes bibliographical references and index.
    ISBN 1-57660-072-6
    1. Small capitalization stocks. I. Ungar, Elizabeth Merrifield, 1951– . II. Title. III. Title: Small-cap stocks. IV. Series.
    HG4751.G7   1999
    332.63'2044—dc21   99-16922
                                    CIP

Book design by Don Morris Design
Sponsoring editor: Jared Kieling

To Jennifer and Claire,

for their love,

friendship,

and encouragement

—C.G.

ACKNOWLEDGMENTS

THIS BOOK HAS BEEN A LOT OF FUN to write, thanks to the support and enthusiasm of countless people. Here's where my coauthor and I get to actually say thanks to a few of them.

From concept through research, writing, and revising, Bill Inman, who manages Bloomberg's publishing group, has given us his complete support and nearly unlimited resources to produce the best book we could. That task was made easier by the fact that we work for an organization and a boss as well respected as Bloomberg Financial Markets and Mike Bloomberg, whose name opened doors and data banks for us. Among the market professionals who answered our questions, offered ideas, and provided research and charts, we owe a particular debt to Bill Berger, founder of the Berger Funds; Mike Berry at Heartland Advisors; Dan Coker, author of *Mastering Microcaps;* Michael Gerding of Founders Funds; Roger Ibbotson of Ibbotson Associates; Steve Kim at Merrill Lynch; Claudia Mott at Prudential Securities; Michael Murphy of the *California Technology Stock Letter;* Steven Shapiro at Scudder Kemper Investments; Bill Nasgovitz of Heartland Advisors; Steve Norwitz at T. Rowe Price; Jim Oberweis Jr. of Oberweis Funds; Terianne Petzold of Heartland Advisors; Satya Pradhuman at Merrill Lynch; Robert Rodriguez of First Pacific Advisors; Tom Dorsey of Dorsey, Wright & Assoc.; Chuck Royce of The Royce Funds; John Spears of Tweedy, Browne Co.; and Matt Wright at First Investors.

Our colleagues, past and present, at Bloomberg deserve particular thanks. We're grateful for the help and encouragement given by Mike Tonrey, Roy Thoden, Bill Merk, and the library staff; Jon Heller, Seth Pitkow, John Place, Joe Schmitz, Scott Darvin, and Noel Cook from the Bloomberg Equity group; the Bloomberg Teledata department; Matt Winkler and Tim Quinson of Bloomberg News; and John Aubert, Stuart Bell, Mike Hastings, Fred

Mitchell, Erin Sanders, Kevin Foley, and Tom Heebink, able managers all.

We'll be picking up the tab well into the 21st century to repay the Bloomberg Press people for their fine editing and assistance, as well as fellow magazine staffers, for their research, opinions, and suggestions. So thank you, Ellen Cannon, John Crutcher, Barbara Diez, Christopher Floersch, Steve Gittelson, Matt Goldenberg, Melissa Hafner, Bill Hester, Jared Kieling, Mark Kociscin, Laurie Lohne, Mary Makarushka, Mary Ann McGuigan, Chris Miles, Russell Morgan, Anne Taylor, Priscilla Treadwell, Andy Treinen, and Maris Williams.

And finally, thanks to our parents, who raised us well.

PREFACE

"I F YOU LIKED a company at $10, you'll love it at $6." That's a classic line brokers use to talk clients into buying more shares of a stock that has lost money. I can sympathize with the sentiment after watching small stocks underperform large ones for most of the time the first edition of *Investing in Small-Cap Stocks* was in the bookstores.

Friends have joked that my timing couldn't have been worse. But I actually feel pretty good about it. This isn't a get-rich-quick book, and it doesn't advise immediately putting every cent into small caps. I think these stocks will offer superior returns over the next ten to twenty years. But superior returns go hand in hand with considerable risk, and to earn them you need to keep your wits (and your small caps) during tough periods like the one we've been experiencing. The first edition laid out a strategy for doing just that; the second improves on it.

The tools and indicators described in the first
edition have helped a lot of readers understand what's
been happening in the economy and how this should
enter into their portfolio decisions—whether to hold,
fold, or raise the stakes on which positions. That book
opened doors for me, allowing me to meet and
interview more people and add new investment
strategies. Some of the most exciting additions to the
second edition came out of an exclusive 1998 interview
with Peter Lynch. Other strategists and researchers
have offered insights into how they've managed to
keep their clients' billions growing through fat times
and lean.

Included as well in the new edition is information
about investing in technology and Internet stocks,
which have exploded during the past two-and-one-
half years. Like the small-cap asset class as a whole,
these sectors offer extraordinary profit potential at

the expense of some sleepless nights. You'll find tips on realizing that potential, while easing your insomnia, from professionals like Alberto Vilar. Vilar turned an investment in a little company called Cisco Systems into a fortune and then, when Cisco got too big, traded his shares for a position in Yahoo!, of which he is the fifth-biggest stockholder. You'll also find tips on determining whether companies are inflating their earnings, advice for profiting from international small-cap markets, as well as more information sources.

The first edition helped thousands of investors negotiate a very difficult market. With luck, the second will be a guide through a period of tremendous profits. The potential is there. In October 1998, Peter Lynch told an audience in San Francisco that small stocks had declined in price far enough below large stocks to look like bargain buys.

There is nothing easy about building wealth. It requires sacrifice, hard work, and discipline, but it can also be fun!

CHRISTOPHER GRAJA

INTRODUCTION

HIS IS A NO-NONSENSE GUIDE to making
money. It's for long-term investors, not speculators,
people who want to beat inflation but aren't willing
to stake their life's savings on the slim chance of
making a killing. And the best way I know to achieve
superior returns with reasonable risk is to put part of
your savings into stocks having small market
capitalizations—companies like the Scotts Co. and
La-Z-Boy, whose issued shares have market values that
are dwarfed by those of IBM and General Electric.

You probably already know that in the long run,
stocks beat out investments like bonds and money
market accounts. You may also have heard that small
stocks trounce larger ones. If not, here are a few stats
to convince you: According to a study by Chicago-
based consultants Ibbotson Associates (whose findings
are summarized in the chart on pages 10 through 11),
stocks outperformed bonds in every one of the twenty-

year periods from 1926 to 1998 and in 93 percent of those periods, the smallest stocks did better than larger ones. Twenty years is probably a suitable investment horizon for most working people. But even if you're retired and most of your biggest bills lie behind you, you may well need to keep your savings growing for another ten years or more. So you should know that Ibbotson also concluded that stocks beat out bonds in 88 percent of the ten-year periods between 1926 and 1998, and the smallest stocks outshone all other investments in 55 percent of those periods.

With comparisons like that, why am I telling you to put just part of your savings in small stocks? Why not the whole wad? Because, as you probably also know, there's no free lunch. Higher returns come with greater risks. That's the curse of an efficient market.

Investors in U.S. Treasury bills, notes, and bonds may barely beat inflation, but they know that if they hold on to their securities till maturity, they'll get their principal back; equity investors can lose their shirts. In addition, the small-cap performance figures quoted above have been averaged over a seventy-two-year period, a process that smoothes out some heavy-duty price volatility and variability. During certain months, years, even decades, the small-stock group lagged giants like Intel Corp. and Microsoft. And for the entire period, the triple-digit growth of a few stars pulled up a large number of stocks that went nowhere or failed altogether. Small companies, which often have only a few products and limited reserves against hard times, are particularly vulnerable to recessions,

20-YEAR ROLLING PERIOD RETURNS

TYPE	MAXIMUM VALUE	
	RETURN	YEARS
Small Company Stocks	21.13	1942–61
Large Company Stocks	17.75	1979–98
Long-Term Government Bonds	11.14	1979–98
Long-Term Corporate Bonds	10.86	1979–98
Intermediate-Term Government Bonds	9.85	1979–98
U.S. Treasury Bills	7.72	1972–91
Inflation	6.36	1966–85

SOURCE: STOCKS, BONDS, BILLS AND INFLATION® 1999 YEARBOOK, ©1999 IBBOTSON ALL RIGHTS RESERVED. USED WITH PERMISSION.

rising interest rates, or the loss of key executives; it takes only a few spooked investors to send their sparsely traded shares down the tube.

In short, small stocks are risky. Pick the wrong one or the wrong time to buy it, and you can kiss part of your nest egg goodbye. "Certainly in any study that you ever read about how small caps have performed, you are going to see that you get that extra return," says Prudential Securities director of small-cap research Claudia Mott. "But it doesn't come without a lot of added risk. And, certainly, the smaller you get in size, the worse the risk tends to get."

The lesson is to be cautious, not afraid. Despite their

MINIMUM VALUE		TIMES POSITIVE (OUT OF	TIMES HIGHEST
RETURN	YEARS	54 OVERLAPPING 20-YR PERIODS)	RETURNING ASSET
5.74	1929–48	54	50
3.11	1929–48	54	4
0.69	1950–69	54	0
1.34	1950–69	54	0
1.58	1940–59	54	0
0.42	1931–50	54	0
0.07	1926–45	54	0

ASSOCIATES, INC. BASED ON COPYRIGHTED WORKS BY IBBOTSON AND SINQUEFIELD.

volatility and principal imperilment, these investments are still your best buffer against what Bill Wilson, economist at Comerica Bank, has characterized as the real danger facing low-saving Americans: having to spend their underfunded golden years flipping burgers under the Golden Arches. Small stocks have offered better returns over the past seventy years than any investment except stakes in start-up private businesses. You need the kind of reward they offer to reach your long-range goals. And you can reduce the risks that go with it by just planning your portfolio properly, doing a bit of homework, and sticking to a few well-thought-out strategies. That is what this book is about.

In the following chapters my coauthor, Elizabeth Ungar, and I will explain how to incorporate the high performance of small stocks into your portfolio without high anxiety. The exact method you choose will depend on what kind of investor you are. You might feel most comfortable, for example, leaving the detailed decisions to a professional. In that case, you would probably do all your small-cap investing through mutual funds. A good fund manager can earn you returns of 15 percent a year. That's after expenses, which can be steep—usually about 1 to 2 percent of the assets you invest. But doing it right yourself isn't cheap, either: One percent of a $100,000 investment is $1,000, which disappears pretty fast when you start buying a souped-up computer and subscribing to a few periodicals and Web sites. And that doesn't count the time you'll need to spend.

On the other hand, you might be someone who likes to take matters into your own hands. You should still probably put a large part of your small-cap portfolio into funds. But you might want to devote a small portion to individual stocks, picking and following these by yourself or with the help of a broker specializing in the small-cap market.

Whichever route you choose, this book will help you on your way with information, advice, and strategies—all supplied by experts in the field and expressed whenever possible in their own words. (One cautionary note: A disadvantage of letting people speak their own minds is that you also allow them to cite their own pet statistics; as a result, the same point made in different places in the book may be bolstered by different data, none necessarily inaccurate, just derived from diverse time periods or sets of securities.)

Each chapter builds on the previous ones. The opening chapter lays the groundwork, presenting definitions and discussions of basic terms and concepts. Chapter 2 addresses mutual funds and how to use them in your small-cap investing. The third discusses how to create and care for a portfolio of small stocks; Chapter 4 presents some strategies to use in picking and weeding out your investments. Finally, following these chapters are a resources section, containing the names and phone numbers of regional brokerages as well as sources for further reading and research, and an appendix, listing small-cap companies alphabetically and broken down by state.

The book is written for a range of readers, from relative market novices to those who, though not professionals, have experience with stocks and perhaps have dabbled in derivatives. Sophisticated investors may want to skip the introductory material and concentrate on the strategies section. Less experienced ones should probably start at the beginning, to ensure they have the background they need at each stage to apply the recommendations and schemes described. They may then decide to stop at the funds chapter but later dip in again to learn more about investing in individual small stocks.

So turn the page or flip to the chapter that interests you most. The one ground rule is to enjoy yourself. Sure, investing, by definition, means giving up something: stuff you won't allow yourself to spend money on right now, time devoted to tending your nest egg instead of relaxing. But don't let it drive you nuts. A reporter once asked Tom Kite (at the time, golf's all-time money winner) how he dealt with the pressure of a putt on which several hundred thousand dollars were riding. He answered that having the chance to win that much money wasn't a burden; it was the culmination of everything he'd worked for. We all dream of being able to do something to make life better for our families. You should feel good about investing. Just by doing it, you're miles ahead of the rest of the world.

CHRISTOPHER GRAJA

CHAPTER

1

LAYING THE
Foundation

SUCCESSFUL INVESTING HAS two components. One is finding areas where you have an edge and putting your money there. The other is integrating the investments you make into a diverse portfolio that has been constituted to reflect both your long- and short-term savings goals.

In this chapter, you'll see that the small-cap sector is one area in which an individual investor can find an edge—where, in fact, small players have distinct advantages over large institutions. You'll learn as well how small stocks fit into a general investment strategy, both boosting the returns of your portfolio and reducing their variability, or volatility. Along the way, I'll slip in a few definitions of concepts you will need to understand in order to apply the tips and advice given in later chapters.

A SMALL CAP IS NOT A BEANIE

"I would tell every individual investor not to spend a whole lot of time analyzing Coca-Cola. If they're going to put their efforts on something and do stock analysis, it should be in the microcap, small-cap area."
—JOHN MARKESE, *president of the American Association of Individual Investors, during a February 1996 episode of* Adam Smith's Money World

YOU'VE PROBABLY GOT THE IDEA by now that small-cap companies can be a good investment. But what exactly are they? First, you should know that *cap* is shorthand for *market capitalization,* which refers to the market value of a company's common stock. It is equal to the number of shares outstanding times the price per share. So a small-cap company is one that either has issued only a few shares or trades at a low price in the market. It may not be diminutive by any other measure—sales, assets, staff—though just about everyone in the field, including me, uses *small stock, small company,* and *small cap* interchangeably.

Microsoft, which has about 2.5 billion shares outstanding, each priced as of March 1999 at $169, is obviously a large-cap stock; Nathan's Famous (a franchiser that grew out of the Coney Island hotdog stand) is just as indisputably small, with 4.7 million $3.50 shares. Somewhere in between lies the cutoff—exactly where depends on who's counting and whether the market as a whole has been growing or retrenching.

Complicating matters, non-large stocks are often subdivided into *mid-, small-,* and *microcap.* The fluidity of the boundaries between all these categories is one reason why analysts often refer not to dollar ranges but to *deciles* and *quintiles*—10- and 20-percent segments, respectively, of a universe of stocks ranked according to some criterion, such as market cap. That's a useful solution for academic studies that generalize across periods in which share prices and market size vary considerably. But for you and me, it's easier to talk in concrete dollars. So I settled on the following cutoffs, which more or less reflect the current consensus. When I say "small," I mean any stock with a capitalization less than $1 billion. I'll use "micro" only when I

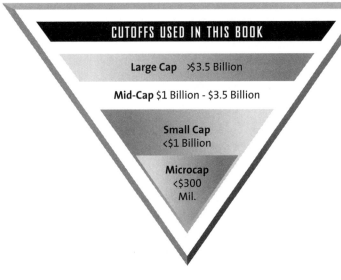

CUTOFFS USED IN THIS BOOK

Large Cap >$3.5 Billion

Mid-Cap $1 Billion - $3.5 Billion

Small Cap <$1 Billion

Microcap <$300 Mil.

need to distinguish the subset of small stocks having caps below $300 million. "Mid-cap" denotes stocks between $1 billion and about $3.5 billion in size; anything above that is "large." *(For a graphic representation of the cutoffs, see the diagram, left.)*

The smaller the cap size of the category, the more companies it contains, a fact captured by the major associated indexes *(illustrated in the chart below).* A stock index provides a measure of the performance of a particular market segment using the combined weighted performances of a group of companies that are considered representative. Weightings are assigned according to various criteria, including capitalization, and members are replaced as their defining characteristics change. The index most commonly used as a proxy for the large-cap universe is the Standard & Poor's 500, which tracks a group of 500 companies that, as of November 1998, had a total market capitalization of more than $9.3 trillion. The Russell Mid-Cap Index has about 800 members, but their combined market cap is only $2.5 trillion, less than one-third as large as that of the S&P. The total market cap of the Russell 2000, widely cited as a small-cap benchmark, is $810 billion, one-tenth the size of the S&P's and equal to less than twice the assets under management of mutual fund company Fidelity Investments. The CRSP

FOUR OF THE MAJOR INDEXES

NUMBER OF COMPANIES	S&P 500	COMBINED MARKET CAP
500 Companies		$9.3 Trillion
	RUSSELL MID-CAP	
769 Companies		$2.5 Trillion
	RUSSELL 2000	
1,944 Companies		$810 Billion
	CRSP 9-10	
3,506 Companies		$228.5 Billion

9-10 index, compiled by the Center for Research in Securities Prices, contains 3,506 microcap stocks (in the 9th and 10th deciles). In November 1998, their combined market cap was a tiny $228.5 billion—less than Microsoft's.

However you define them, small caps are profitable. According to data compiled by Prudential Securities, Inc. *(displayed in the table below)*, small stocks have outperformed the big ones by an average of 1.7 percent a year since 1926.

But bear in mind a couple of caveats. First, Prudential defined small-cap stocks for its survey as those in the lowest quintile in terms of market cap; in 1998, that would produce a cutoff of about $250 million, well within my *microcap* category. In fact, it seems that much of the outperformance of the small-cap sector is produced by the very smallest, and riskiest, segment.

Second, the returns cited are averages. In each of the decades studied, a sizable number of small companies not only failed to grow at the rate shown in the chart but actually failed altogether. Of course, those failures mean at least a few other stocks far outstripped the average. To see how variable the results of a small-cap portfolio—even one put together by well-informed experts—can be, consider the one-year results for *Individual Investor's* "Magic 25." This is a portfolio of twenty-five very small stocks that the magazine's market-savvy editors believe have tremendous growth potential. According to *II*'s Web

RETURNS FOR LARGE AND SMALL CAPS*

	1920s	'30s	'40s	'50s
Small	-3.9	6.9	20.6	19.0
Large	16.9	-.5	8.8	18.2

* "SMALL CAPS" = STOCKS IN THE LOWEST TWO DECILES IN TERMS OF MARKET CAP

site, in 1997 the portfolio as a whole rose 6.1 percent. Individual stock performance, however, ranged from a 263.7 percent gain for THQ Inc. to a 94.9 percent *loss* for Physician Computer Network.

Bob Barker—the "Warren Buffett of small-cap stocks," according to *Adam Smith's Money World*—feels the sector's extreme variability can work to investors' benefit. The venerable head of the investment firm Barker Lee & Co. pointed out in a February 1996 *Money World* appearance that "if . . . half your companies are mistakes, and you lose everything in them, and the other half go up between 5 and 10 times, that's all you need." Barker tested this insight by putting together a theoretical portfolio of twenty companies and leaving it alone for five years. At the end of that time, nine stocks had fallen, four of them by 80 to 90 percent. But the portfolio as a whole had an annual compound rate of return of 23 percent, because the winners had risen between 80 and about 1,000 percent.

Barker's point was illustrated in a family story that Bill Sams, manager of the First Pacific Advisors Paramount fund, told at a 1996 conference sponsored by Morningstar Mutual Funds, the Chicago rating service. "My father bought $700 worth of Frito in the old days," Sams said. "Frito got bought out by Lay's, and then Lay's got bought by Pepsi. That investment turned into more than $6 million. Every other stock he bought lost money, but that one made up for it."

'60s	'70s	'80s	THRU 1998	VALUE OF $1.00 INVESTED IN 1926
13.7	8.6	12.5	15.7	$5,104
7.4	5.2	17.0	16.6	$1,742

WHERE'S THE EDGE?

"There was a two-tier market: You had large compa-
nies selling at 20 times earnings, and small companies
with prospects similar to large companies selling at
12 times earnings. There seemed to be a lot more
value in the smaller companies, so I learned that way.
And back then there were a lot of small companies not
followed by analysts. You could call on somebody and
get information that had not been widely published."
—RALPH WANGER, *manager of Acorn Fund, telling*
Kiplinger's Personal Finance Magazine *in a February 1995 inter-*
view why he started his small-cap fund in the 1970s

VALUATION VS. COMPANY SIZE AND GROWTH RATE

Small and mid-sized growth companies are cheaper than large growth companies,
relative to expected earnings per share growth.

	AVERAGE MARKET CAP (\$ MILLION)	QUINTILE BY MARKET CAP
Large	\$24,495.61	1
Mid	1,846.76	2
Small	752.86	3
Small	334.69	4
Micro	123.19	5

◆ Sample—1,100 U.S. companies as of December 31, 1998. ◆ P/E based on
consensus 12-month forward EPS estimate. ◆ Long-term growth = projected
five-year EPS growth rate. ◆ Companies in sample include only those with

NOW THE REALLY IMPORTANT QUESTION: Why are stocks with small market capitalizations particularly good for individual investors like you?The answer: Because, as Ralph Wanger found during the early days of Acorn, you have a better chance of finding real value in small stocks than in larger ones.

First, as the table below illustrates, the prices at which small companies trade are generally lower in relation to their expected earnings growth than those of larger companies. I'll discuss the price-to-earnings ratio later, in the section on growth and value, but for now, you should know that this measure indicates that the smallest stocks, as a group, deliver the best value.

Second, more good values exist among these companies because so many of the big players give the sector

AVERAGE P/E RATIO					
43.97	42.99	22.02	24.33	16.71	
29.65	23.20	15.72	14.42	15.34	
21.57	16.36	14.03	14.06	15.61	
19.20	13.67	12.52	12.22	13.55	
14.39	11.77	10.05	10.14	12.08	
1	2	3	4	5	QUINTILE BY LONG-TERM EPS GROWTH
Fastest Expected Growth				Slowest Expected Growth	
33.08	21.85	16.62	13.30	9.26	AVERAGE LONG-TERM EPS GROWTH

positive increasing earnings for last year, current year (projected), and next year (projected), with market capitalization in excess of $50 million and share price above $5.

SOURCE: T. ROWE PRICE ASSOCIATES, INC., I/B/E/S

short shrift. It's a matter of economics: Large institutional investors can't earn enough on small stocks to recover their research costs. An institution must know a lot about a company to feel comfortable buying a stake in it. That can take many hours of a researcher's high-priced time and probably an on-site visit. Any purchase the institution makes must have the potential to boost its returns enough to cover these expenses and then some. But to move a $10 billion portfolio requires an investment of at least $100 million. That would amount to 10 percent of a company with a market cap of $1 billion. Many portfolio managers are limited by their mandates to 5 percent stakes. Even those not so limited might find it impossible or imprudent to amass a large number of shares of small-cap companies, which generally trade infrequently, in small blocks, and among a limited number of buyers and sellers.

Brokerages also neglect small stocks, as illustrated in the bar graph below. Although the 450 U.S. companies with market caps larger than $2.4 billion are covered by an average of twenty-two analysts each, according to Merrill Lynch, the 2,600 companies between $60 million and $600 million are each followed by about three: "the underwriter, the co-underwriter, and usually the third is a total fool," jokes a money manager at a New York–based mutu-

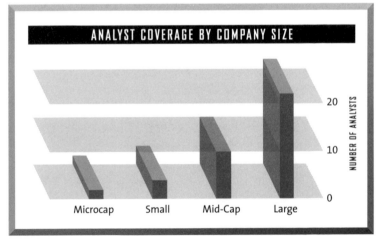

ANALYST COVERAGE BY COMPANY SIZE

NUMBER OF ANALYSTS

20

10

0

Microcap   Small   Mid-Cap   Large

SOURCE: MERRILL LYNCH QUANTITATIVE ANALYSIS

al fund. The even tinier microcap issues average about two analysts each; it's your guess if the dropout is the co-underwriter or the fool.

The reasons for this neglect are again economic. "It does not pay [a broker] to have an analyst research a company where a buy recommendation will not generate orders for hundreds of thousands of shares," investment adviser Tweedy, Browne Co. says in a February 1996 letter to its clients explaining why the firm likes the small sector.

The result: Many fine companies remain undetected, their share prices far below what their intrinsic value would justify. You—or the manager of a mutual fund nimble enough to profit from small-cap research—gain an edge by discovering these gems before other investors can bid them up.

Finding them, moreover, does not take a jeweler's loupe. Again according to Tweedy, smaller companies are often easier to analyze than larger ones: They tend to have fewer products and lower debt levels, since borrowing is more difficult for them.

The relative simplicity of small caps means that the professionals' huge staffs and technical support give them less of an advantage over individuals here than in the large-cap sector. Back in 1996, I asked Peter Kris (managing director of the Van Wagoner funds and no relation to the drummer from Kiss) if an ordinary investor could replicate any part of the strategy followed by star small-stock picker Garrett Van Wagoner. "All of it," he said. "Garrett is just an individual investor who has decided to devote his life to it. He has no analysts and finds that he can uncover new developments before Wall Street analysts [do]." (Since that conversation, ironically, Van Wagoner has added analysts to his staff, along with other professional trappings—and has yet to match the returns he generated when going it alone.)

ALL PART OF A GRAND PLAN

"Two are better than one; because they have a good reward for their labour. / For if they fall, the one will lift up his fellow: but woe to him that is alone when he falleth; for he hath not another to help him up."
—ECCLESIASTES *4:9, 10*

SMALL-CAP STOCKS ARE a crucial investment if you want to get the most value out of your research and grow your wealth faster than inflation eats into it. But crucial as they are, they should still be just one part of a larger, diverse portfolio whose composition is determined by an overarching savings strategy.

The key word here is *diverse.* You never want to put all your eggs in one basket, whether it's one U.S. Treasury bond or a selection of Pacific Rim equities. Only by diversifying can you ensure both the growth you'll need for a prosperous future and protection against the economic and company-specific bumps you'll inevitably hit.

Lately, this philosophy has taken some hits. Some people hate the fact that one component of their diversified (or, as they call it, "deworseified") portfolio is always dragging down returns. Well, that is a fact of life. Diversifying is an admission that you won't always be perfectly right. The good news is that you'll never be perfectly wrong, either.

Your portfolio, of course, shouldn't look like your grandfather's (unless you're 75 and he's 110). Different goals, outlooks, and stages of life demand different investment classes in different proportions. The pie charts on pages 30–31 show the asset allocations that experts typically recommend for the main stages of a person's financial life cycle. These are just guidelines. If you need pointers on modifying the mix to suit your particular needs, you should turn to a book such as Burton Malkiel's *A Random Walk Down Wall Street,* or go to www.russell.com, the Web site run by the same folks who compile the Russell 2000 index of small-cap stocks *(see Resources).* But whatever your stage in life and specific needs, the same general principle applies: To get good growth with a minimum of risk, you should divide your investments between debt and equity; your equities between large and small stocks; and your small stocks among different size, regional, and style segments. (Your portfolio should also contain both domestic and international components; I'll get into global investing later.)

DEBT AND EQUITY

"By mixing bonds with small stocks, a portfolio can have higher returns yet no greater volatility."
—PETER L. BERNSTEIN, *author of* Against the Gods: The Remarkable Story of Risk

NO MATTER HOW CAUTIOUS or aggressive you are as an investor, your portfolio should contain both instruments that conserve principal and those that, in the long run, increase it. The prototypical principal conservators are government debt instruments such as Treasury bonds, bills, and notes; the standard growth producers are equities, or stocks. These two types of securities serve two distinct purposes. Treasuries are best for funding a fast-approaching goal, since you know exactly how much money you'll have if you hold them until maturity. They provide a cushion that allows you to put money you don't need immediately into stocks, whose earnings tend to be higher but more variable (*see the graph on page 32*). Stocks are used to beat inflation and ensure that you have the funds you need to meet expenses in the more-distant future.

Diversifying your investments thus enables you to provide for both imminent needs and far-off goals. It also serves to stabilize the value of your portfolio. Different types of investments tend to prosper in different economic climates, so while one part of a diversified portfolio is taking a breather, another may be coming on strong (*see the chart on page 33*). Stocks and bonds, for instance, do not generally move in tandem, as they did during the unusual period of economic growth paired with low inflation we

TYPICAL RECOMMENDED ASSET ALLOCATIONS

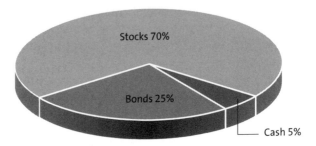

AGE: Mid-Twenties

LIFESTYLE: Fast, aggressive. With a steady stream of earnings, capacity for risk is fairly high. Need discipline of payroll savings to build nest egg

CASH (5%): Money-market fund or short-term-bond fund (average maturity 1 to $1\frac{1}{2}$ years)

BONDS (25%): Zero-coupon Treasury bonds; no-load GNMA fund; or no-load high-grade bond fund

STOCKS (70%): 20% small-company stock fund; 20% growth stock fund; 15% international stock fund; 15% growth and income or "value" fund

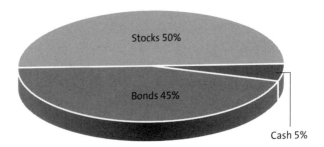

AGE: Mid-Fifties

LIFESTYLE: Many still reeling from college tuitions. No matter what the lifestyle, this age group must start thinking about retirement and the need for income protection

CASH (5%): Money-market fund or short-term-bond fund (average maturity 1 to $1\frac{1}{2}$ years)

BONDS (45%): 10% zero-coupon Treasury bonds; $17\frac{1}{2}$% no-load GNMA fund; $17\frac{1}{2}$% no-load high-grade bond fund

STOCKS (50%): 10% international stock fund; 20% high-income stock fund; 20% growth and income or "value" fund

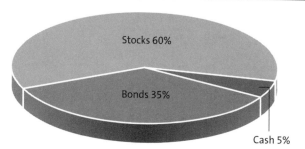

AGE: Late Thirties to Early Forties

LIFESTYLE: Midlife crisis. For childless career couples, capacity for risk is still quite high. Risk options vanishing for those with college tuitions looming

CASH (5%): Money-market fund or short-term-bond fund (average maturity 1 to 1½ years)

BONDS (35%): 10% zero-coupon Treasury bonds; 12½% no-load GNMA fund; 12½% no-load high-grade bond fund

STOCKS (60%): 10% small-company stock fund; 10% growth stock fund; 10% international stock fund; 30% growth and income or "value" fund

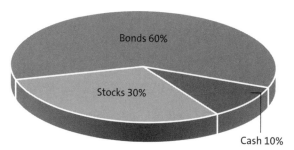

AGE: Late Sixties and Beyond

LIFESTYLE: Enjoying leisure activities but also guarding against major health costs. Little or no capacity for risk

CASH (10%): Money-market fund

BONDS (60%): 20% no-load short- or intermediate-term bond fund; 20% no-load GNMA fund; 20% no-load high-grade bond fund

STOCKS (30%): 15% high-income stock fund; 15% growth and income or "value" fund

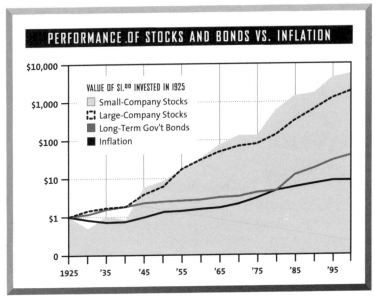

SOURCE: PRUDENTIAL SECURITIES, INC.

enjoyed from 1995 through 1998. In a low-inflation recession, bonds might rally as stocks slump. An opposite reaction would follow the early stages of an expansion. By holding both instruments, you position yourself to win either way. That's a lot safer, and cheaper, than trying to time the market, constantly jumping out of one period's losers and into its winners.

LARGE AND SMALL

"I now favor investing in an index that contains a much broader representation of U.S. companies [than the S&P 500], including large numbers of dynamic companies that are likely to be in early stages of their growth cycles."
—BURTON G. MALKIEL, *in* A Random Walk Down Wall Street

IT IS AS IMPORTANT TO diversify your equity holdings as it is to diversify your overall portfolio, and for the same reasons. By investing in both small and large stocks in a variety of industries, you stabilize your returns while also giving them a boost.

HISTORICAL ASSET ALLOCATION PORTFOLIOS: 1926–96

YOUR ASSET ALLOCATION	AVERAGE ANNUAL RETURN	AVERAGE OF DOWN YEARS*	TWO YEAR RETURN 1973–74	WORST ANNUAL LOSS	BEST ANNUAL GAIN
Aggressive Growth Portfolio 15% / 85% 15% bonds, 85% stocks	10.1%	-10.9%	-30.9%	-37.2% (1931)	46.2% (1933)
Growth Portfolio 5 / 25% / 70% 5% short-term instruments 25% bonds, 70% stocks	9.4%	-8.8%	-24.0%	-30.9% (1931)	38.3% (1933)
Balanced Portfolio 10% / 50% / 40% 10% short-term instruments 40% bonds, 50% stocks	8.3%	-5.8%	-14.5%	-22.5% (1931)	27.8% (1933)
Capital Preservation 20% / 50% / 30% 30% short-term instruments 50% bonds, 20% stocks	6.2%	-2.4%	1.4%	-9.5% (1931)	22.0% (1982)
Short-Term Portfolio 100% 100% short-term instruments	3.7%	0.0%	15.5%	0.0% (1938)	14.7% (1981)

* AVERAGE OF YEARS WHERE RETURN IS NEGATIVE.

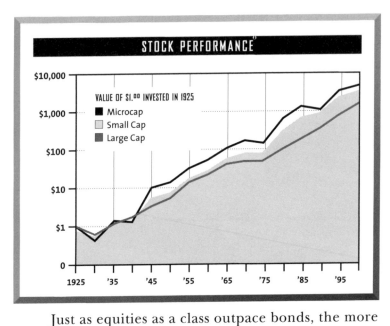

STOCK PERFORMANCE

VALUE OF $1.⁰⁰ INVESTED IN 1925
- Microcap
- Small Cap
- Large Cap

SOURCE: PRUDENTIAL SECURITIES, INC.

Just as equities as a class outpace bonds, the more volatile small stocks outperform slow-but-steadier large ones. This is illustrated in the graph *(above)*. Of course, extra return usually involves extra risk. But time tends to reduce the trade-off, as statistics compiled by Ibbotson Associates demonstrate. Ibbotson studied the one-, five-, ten-, fifteen-, and twenty-year returns of government and corporate bonds and large and small stocks from 1926 through 1998, noting both the maximum and minimum figures generated by each security type. The gap between the highest and lowest figures decreases steadily as you move from risky small caps to conservative U.S. Treasury bills, but so does the size of the greatest gains: the one-year returns of small caps during this period ranged from 142.87 to -58.01; U.S. Treasury bills, meanwhile, earned from 14.71 to -0.02 annually. As the holding period lengthens, differences in variability decline while growth rates continue to diverge: The maximum and minimum twenty-year returns for small stocks were 21.13 and 5.74 percent, respectively, versus 7.72 and 0.42 percent for T-bills.

Given those performance figures, small stocks can clearly play a specific role in your portfolio: funding goals that lie in the relatively distant future and that will require outlays well beyond your current cash reserves and income. For example, they're suited to saving for a far-off retirement or your baby's college tuition.

Adding small caps to your investment mix also provides the second benefit of diversification: stable returns in a variety of environments. Small and large stocks, like equities and bonds, tend to perform best at different times and in response to different economic factors. "It is generally accepted that big-cap and small-cap stocks perform in alternating multiyear cycles," Kenneth Fisher and Joseph Toms, president and senior vice president of Fisher Investments, point out in the book *Small Cap Stocks*. These cycles of under- and overperformance *(discussed more fully in Chapter 4)* last anywhere from three to more than seven years.

In addition, smaller companies generally react more quickly to changes in the economy than larger ones, according to Susan Belden, former senior editor of the newsletter *No-Load Fund Analyst*. Because of their extra sensitivity, small stocks will outperform large ones at the beginning of an economic recovery and underperform when recession is looming.

Different-size companies also respond differently to inflation. When the rate is rising, nimble businesses that have near monopolies in fast-growing niches generate better earnings than more unwieldy corporations operating in broader, highly competitive markets. And better earnings translate into higher stock prices. In his book, *Market Timing for the Nineties,* Stephen Leeb notes that during periods of high inflation, small stocks have returned 21 percent a year, far more than the 16 percent return of gold, the traditional inflation hedge.

Because their performance cycle complements that of large stocks, a moderate allocation to small caps may reduce (or, at worst, add little to) the overall volatility of a portfolio. Satya Pradhuman, director of small-cap research at Merrill Lynch, says that by devoting 10 percent of your equity funds to the smallest stocks, you can boost returns

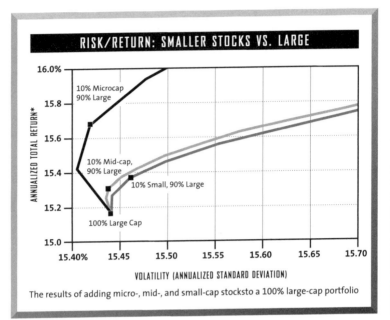

by 40 to 100 *basis points* (hundredths of a percent) without increasing risk *(see the chart, above)*. Pradhuman's point was demonstrated in a Fidelity study comparing the performances, over twenty-five years ending June 30, 1998, of two balanced portfolios: one consisting of 60 percent large-capitalization stocks, 5 percent cash, 20 percent long-term corporate bonds, and 15 percent long-term government bonds; the other reducing the large-cap portion to 48 percent and adding 12 percent small stocks. The first allocation earned an average annual return of 13.02 percent with 11.08 percent volatility; the second returned 13.6 percent, or 60 basis points more, while increasing volatility by only 10 bp. In dollar terms, after twenty-five years, $10,000 invested in the second portfolio would have become $221,079, versus $195,536 for the first portfolio.

Pradhuman warns that if you boost your small-cap allocation above 20 percent, the extra returns come with considerable extra risk. So if you're considering a larger proportion of small companies, ask yourself if you can stomach the tailspins along with the vertical climbs.

PBHG fund-family manager Gary Pilgrim advises investors to "be very conservative about money you think you might need over the next few years," using small-fry funds to help put some punch into the rest of your portfolio. Another way to reduce risk is to mix stocks that are insensitive to the economy—among large caps, Campbell Soup Co. is an example—with some that are very sensitive, such as a steel company.

DIVERSIFICATION NEEDN'T STOP at the small-cap level. Small stocks are themselves a disparate lot, and your portfolio should probably contain both growth and value companies and possibly also microcaps and regionals.

GROWTH VERSUS VALUE

"Nobody would claim to be a nonvalue investor. It is certainly not the opposite of growth."
—CHARLES ROYCE, *president of the Royce family of funds,* in an October 1992 interview with Institutional Investor

THE TERMS "GROWTH" AND "VALUE" may apply less to companies and stocks than to different ways of looking at and evaluating them—that is, to different investment styles. A stock cannot be both small and large (though two investors may place the cutoff at different points); it might, however, be categorized as both growth and value. That's because size is measured along one dimension—market capitalization—whereas growth and value involve two different axes: earnings growth and asset value. A stock's categorization, therefore, depends in part on the perspective from which it is being studied and on the emphasis given different factors. This section defines the growth and value perspectives in general terms. You'll get a more detailed look at the analyses they translate into in Chapter 3.

The growth approach to investing was popularized in 1939 by T. Rowe Price, founder of the eponymous fund company. Price believed that companies, like organisms, pass through three major phases: growth, characterized by increasing earnings; maturity, when earnings stabilize; and decline, when they fall off. The first phase, he felt, offers investors the greatest opportunity for gain with the least risk. Price's followers look for companies with expanding profit margins, quarter-to-quarter sales increases, and a history of accelerating earnings growth, year over year and quarter over quarter. If these criteria are met, growth investors are willing to accept a high share price relative to earnings, a measure known as the *price-earnings ratio*, or *p/e*. They believe that the market

ONE STOCK, TWO PERSPECTIVES

IN THE COURSE of a 1996 analysts round table, I asked growth advocate Jim Oberweis Jr., of the Oberweis funds, and value investor Bill Nasgovitz, of Heartland Advisors, to discuss Just for Feet. The footwear superstore operator appears in both their portfolios, but in opposite positions: Oberweis is *long* the stock, meaning he actually holds it in his portfolio; Nasgovitz has *shorted* it— that is, he sold shares borrowed from a broker, planning to replace them with others bought later at a lower price. Why the different approaches?

Oberweis: When we bought Just for Feet, it really was at an attractive valuation. . . . We look for 30 percent growth in revenues. . . . That's actually the bare minimum; in fact, in our portfolio, the average companies grow at a rate of 70 percent. The second thing we look for is 30 percent growth in earnings. Again, an average of about 70 percent in the portfolio.

Graja: So they can't get their earnings by simply laying people off or cutting costs.

Oberweis: Right. These are the most successful, best-managed companies in the business. However, like Bill, we don't want to pay a ridiculous price for the company. I would call us not so much growth investors as growth-value investors. We're looking to buy companies for a p/e not higher than half the rate of growth. So if a company is growing at 50 percent annually, we don't want to pay tends to underestimate the growth potential of truly great companies, reasoning that when earnings have been growing at an ever-faster pace, they should continue to grow strongly enough in the future to narrow the gap with the share price in a short time.

Value investors, in contrast, generally shy away from overblown p/e's. That doesn't mean they discount the importance of earnings. They are merely wary of accepting high market valuations now on the basis of achievements yet to come, which, unlike the growth crowd, they feel are apt to be overestimated. (In fact, research by David Dreman,

a p/e higher than about 25. When we bought Just for Feet, I think we paid no higher than 33 times ever and an average of about 27 times. The company is growing at 100 percent annually, in terms of both revenues and earnings. We had outstanding growth in both. And I think that continues. I think it's pretty much a fully valued company at this point. We wouldn't buy it at these levels. But we continue to hold on to it.

Graja: Bill, what's the other side of that coin?

Nasgovitz: Well, the flip side would be, we think the stock is fully valued. It is a great company. Great concept. They are a retailer of tennis shoes. No rocket science behind that concept. But at $45 a share, the stock is selling at approximately 60 times this year's estimated earnings. You know, 60 times earnings . . . if you bought the whole company at that price, you'd be getting 1.6 percent on your money. That just doesn't make sense to us.

Graja: That's the earnings yield, 1 over the p/e of 60.

Nasgovitz: That's the earnings yield. . . . When 2-year Treasuries are yielding a lot more: 6.4 percent. So, the stock has had a big move. We think it's a concept that has worked, but margins will be squeezed as the company continues to grow and competitors step into the market. Now, we haven't made any money on the short side yet. It just went into the 50s and we shorted some more. But at this price, we think it's fully priced.

a value investor and one of the past decade's best fund managers, shows that analysts often blow their forecasts.)

Instead, value advocates look at the present (and, to some extent, the past) situation for elements that support a price higher than the current one—for instance, low p/e and low *price-to-book* (the company's market cap divided by its total assets net of liabilities).

"We determine the enterprise's value, [which] may mean looking back a couple of years to when circumstances were better or considering the result of the sale of certain assets or the elimination of losses in certain divisions," Charles Royce explains in the October 1992 *Institutional Investor* interview. "And we try to invest at a discount to that value."

The market should eventually push the stock price up to, or even above, the company's true, intrinsic worth. When this happens, the value investor is gone.

"We like to come in early, when these things are undiscovered or unloved," says Bill Nasgovitz, manager of the small-cap Heartland Value fund. "And when they attract attention or move up in price, we'll gladly part with our stock."

Nasgovitz, Royce, and their fellow value investors are apostles of the almost-legendary Benjamin Graham, whose methods form the basis of the fundamental stock analysis employed today. Since the 1940s, when Graham's ideas started gaining acceptance, and largely because of his teachings, the market has become considerably more efficient, making it nearly impossible to find large stocks that meet his strict criteria. Today's value candidates are found primarily in the small-cap market, which is generally less well followed on Wall Street and is therefore less efficient.

Distressed companies constitute another major group of value candidates, mined mainly by contrarians. Michael Price, a value investor who until November 1998 managed the Franklin Mutual Series funds, described the scavenger style in a May 1996 interview with Bloomberg News's Tim Quinson: "Lawsuits, environmental spills, wrong part of

the business cycle, companies with disappointing earnings—those are the ponds we fish in."

The rationale is that investors tend to overreact to bad
news. David Dreman, a dyed-in-the-wool contrarian, has
stated that while in-favor stocks are notoriously overpriced, out-of-favor ones are just as notoriously under-
priced. The trick is to find fallen companies with both
low debt and balance sheets strong enough to keep them
solvent while good management teams figure out what
went wrong and fix it.

Royce, showing that the distinction between growth and
value is one of style rather than substance, finds some of
his value prospects among "fast-growth companies . . . that
have stopped growing as quickly as Wall Street wanted
them to. The company may get its act together and be a
20 or 25 percent grower again . . . . But in the process of
that shift, there are a lot of growth investors that become
highly agitated." As an example, he cites women's apparel
retailer Charming Shoppes, a onetime highflier that he
picked up cheap when its earnings flattened. The chain
rejoined the fast track after a short breather, and his fund
got a nice boost.

BOTH THE GROWTH AND VALUE approaches have advantages. Each also has limitations, which the other side is
quick to point out.

Value investors claim their style generates the best long-
term results. They cite evidence like that illustrated in the
graphs on the following page, showing that a $1 invest-
ment in 1975 would have become $57.72 by the end of
1998 if put in small-cap value stocks, compared with only
$30.91 in small-cap growth, $19.10 in large-cap growth,
and $33.15 in large-cap value stocks.

Going further, researchers at Tweedy Browne and
investment firm Sanford Bernstein have stated that so-
called small-cap outperformance during the past two to
three decades is attributable less to size than to deep
undervaluation. They point out that, except for three years

VALUE VS. GROWTH PERFORMANCE

SMALL-CAP STOCKS

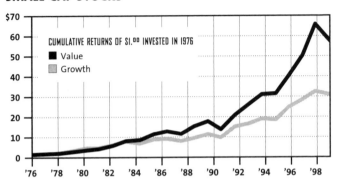

MID-CAP STOCKS

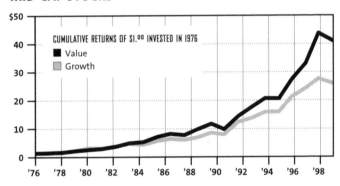

LARGE-CAP STOCKS

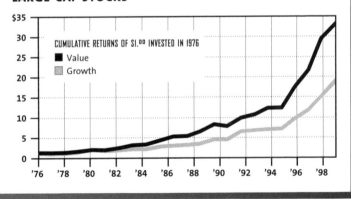

in which small clearly outshone large, returns for both groups have been almost the same. But when the universe is divided between growth and value stocks, the latter have a significant and consistent advantage.

Moreover, if you adjust returns for risk, small-cap growth comes in dead last among the possible size and style combinations. This is hardly surprising, say value investors, since the growth strategy of buying expensive companies can easily fall flat if earnings don't increase as fast as expected.

"The way some of these companies are priced, they better become the next Microsoft," Nasgovitz says, "because at a 100 or 150 times earnings, one disappointment is going to be extremely painful."

Of course, not every small-cap growth company is a potential Microsoft. The chance that a $50 million company will become a $50 billion one is slim. Just look at the technology sector: Research by Morgan Stanley found that, of 12,993 tech businesses that received venture capital (the first step in becoming a real company) from 1980 through September 1997, only 1,099 subsequently issued stock and a minuscule 45 have become major players. So, you could put the odds of that little enterprise you spotted becoming the next Microsoft at about 1 in 250.

Why is it so hard? First, the founders need to turn a brilliant idea into a product the whole country knows and uses. Then, when the company really takes off, they need to mutate from hands-on garage inventors to macromanagers. The biggest turning point, though, occurs when the up-and-comer is large enough to attract the attention of the big guys—well-managed competitors with rock-solid balance sheets that can afford to devote some of their resources to putting an upstart out of business.

Growth advocates, for their part, might counter that the statistics showing value's superiority are biased. The studies cited assume a "black-box" style of investing, in which someone blindly buys all the stocks ranked in particular quintiles by their p/e's. This is artificial. Even the most rabid growth investor will avoid the highest ratios. In fact, Claudia Mott, director of small-cap research at Prudential Securities, points out that small-cap growth funds on average outperform small-cap value funds; even Tweedy Browne concedes this in its September 1996 semiannual report.

The growth people also note that though one of their winners could well grow a thousandfold, percent increases for the top value picks are more commonly in the hundreds. Many value stocks, moreover, turn out to be "permacheap," their prices doomed to languish in the low figures. The fact is, most cheap stocks are cheap not because they have been overlooked but because something is gravely wrong with them. And even truly undiscovered stocks may stay underpriced for a long, long time. As Merrill Lynch's Pradhuman puts it, many value investors see value long before anyone else does and, as a result, end up hanging on to stocks through a long unprofitable period.

"When you talk about errors on the value side," says Nasgovitz, "we're generally there a little bit earlier than the rest."

WHERE DOES ALL THIS LEAVE YOU? On the fence, if you're smart. Neither the growth nor the value style of stock picking is infallible, but both are capable of producing winners. And though it's possible for one stock to attract both types of investors, the two groups generally have different takes and make very different choices. So if you combine both growth and value styles in your portfolio, you'll increase both its diversity and your chances of making successful investments. In fact, Peter Lynch attributes a major part of his investment success to his flexibility, a refusal to follow blindly any particular dogma.

Because of their different characteristics, growth and value stocks can perform different roles in your portfolio. The former produce spectacular price rises (and just as spectacular falls); the latter, less spectacular but more consistent gains. So growth stocks can provide momentum,

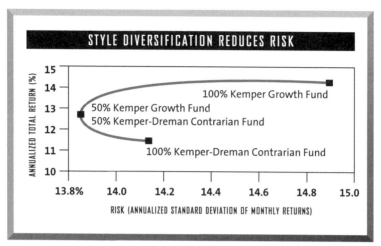

STYLE DIVERSIFICATION REDUCES RISK

100% Kemper Growth Fund

50% Kemper Growth Fund
50% Kemper-Dreman Contrarian Fund

100% Kemper-Dreman Contrarian Fund

ANNUALIZED TOTAL RETURN (%)

RISK (ANNUALIZED STANDARD DEVIATION OF MONTHLY RETURNS)

while value picks furnish downside protection.

Growth and value also thrive in different market situations. Though value, as I said above, seems to do best over the long term, in certain economic environments growth is dominant. Value, for example, is generally soundly beaten by growth when the economy is slowing, when interest rates are rising, and when the U.S. Treasury yield curve is flat *(see Chapter 4 for details)*. So my advice here is the same as it was for debt versus equity and large versus small stocks: If you want consistent and reliable returns, make sure both groups are represented in your portfolio. The proportions will depend on your goals and risk tolerance. The chart above shows the risks and returns of different combinations of growth and value stocks, represented respectively by Kemper Growth and Kemper-Dreman Contrarian funds.

If you're in a high income-tax bracket and hold individual stocks in a taxable account, small-cap growth may have an edge.

An article in the September 1996 issue of *SmartMoney* pointed out that if you assume federal and state tax rates of 31 and 6 percent, respectively, small-cap stocks had outperformed large-cap ones during the past fifteen years, and growth had beaten out value. Specifically, the average tax-adjusted annual return of the Russell 2000 index of small-cap stocks was 15.1 percent for the period, versus 14.5 for the large-cap S&P 500. During the same period, value stocks in the mostly large- and mid-cap Russell 1000 returned 14.7 percent, versus 14.9 for growth stocks in the same index. The reason for the relative success of the small and growth sectors is that returns of large-cap and value companies derive in great part from the reinvestment of taxable dividends; in contrast, small-cap and growth companies rely more on capital appreciation, which is taxed at a lower rate than income.

BOTH VALUE AND GROWTH INVESTORS hope their small-cap stocks will get bigger fast, either by maturing or by recapturing past glories. Investors in small regional and niche companies generally have more modest aspirations. They're content with solid, steady earnings in relatively noncompetitive environments. Regionals are usually not glamorous, but they may be the friendliest for you, the small investor. They're the ones most likely to be sitting in your hometown, or where your Uncle Bill works. In either case, you're in a position to get some perfectly legal inside information that could give you an edge over the big guys. All you have to do is read the local newspapers, drive by the plant, talk to employees and neighbors, customers, and suppliers.

SMALL AND SMALLER

"During the forty-three years of our study, $10,000 invested in all the stocks in the Compustat database with a market capitalization below $25 million would have grown to over $29 million! Unfortunately, no professional money manager can realistically buy these stocks."
—JIM O'SHAUGHNESSY, *in* What Works on Wall Street

REGIONAL, GROWTH, AND VALUE stocks differ in the reasons they're small: because they're parochial, young, or misunderstood. Small stocks can also differ in their degree of smallness. The tiniest of the tiny are the microcaps.

I've defined microcaps as companies having market capitalizations under $300 million. Some in the business put the bar even lower. The Fremont U.S. Micro-Cap fund, for instance, has a median market capitalization of $149.10 million. As I've said before, boundary disputes are common. What isn't disputed, though, is that when you're talking returns, smaller is better. Over the past twenty years, Merrill Lynch's Pradhuman states in a 1995 *Business Week* article, companies with market caps of $60 million or less have produced average annual returns of 21 percent, compared with 17 percent for small-cap stocks and 13 percent for large caps.

"Historically, this is the group that has given you the biggest bang for the buck," says Prudential's Mott.

Microcaps are even less well followed on Wall Street than the larger small caps. There are a lot of microcap companies, for one thing: Estimates range from 3,000 to more than 6,940. And they cost at least as much to research as larger companies in which institutions can take bigger stakes and make bigger profits. As a result, about 45 percent of the tiniest stocks have no analyst coverage at all, according to Daniel P. Coker, former quantitative analyst and strategist of emerging-equity research at Schroder & Co. Even those companies that are covered aren't exactly smothered: Coker figures they average around 1.4 analysts each; the average is less than 1 for caps below $100 million.

That leaves the field pretty much open for you. Digging up what's going on at an underfollowed company takes a fair amount of time and effort. But think of it as fun, and remember that this is one area where an amateur with a little horse sense and patience can sometimes outsmart an MBA with five investing theories.

"The world has adopted small cap as a real genre," Quest Advisory's Royce, who specializes in small- and microcap stocks, told *The Washington Post*. "What's remaining [at the lowest levels of capitalization] is below the radar screen, and it's a large area for opportunity."

It's also an area where research really pays off. That's because a small company's performance is determined largely by its own actions and condition, rather than by the economy at large. "As you go down along the scale of size of companies, the success of the company and the investment are much more dependent upon individual company developments," says Robert Kern, portfolio manager of Fremont U.S. Micro-Cap. "I like that the things you are analyzing are closely tied to the company, as opposed to some macroeconomic variable."

Mammoths like AT&T, which spread themselves over many businesses, can't grow much more quickly than the economy itself. Tiny companies, limited to a small slice of one niche, grow principally on the strength of their own products. Of course, if they rely on a few giant customers and these suffer a slowdown, the small suppliers will suffer, too. But really innovative products will always be in demand. Because microcap companies are relatively independent of macroeconomics, good research provides a real edge in this sector: You need a crystal ball to predict where the economy is headed, but a little hard work can uncover customer base and product innovation.

Still, this is a very risky area. The failure rate is much higher for microcap companies than for their larger cousins. Bigger businesses generally have a few past successes to build on, as well as decent managers, capital, and a few long-term contracts to stabilize their earnings. Call it the "survivor effect"—the same inertia that holds giants back in a rising market keeps them afloat in a sinking one. Tiny companies are more agile, but also more vulnerable.

In addition, microcaps are almost invisible and their market consequently illiquid. Want to sell Coca-Cola? Done. Want to sell Lifetime Hoan? Who's the buyer? For microcaps, the average daily trading volume is just 18,000 shares, compared with 54,000 shares for small caps and 505,000 for large stocks, says Pradhuman. Because demand is so low, a seller with an oversupply of micro shares will have to drop his or her price. By the same token, a would-be buyer may have to bid the price way up. This amplifies price swings. According to Ibbotson chief economist Paul Kaplan, microcaps are twice as volatile as large-cap stocks and a third jumpier than small ones.

PUTTING IT TOGETHER

NOW YOU KNOW YOUR PORTFOLIO should be divided into stocks, bonds, and money markets, and the equity portion between large and small stocks. You might also want to divide your small-cap investments between micro and somewhat larger companies, and among value, growth, and niche stocks. Fine. But how do you go about choosing what exactly to buy in each of the small-cap categories? The following chapters will provide specific tips. For now, though, here are some general rules and strategies.

Allocate a portion of your small-cap portfolio to mutual funds. Consider making that 100 percent if you don't have enough time to research your picks thoroughly or enough money to spread your risk around. Jim Oberweis Jr. feels that anyone who can't afford to buy twenty individual small-cap stocks should stick with funds. I'd modify that a bit: If you have only $10,000, say, to allocate to this sector, you could invest about $3,000 in one or two well-researched individual stocks and turn over the rest to the professional managers. Investors looking at small caps only for the diversification they provide might do best with an index fund, such as one of those discussed in Chapter 2.

Whatever you do with the rest of your small-cap investment money, mutual funds should probably be the vehicle for your microcap investing. A fund gives you diversification, which keeps any one failure from ruining your returns. If you choose well, you also get a skilled manager who has access to the companies' management and the research clout to keep you out of trouble.

Fund management is especially important in the

microcap sector, with its relative independence from macroeconomic movements. Since managers can't just ride the trends, their fundamental analysis and business research can make a real difference. As a result, the gap between the best and worst performers in the microcap sector tends to be much greater than in other specializations. In 1995, for instance, Perkins Opportunity, which invests in upstart companies largely from the same upper-Midwest region where the fund is based, returned a stellar 70 percent; at the other extreme, Frontier Equity lost 1.26 percent.

Research, research, research. This advice applies no matter how you decide to invest your small-cap money. As will be explained more fully in the following chapter, research is important in finding funds with good track records and, once you've invested, making sure they hold to their stated objectives. It is crucial, though, when you're looking at individual stocks. As I've said before, the investor with more knowledge always has an edge over the one with less; small caps are one sector where you can glean information not known by the whole world. You also reduce your risks by researching your prospects' finances and weeding out ones that could be toppled by a bad quarter. All this is covered in Chapters 3 and 4.

Stay small. You don't have the time to analyze all 5,000-plus small companies. For your individual stock investing, you need to reduce your universe to segments in which you have an edge and that you can research thoroughly. Many brokerage firms succeed by following very closely companies in one industry or geographic region. Alexander Paris, the president of Barrington Research, for example, focuses on companies based in the Midwest. The small-cap mutual funds you buy should probably also be small, limiting the assets they will accept to manage. Remember, this is an area where big guys often have trouble maneuvering.

Keep your costs low. One sure way to lower costs is to minimize your transactions. Trading stock costs you money in commissions and in the bid-ask spread—the difference between where market makers will buy (the bid) and where they'll sell (the ask).

Small-cap transactions are particularly expensive, since spreads tend to be wide. Most small- and microcap stocks are traded over the counter, on the National Association of Securities Dealers Automated Quotations system, or Nasdaq. When you buy or sell shares of these companies, you're dealing not with other investors (as you do on an exchange) but with market makers, such as brokerages. These market makers enter the prices at which they will buy or sell a stock onto an electronic system. The highest buy price and lowest sell price become the bid and ask you see when you get a quote. The difference between the two prices represents the brokerage's compensation for making a market in the stock. The smaller the volume of shares changing hands, the greater the market maker's risk and the wider the spread they accept in compensation.

Despite recent reforms, Nasdaq spreads are often as large as half a point. That means you're buying shares for 50 cents more than you could turn around and sell them for. So if you are to make any money on the trade, the stock's ask must rise more than a half point. On a $10 stock, that represents a 5 percent increase—huge in a market where the average annual return is just 12 percent.

Have a plan for when to buy and when to sell. This is important for funds, but critical for stocks.

Buying is easier. Your goal is to acquire stocks that Wall Street will latch on to a short time later, thus creating demand that will push up their prices. Not every company that produces a fine product and has sound finances fits the bill. Dozens of research studies have shown that stocks go in and out of favor. If you follow your collection of companies carefully and apply a few of the strategies described in later chapters, you should be in a position to scoop up bargains.

Selling is a tougher call; you'll find specific advice in Chapter 3. For now, just remember that you can lessen the pain of your sell decisions by setting both a goal and a cut-loss point for every stock when you buy it. If the share price reaches either level, you should reevaluate the company's prospects and its fit with your portfolio to see if there are any new reasons to hold it.

THAT'S JUST A QUICK TASTE. The following chapters will give you more detailed information and recommendations to really sink your teeth into. For advice on building a small-cap mutual-fund portfolio, turn the page. If you're eager to start on individual-stock investing, skip to Chapter 3 or, to get straight to the more sophisticated strategies, Chapter 4.

CHAPTER

2

Mutual
FUNDS

O MATTER HOW you handle the rest of your investments—carefully researching and selecting every bond and blue chip yourself or handing the whole thing over to a financial manager—when it comes to your small-cap allocation, you should seek professional help. That means mutual funds. As I said in the previous chapter, most individual investors should have a portion of their small-stock portfolio in funds. The minimum is probably 50 percent. You might even decide to go for 100.

Mutual funds represent the easiest and cheapest way to buy diversification and good asset management. That's true for most investments, and it goes double for small stocks. Make that quadruple for microcaps.

This chapter won't tell you everything you need to know about investing in funds. For that, I'd suggest you look at *The New Commonsense Guide to Mutual Funds,* by Mary Rowland. What I hope to do here is to convince you of the benefits of incorporating funds into your small-cap strategy and give you some pointers on how to accomplish that.

DIVERSIFICATION

"There are a small number of people, like [Warren] Buffett or Sam Walton, who become incredibly rich from one or just a few holdings. But you never hear stories about the people who go broke. Think of it this way: There are no guarantees when you invest in stocks. If you had $100 to play the lottery, would you put all the money on one number? Or would you want 100 different numbers? I think you're better off with more lottery tickets."
—CHRIS BROWNE, *a partner at investment adviser Tweedy, Browne Co.*

THE WAY I'VE BEEN thumping this theme, it could be a tax-cut plan in an election year. But believe me, diversification is a lot easier to execute, and the cost/benefit trade-off is a lot clearer.

There's a cost? Well, yeah. If you spread your investments among a bunch of different sectors and stocks, you're going to get less of a bang when one stock takes off than if you had made a concentrated bet on it. That's investor Warren Buffett's view. And that's why his strategy is to put all his eggs in one basket and watch that basket really carefully.

The trouble is, a concentrated bet that goes wrong can crack your nest egg. Buffett's strategy works only if you pick stocks as well as he does; most of us don't. We also can't take the huge stakes in companies that Buffett does and so don't have the same leverage with management to challenge decisions not in shareholders' interest.

Splitting your bets diffuses your risk, keeping any one failure from ruining you. That's an important consideration when you're dealing with small companies, which often don't have fat reserves to carry them through lean times. (Buffett, of course, buys huge companies that not only have ample financial padding but are themselves diversified across a number of businesses operating in a number of countries.)

"It's somewhat like trying to know when lightning will hit which trees," Royce & Associates president Charles Royce told *Institutional Investor* magazine in an October 1992 interview. "If you have enough trees, you'll still have firewood at the end of the season." Diversification also stabilizes your returns, since different sectors and styles tend to prosper at different times and in response to different economic factors.

But spreading your wealth among individual stocks is tough unless you have a lot to invest. A thousand dollars isn't going to buy you much of a stake in fifteen to twenty companies—the minimum number you should hold, according to Jim Oberweis Jr., portfolio manager of the Oberweis funds. A thousand dollars is all you need, though, to make an initial investment in the average small-cap mutual fund and a stake in its portfolio of upwards of seventy-five stocks.

PROFESSIONAL MANAGEMENT

"Individuals should own stocks. Then they'd see how hard it is and let professionals do some of the work for them."

—BILL BERGER, *retired manager of the Berger Funds*

IN EVERY BUSINESS, THERE ARE artists and hackers. The man who painted my house is an artist. He could spackle and prime the dining-room ceiling while you were eating Thanksgiving dinner, and you'd never know he was there. Last summer I painted some Adirondack chairs and wound up ruining a pair of shoes, wrecking my new shorts, and splattering paint in my hair. A lot of small-cap mutual fund managers are artists; most of the rest of us are paint-spillers.

Wait a minute, you say, aren't we the little guys that are supposed to have an edge in this sector? Sure, but many of the best small-cap funds are little guys, too, relative to the industry. Just compare the $6 million or so in assets that Bjurman Micro-Cap Growth was managing in October 1998 with Fidelity Magellan's more than $65 billion under management.

With less investor money that must be kept working, funds like Bjurman can keep their portfolios relatively small. This helps them avoid one of the most serious problems large investors face in the small-cap sector: To juice returns enough to offset research costs, a big institution with a huge portfolio must hold a sizable block of a successful stock. That's tough when you're dealing with a company that has a small market cap. A "sizable block" of its shares may represent a larger percentage of the total outstanding than a fund's mandate—or a manager's prudence—allows it to hold. A much more modest stake does the job in a Bjurman-size portfolio, whose manager can thus afford to spend the time and money necessary to find the best small companies.

So small-fund managers are little guys. But they're artistic little guys, with more research money and experience, not to mention better connections and backup, than us hackers. Daniel Coker, most recently a quantitative analyst and strategist of emerging-equity research at Schroder & Co., notes that huge information gaps exist between institutional money managers and even the best stockbrokers, and between brokers and most individuals. A manager like Michael Gerding, of international small-cap fund Founders Passport, will visit 300 companies a year. Others, like Jim Oberweis Jr., avoid direct contact with company management but have their own ways of digging up the reams of data they need. Just as important, from having studied thousands of these companies, the pros know what to look for in the piles of numbers and facts they gather and usually have both a talented staff and sophisticated models to analyze the data.

You might still be able to unearth some small gems that escape the pros' notice—the well-run factory down the street, say, or the company that makes the snowboards all of your kids' friends are bugging their parents to buy. The searching, though, takes time, effort, and more than a little luck. To figure out if the potential profits are worth the trouble, ask yourself whether your edge is greater than the average investor's—do you have special sources of information, and if so, how reliable are they? If you aren't too sure, spend extra time with your kids and let a fund manage your money. If you think you do have a bit of an advantage, you should still spend as much time as you can with your kids— the *only* risk-free investment—but maybe give up some sleep or devote one lunch hour a week to doing the research for the nonfund part of your small-cap portfolio.

CONVENIENCE AND COST

"Transaction costs are very high for small stocks, especially if you are wrong. When the stock is doing poorly and everyone wants to sell, that is where you really get hurt."
—ROBERT KERN, *portfolio manager of Fremont U.S. Micro-Cap*

YOU SHOULDN'T DO A LOT OF TRADING, in either mutual funds or individual stocks. But even buying to hold involves buying, and you can't hold forever. So bear in mind that shares of a mutual fund are much easier and cheaper to purchase and redeem than shares of a small-cap stock. Consider, also, that every fund share represents multiple stocks—if you had to buy or sell all of them individually, your transaction costs would be multiplied, too.

When you trade stocks, both your principal in a purchase and your profit from a sale are eroded by commissions, fees, and spreads. The bite is particularly big in the small- and microcap markets: The limited numbers of available shares and of investors willing to buy or sell them make for very wide bid-ask spreads. The same factors can lead to delays in execution, particularly in sales of lesser-known microcaps.

In contrast, you always have a ready buyer for your mutual-fund shares: the fund itself. And if you deal directly with the fund or trade through a supermarket broker such as Charles Schwab, Jack White, or Fidelity, you may pay no transaction fee, or load. *(For more on fund fees, see "Masters of Their Domain," below.)*

That doesn't mean you get off scot-free. Funds have to pay commissions and deal with spreads when they trade for their portfolios, and those transaction costs (along with manager salaries and administrative fees) reduce your returns. On the other hand, because they buy in bulk, managers usually get breaks from their brokers that you and I will never see.

NOW THAT YOU'RE SOLD, I hope, on putting at least some of your small-cap money into mutual funds, the next step is to choose one, or maybe a few. Ten years ago, that would have been easy. You were limited to forty-five or so funds specializing in small companies. Times have changed, though. In 1999, according to Bloomberg Fund Performance, there were 614 funds investing in small-company stocks. To find the ones among this multitude that are right for you, you have to do some research. It may not be as rigorous as when you're picking a stock, but you can't just stick a pin in your newspaper's fund listings. Look into who manages each fund's portfolio and how, what its record is, and the fees and other costs you'll have to pay.

THE NO-BRAINER APPROACH

Here's a good rule of thumb:
Too clever is dumb.
—OGDEN NASH

IF YOU WANT TO MINIMIZE your research time, stick to the type of fund that minimizes management. In other words, put your money in an *index fund,* one whose holdings—and, consequently, returns—mimic the composition of a market index such as the Russell 2000. The only thing these funds' managers have to do is keep up with changes in the companies making up the index. So trading and administrative costs, not to mention management fees, should be minimal: The Vanguard 500 Index Fund, for example, charges less than 0.2 percent in management expenses, compared with 1.33 percent for the average stock fund. The lower a fund's total expenses, the more of your money gets invested and generates returns. This is especially important in the small-cap market, where "round-trip" costs on stock trades can be 4 to 6 percent, according to Satya Pradhuman, director of small-cap research at Merrill Lynch.

Because indexing managers have so little leeway in managing, you don't have to worry as much about their investment philosophies and records as you would with an actively managed fund. Specifically, you don't have to worry that they'll stray from your objective, which in this case is to stay small. The organization that creates an index will remove stocks that no longer fit its defining criteria—such as market-cap size—and the funds that match the index must follow suit. As I'll discuss later, active managers often aren't as disciplined about cleaning house, tending in particular to let their average market cap drift upward.

An index fund also supplies automatic diversification. Since the market includes both growth and value stocks, for instance, the fund will, too. Different styles cycle in and out of favor. Combining them in one portfolio, as an index fund does, should provide more consistent returns over the long run.

THAT SAID, INDEXING HAS NOT BEEN the bonanza in small caps that it has in the large-cap arena. This is largely due to the differences between the indexes used in the two cases. For almost twenty years the leading small-stock benchmark has been the Russell 2000, which contains not only 4 times as many companies as the large-cap Standard & Poor's 500 index but also many that are tiny and hard to trade. Both those characteristics mean that good active management can add more value in small than in large stocks.

First, a large-cap portfolio of 100 stocks contains a full one-fifth of the S&P and is bound to overlap considerably with competing portfolios. In contrast, a holding of 100 small caps accounts for only one-twentieth of the Russell and probably includes stocks not owned by other institutions.

Second, indexing's cost advantage is greater for large caps than for small. Mirroring the S&P is relatively inexpensive, since the index's components change seldom and, when they do, are easy to buy and sell. The Russell, in contrast, is rebalanced annually, and many of the stocks are very illiquid, with large spreads. So the cost difference between indexing and active management is greater for large caps. Moreover, given the fact that large-cap portfolios tend to hold many of the same stocks and thus get similar returns, expenses play a greater role in differentiating performance.

To circumvent some of the problems of indexing to the Russell 2000, a few small-stock index funds have chosen instead to mirror the S&P's SmallCap 600 (discussed in more detail in Chapter 3). The 600 index comprises slightly larger, more liquid stocks (with no real estate exposure) and has lower turnover. On the other hand, by excluding the tiniest companies, the S&P 600 eliminates a segment that has produced outstanding returns. And though the index's 600 stocks are easier to trade than many in the Russell 2000, managers tracking it need to own 3 times as many shares of each, which critics say takes them right back to square one.

Some experts believe investors can achieve better returns by indexing only the value portion of their portfolio, seeking active managers for the growth part. They reason that returns of growth indexes are dragged down by so-called glamour stocks, whose inflated valuations reflect equally inflated expectations and whose prices, as a result, tend to crater at the slightest hint of bad news. Active managers who have an effective discipline for selling shares can sidestep this problem.

Call Vanguard. Its Extended Market Index Fund invests in the Wilshire 4500, which contains all exchange-traded stocks not included in the S&P 500.
The Extended Market Index Fund, often tacked on to the firm's famed 500 Index Fund to mimic the returns of the entire market, can be used alone as a low-cost way to gain exposure to small stocks. However, it includes many midcaps, and even a few large stocks that aren't in the 500, and so is not a pure small-stock play. Vanguard also offers the Index Small-Cap Fund, which matches the Russell 2000. You might in addition check out Dimensional Fund Advisors' 9-10, 6-10, and small-cap value funds (though they require a $50,000 minimum investment, far higher than Vanguard's). Then there's Charles Schwab's Small Cap Index Fund, which invests in the second 1,000 largest U.S. stocks (excluding investment companies).

As long as we're talking indexing, why not go the whole hog and match the performance of the entire U.S. equity market?
If you have $10,000 to invest, put $7,000 of it in the Vanguard 500 Index Fund and $3,000 in the Extended Market Portfolio. According to Burton Malkiel's classic, *A Random Walk Down*

Wall Street, a similar portfolio has outperformed the S&P 500 since 1973, with lower volatility. How's that for a free lunch? This one step will give you better returns than most of the Hermès-tie-wearing money managers get. Depending on your investment goals and the amount of risk you can tolerate, you may want to raise or lower the small-cap exposure very slightly. You'll also need to decide, when the outperformance of one sector changes the original allocation, whether to trade around and restore it—a process called "rebalancing"—or just let the investment ride. I'll return to this question below, in "To Balance or Not To Balance."

MASTERS OF THEIR DOMAIN

"Some individuals can invest successfully, but most don't have the patience or discipline to really be successful. That's what they are paying us for."
—CHARLES ROYCE *of Royce & Associates*

INDEXING HAS DEFINITE ADVANTAGES. But if you want high performance, not merely low maintenance, it may not be for you. Although actively managed small-cap funds have higher expenses and take more monitoring than index funds, their returns can be greater as well.

Good managers who can exploit the inefficiency of the small-cap market to pick up undervalued treasures should outperform the Russell 2000, the Nasdaq Composite, or any other small-stock index. The catch is that you have to do a little homework to find these whizzes.

What do you look for, and where? Mary Rowland's book has most of the answers. For now, though, here are a few pointers.

Figure out what investment roles you want small-cap funds to play. You may use them to fill specific slots—growth, value, aggressive, contrarian, micro—in your otherwise individual-stock portfolio. Or they may be your only small-cap holdings; in that case, try to cover a range of styles and subgroups, either through a few diversified funds or through several more-specialized ones. Whichever strategy you follow, be sure that the funds you buy will do the jobs you chose them for.

Don't rely on a fund's name to tell you how it will function in your portfolio. Names are marketing tools, and there's no truth-in-labeling law here. For example, 39 percent of Fidelity Blue Chip Growth's assets in the first part of 1995 were in small and medium-sized technology companies, not typical blue-chip fare. And the second-biggest holding in the Legg Mason Value fund is America Online, which trades at almost 400 times earnings (though, to be fair, the manager bought AOL when it was beaten down and wisely held on as the shares soared). Even worse, many funds that include "small cap" in their titles include some pretty large caps in their portfolios.

So look past a fund's name and read up on it in *Morningstar Mutual Funds,* a collection of reports on 1,600 funds published by the well-respected Chicago rating company *(see Resources).* A fund's report indicates such information as its median market cap, how its portfolio is allocated among various investment categories, and, in a short review section, how its manager has been implementing its stated goal. For more details, including what companies the fund holds, the size of its stakes, and comments about its performance, get its semiannual report from the fund company.

Look for good performance over a long period. You want to gauge how a fund performs—both in absolute terms and relative to other funds in the same field—in bad markets as well as good. You'll find this info in Morningstar's newsletters and in the quarterly reports that the fund mails to shareholders. Some funds will be slow and steady; others will vary between stellar and dismal showings. Ask yourself how much volatility you can stomach. If a fund's average five- and ten-year returns are good despite periodic dips and you won't need the money you put in too soon, you may decide to buy it and just lay in a supply of

Maalox. Or you might opt for another fund that's consistently middle of the road and hold the antacid.

Make sure you understand the fund manager's general investment philosophy and are comfortable with it. Professional investors fall into two camps. Some, like the managers at Tweedy Browne, are big fans of spreading around the risk and the wealth; in summer 1998 their American Value fund owned about 250 stocks, only one of which accounted for more than 3 percent of the portfolio's total. Other investors prefer to concentrate their resources; the Janus 20 fund, for instance, has only about—you guessed it—twenty holdings. Big bets often win big; the Janus 20 was one of the best performers in 1998. But concentrated funds can also lose big: From October 1997 to October 1998, the Robertson Stephens Contrarian fund, which had 15 percent of its assets invested in one stock and 36 percent in the mining sector, lost almost 50 percent.

More and more managers are taking the big-bet route, figuring it's the way to become rich and famous (not necessarily in that order). Decide whether you're comfortable with this style: Do you worry more about losing the farm or missing the boat? In any case, you shouldn't own more than one or two funds whose managers can take outsize stakes. Ten percent in one company is extreme (even for sector funds, which focus on one industry group), as is more than 30 percent in a single industry. And concentrated managers should have superb track records picking winners. If you own more than one such fund, make sure they aren't putting your money on the same horse, like tech stocks.

Check the investment policies in a fund's prospectus to see how much latitude the manager is given to concentrate investments, to short stocks, and to use derivatives. Then check fund holdings—detailed in the semiannual reports—to see if he or she actually does any of this. Remember, though, that funds disclose these facts only twice a year; what they do in between is anybody's guess.

Get copies of funds' newsletters. In these publications, managers will often discuss economic issues and the techniques they use in tending to their portfolios. Check whether any of the stock strategies described in the following chapters are utilized and how they are implemented.

Diversify, but don't dilute. You're paying a manager, whom you've supposedly screened carefully, for his expertise, so let it shine through. If you spread your investments among too many funds investing in too many styles and sectors, the effect of any one manager will be diluted. In that case, you might as well save on fees and put the whole shebang in an index fund.

Check expenses. Just because you decide to pay for active management doesn't mean you should get soaked. The higher a fund's expenses, the better it has to perform relative to its benchmark index to make investing in it worthwhile. Look for combined operating costs (administrative, management, and marketing) that are lower than 75 basis points. And go no-load. The load is the sales commission you pay when you buy or sell through a broker and sometimes even when you deal directly with the fund family: Front-end loads are deducted from the amount you invest; back-end loads (also known as *deferred sales charges* or *redemption fees*) are skimmed off the money you take out. Some firms even charge for reinvesting dividends or for transferring money from one fund to another. Any fund with such fees had better have a manager who is the Vermeer of small caps.

Look for a low turnover rate. This refers to the percentage of the portfolio that is traded each year; for instance, a 50 percent turnover indicates that half the fund's holdings change annually. The higher the rate, the higher the transaction costs and capital gains taxes, which reduce your returns. Turnover is particularly important in the small-cap market, where trades tend to be more expensive.

Keep it small, especially when choosing a microcap fund. Any fund can become unwieldy when it becomes too large— even Warren Buffett's Berkshire Hathaway. In spring 1996 Buffett told investors in his enormously successful investment pool that neither he nor his vice chairman would buy Berkshire shares at their current price. Buffet said he felt his fund had grown to the point where performance might begin to suffer.

That point is much lower for small-stock funds. "As a small-cap stock fund gets bigger, it has two choices," says Acorn's Ralph Wanger. "It can own more stocks and risk becoming nothing more than an index fund, or else own larger stocks and become a mid-cap fund."

It's a matter of simple math. Many funds are prohibited by their mandates from owning more than 10 percent of a company, and prudence usually dictates much more modest stakes, particularly in small businesses. A small-cap manager might well keep his or her average investment to 2 percent. Given that the average small stock has a market cap of around $500 million, that comes to $10 million. So a fund like Acorn, with $2 billion to put to work, would have to spread its assets among 200 small stocks.

But could the manager find that many exceptional stocks, and would he or she have the resources to stay on top of them all? Laura Lallos, senior analyst at Morningstar, notes in the January 30, 1996, issue of *Financial World* that the difficulty of researching small companies limits the number that a fund manager can reasonably follow and invest in. In the same article, Bill Nasgovitz, manager of Heartland Value, admits that he and his eight analysts were finding it difficult to do the research needed to put to work all the money flowing into the fund before he closed it to new investors in July 1995 (it has since reopened).

Managers who don't close their funds have two alternatives to expanding the number of companies they invest in. One is to increase the size of their average stake. But that can be risky in the relatively illiquid small-cap market, where it's tough to amass or divest a large block of shares without affecting their price. The other option is to abandon the fund's small-cap focus and look for larger companies.

As an investor, you don't want your small-cap money invested in large stocks, which should already be represented elsewhere in your portfolio. You also don't want to pay an active manager to put together an index fund, nor do you want the fund holding stakes too large to be traded quickly.

Check out the asset size of any fund you're considering. A good rule of thumb—offered by John Bogel Jr., formerly of Quantitative Numeric Advisors—is that the money a fund manages should not exceed its target market cap. By this reckoning, a microcap fund should close when its assets equal $300 million, while one investing in large-cap growth might be able to manage $15 billion or more.

The absolute asset figure, however, may be less important than its relation to the size of the fund's analyst and support staff. Despite a huge asset pool of $4 billion, T. Rowe Price's small-cap New Horizon fund has produced respectable five-year returns because manager John Laporte has twenty to twenty-five analysts and researchers to rely on.

Next, make sure the fund's management is committed to closing its doors before assets get too large for the staffing to support. Bogle Jr., for example, showed he practices what he preaches by shutting off Numeric Investors Growth and Micro Cap funds to new investors at $100 million.

Finally, you want any shutdowns to apply not only to new customers but also to new money from old ones. Additional contributions made by existing investors after a closing can be substantial enough to cause problems. That's especially true if, as often happens, new investors rush to get in before the deadline. When Heartland Value closed after reaching $800 million in assets, it allowed existing investors to increase their stakes; by mid-1996 its assets had grown to $1.5 billion, according to Morningstar. Nasgovitz's fund is still a top performer, but others might founder under such a flood of money.

Players who don't move fast may find all the microcap doors shut: To invest successfully in Lilliputian companies, funds have to stay as lean as supermodels. On the other hand, new microcap funds keep being created. Just hope that there aren't so many that managers can't still pick up plenty of bargains with tweezers.

 Don't buy into a fund immediately before it closes.
In *The New Commonsense Guide to Mutual Funds,* Rowland cites a 1995 *New York Times* article by Timothy Middleton showing that closings are generally followed by downturns in performance. The reason: By the time most managers decide to cut off new investment, they already have more money than they can profitably put to work.

 Do buy when it reopens.
Middleton also points out that managers who close their funds are putting shareholders' interests ahead of their own, since their salaries are based on the size of assets under management. So when managers decide to reopen, it may be because they see opportunities to keep more money at work and more investors happy. Then again, they may be trying to replace money withdrawn by investors dissatisfied with recent substandard performance—check out the funds' returns relative to their sectors.

 Try not to buy any fund immediately before it makes its annual capital-gains distribution to shareholders.
The distribution diminishes the net asset value you just paid for, returning money you wanted invested and making you pay capital-gains taxes on it. It's as though you lent a dollar one day and got it back minus taxes the next. So before you buy in to a fund, check its *record date.* That's the day, usually falling between the end of October and year end, by which you must own shares in order to get a payout. If you find that the record date is near, wait until it passes to make your purchase.

GROWTH AND VALUE

"I think investors, as they're looking at funds, are bet-
ter off to balance between some of the more growth-
oriented funds and some of the more value-oriented
funds, and not really try and say, Is this right time to
get in or the wrong time to get in?"
—CLAUDIA MOTT, *director of small-cap research at Pru-*
dential Securities

PROS CAN MAKE GOOD LIVINGS specializing in either
value or growth. You probably can't. If you want your
small-cap portfolio to work for you in various economic climates, make sure both styles are represented.

Growth and value thrive at different points in the business cycle and under different interest-rate conditions.
The *business cycle* is the period during which the growth
rate of the gross domestic product climbs to a peak, falls to
a bottom, and then moves back up to the base line. At the
beginning of this cycle, when company earnings and
expectations about them are rising, small value stocks tend
to do best; after the peak, as the economy slows, small
emerging-growth companies take the lead. Similarly, a significant drop in interest rates usually presages good times
for value investors, while rising rates mean a small-cap
growth spurt lies ahead. *(For a more detailed discussion of*
the business cycle and interest rates, see Chapter 4.)

Growth and value stocks also complement one another
in the way they perform. Growth companies tend to be
shooting stars: They can rise spectacularly or plummet
sickeningly. Value plays aren't as volatile, since out-of-favor
companies generally trade closer to the worth of their
assets. The downside of low volatility is that these stocks
can be stuck at less-than-inspiring price levels for a long
time. By combining the two styles in your portfolio, you
get growth's momentum tempered with value's stability
and downside protection.

"You don't intend to push out too far on the valuation

spectrum," says Claudia Mott. "You hope that by having a little bit of earnings momentum built in, you're not just looking at very low valuation names that may not necessarily have much to drive them forward."

How you incorporate growth and value in your small-cap portfolio is up to you. If you like choosing your own individual stocks, you may feel more comfortable ferreting out the next Intel than researching turnaround candidates. In that case, leave the value-picking to pros like Charles Royce, whose Micro-Cap fund follows a strict value style and, according to Morningstar, generally produces good returns with low risk. On the other hand, you may be happier selecting companies on the rebound than new up-and-comers. So for your growth investing, you'd enlist a manager like Ron Baron: His Baron Asset fund is on the big side both in terms of total assets managed ($4 billion) and average market cap (just over $1 billion), but it has a low turnover rate for a small-cap growth fund—just 13 percent—and, says Morningstar, "deserves the benefit of the doubt." Or you might want to add both types of managers to your roster, particularly if you do all your small-cap investing through funds. (A list of small-cap growth and value funds appears on page 84.)

BORDER CROSSINGS

"A portfolio isn't efficient without an international component."
—BURTON MALKIEL, *the Chemical Bank Chairman's Professor of Economics at Princeton University*

FOR TRUE DIVERSIFICATION, leave home. Internationalizing your portfolio will stabilize returns while adding some zest. One nation's economy is always peaking when another's is falling off the edge (at least, that was the pattern before the global malaise of 1998, and it's likely to be reprised in the future). If you spread your money around the world, part of it should be working hard all the time.

To gain exposure to foreign economies, the local small

companies are generally better investments than the large blue chips, which tend to operate across borders. A properly diversified international small-cap fund spreads risk among countries, markets, and currencies, Oppenheimer Funds portfolio manager Nicholas Horsley pointed out in a roundtable appearing in the January/February 1998 *Bloomberg Personal Finance.*

Foreign small caps may also represent the last frontier for true stock pickers. Outside the United States, tons of small companies exist that are well managed—and completely neglected by investors. As a result, this market is where that for small U.S. stocks was twenty or thirty years ago: It is enticingly inefficient, enabling someone willing to do the research and shoulder the liquidity risk to gain an edge.

"There's a big world out there," SoGen portfolio manager Jean-Marie Eveillard told the same roundtable. "In the case of international small caps—particularly international small-cap value stocks—there is the opportunity to find extraordinarily undervalued companies."

This, therefore, is an area where a good fund manager can make a real difference. Beyond the three participants in the round table—who included Henrik Strabo, international portfolio manager of American Century Investments, as well as Eveillard and Horsley—some prime practitioners of international small-cap investing are Mike Gerding at Founders Funds and Leah Zell at Acorn. One caveat: Most of these funds have only been around for a few years, so it's hard to judge their managers' track records.

Another consideration to bear in mind in selecting an international small-cap fund is its exposure to emerging markets. Developing countries are expected to outpace the industrialized nations in economic growth over the next decade. That makes the prospects of small companies in the Third World very tempting. But these stocks are also among the riskiest.

"In the emerging markets," Strabo remarked at the

1998 roundtable, "you have to pay attention to macro development, because you could have owned the best stock in Thailand over the last five years and you would still have been down 80 or 90 percent."

 Go international, not global.
They sound the same, but they're not. International funds invest exclusively outside the United States. Global ones can put their assets anywhere in the world—including the U.S., if they see opportunity there. As a result, a global fund could easily duplicate holdings in your domestic funds. That won't give you diversity.

 You can index internationally.
The Vanguard Emerging Markets Stock Index Fund provides exposure to the economies of the developing world by matching a custom benchmark created for the fund by Morgan Stanley. Excluded are countries whose markets are illiquid or that make foreign investment difficult or unprofitable. For a broader international exposure—to developed as well as developing economies—check out Vanguard's Total International. The fund allocates 67.4 percent of its assets to developed markets in Europe, 25.3 percent to developed markets in the Asia-Pacific region, and 7.1 percent to emerging markets.

BACKING THE HOME TEAM

"Why would you send your money anywhere you wouldn't go on vacation?"
—CHRIS BROWNE, *partner in investment advisers Tweedy, Browne Co.*

AN INTERNATIONAL PERSPECTIVE adds diversity to your portfolio. But staying close to home has benefits, too. With small companies, the guy who's there on the ground, ears and eyes open to catch developments as they occur, has a big advantage over the pro slaving at a hot computer hundreds of miles away. Regional funds invest in companies within a few hours' drive of their offices. So the managers and analysts can visit prospects, chat up their neighbors, employees, suppliers, and customers, and read about them in the local papers. With all that info, regionals should be able to dig up overlooked nuggets of intelligence and react to good and bad news before it reaches the Street.

Homestate Pennsylvania Growth fund, for example, has earned top-notch returns with below-average risk by investing primarily in companies located in Pennsylvania, according to Morningstar. This fund finds plenty of investment opportunities in a state with 700-plus public companies and an economy that, at almost $300 billion, is larger than those of many foreign countries. But one of Homestate Growth's greatest strengths, says Morningstar, is manager Kenneth Mertz's ability to search out obscure yet solid local companies that he can buy cheaply.

You can find out if a small-stock fund is a regional specialist the same way you'd determine if it follows a growth or value style: read its *Morningstar Mutual Funds* review, check its aims in the prospectus, and study its holdings in the semiannual report.

FUND MAINTENANCE

"You should make certain that each fund is doing what it is supposed to do."
— MARY ROWLAND, *in* The New Commonsense Guide to Mutual Funds

ONCE YOU PUT TOGETHER a portfolio of small-cap funds whose objectives match yours and whose managers have good records of keeping them on track, your hardest work is over. One of the advantages of investing this way rather than through individual stocks is that it's fairly low-maintenance. But don't just stick the funds' prospectuses and reports in a file and forget them. Nothing is forever—that includes fund managers, management styles, and performance, as well as your goals and portfolio allocations. It's your job to stay on top of changes and take whatever actions they may require. Again, look at Rowland's guide for details. Meanwhile, here are a few tips.

When a manager jumps ship, follow.
Just a suggestion—but give it serious consideration, especially
with small-cap managers. Many of these are inseparable from
their funds: Wanger at Acorn, Nasgovitz at Heartland, Oberweis at Oberweis. Even when the identification is less strong,
the man or woman at the helm is usually responsible for a
fund's track record; you can't be sure the performance will be
the same when someone else starts steering. A friend of mine
just took over the management of a fund. He says he can't figure out for the life of him why the previous manager was holding certain stocks, and it will take him months to get his own
team together.

**The other side of the coin is that by following a
manager you really like, you might get in on the ground floor
of a good thing.**
When Garrett Van Wagoner, the star stock picker of Govett
Smaller Companies, left that fund to set up his own at the
beginning of 1996, many investors moved with him. During the
first half of that year, the defectors had reason to rejoice: Van
Wagoner's young Emerging Growth fund returned more than
49 percent, making it the best-performing small-company
growth fund, according to *Barron's*. Govett, meanwhile, fell into
the lowest percentile of all funds.

Van Wagoner has since suffered setbacks, dropping more
than 20 percent in 1997, as the market turned against his concentrated, tech-heavy style of investing. By 1999 he was back
on top with two funds ranked in the top five. So, all in all, it pays
to keep on top of who's coming and going, when and where.
You can do that by subscribing to a newsletter like *Morningstar
Investor* or *The No-Load Fund Investor (see Resources)*.

**Look in a fund's annual report for its performance stats,
both for the current year and for the past ten years.**
Compare this year's figure with the returns of a benchmark like
the Russell 2000, which should be included in the report. Make
a similar comparison with the fund's peer group; Lipper Analyt-

ical Services, *The Wall Street Journal,* and *Barron's* all publish performance statistics for style and segment groups. Then turn to
the historical performance. You'd like to see steady or improv-
ing numbers.

 But check for patterns, too.

As I've said before, different types of stocks do better in different
environments. Make sure your fund's performance is consistent
with its style, and that at least some of your other holdings
show complementary patterns.

   Read your newspaper's stock pages. If you own a fund that
invests heavily in one sector, check how those stocks are doing,
then compare your fund's performance. If, over a few months,
the individual stocks are booming and the fund is stagnant,
something's wrong. The unfortunate souls who owned Steadman Technology Growth in 1995, for instance, must have won-
dered if they'd warped into a parallel market. Although tech
stocks, which make up a large part of Steadman's portfolio,
soared in the first part of the year, the fund's returns were negative. Definitely time for investors to head for the door—if they
weren't halfway through already.

 **See what your fund managers have to say for them-
selves. They all have a chance to explain their performance in
the annual and semiannual reports.**

Look for a candid appraisal, including an indication of what to
expect from the market and their probable responses. In addition, some funds, such as those in the Heartland, Robertson
Stephens, and Founders families, equip their 800 numbers
with recorded messages in which the managers discuss their
takes on the economy and what they're doing to adapt to any
changes they foresee. Listen in to determine if the explana-
tions make sense to you and if you agree with the general
investment philosophy expressed. This is also a good way to
check for changes in viewpoint that could indicate "style slippage," coming up next.

Don't assume that a fund is going to stay in the slot you bought it to fill.

Small-cap funds with too much investment money flowing in often start loading up on mid- or even large-cap stocks. Managers may drift to whatever style or sector is currently hottest. "Style slippage" would be fine if you were doing all your stock investing through one fund and just wanted to get the best returns currently available. But it is a headache if you buy specific funds to play specific roles in your portfolio—whether to provide general small-cap exposure or to specialize in a segment such as value or growth.

 Check a fund's holdings in its annual report.

If you bought it for the manager's domestic small-company focus and its portfolio contains IBM, Microsoft, and Finnish telecommunications giant Nokia, pull out. Stocks like those may boost the fund's returns, but they don't do anything for your diversification. And they could duplicate other of your holdings if you also own large-cap domestic and international funds.

 Read the proxy statements.

When funds want to change investment policies—raise market cap, leverage, add derivatives, increase fees—they have to spell out the proposal in one of these statements, so that shareholders can vote on it. If you don't like a proposed change and it passes, you can vote again, with your feet, by moving your money to another fund.

TO BALANCE
OR NOT TO BALANCE

"Every crowd has a silver lining."
—P.T. BARNUM

IN SETTING UP A DIVERSIFIED PORTFOLIO you allocate a certain percentage of your funds to each of the styles and segments you want represented; for instance, as I noted on pages 64–65, you might want to duplicate the performance of the entire market by putting 70 percent of your money in Vanguard's 500 Index Fund and 30 percent in its Extended Market Index Fund. But one reason you diversify is that you expect different types of investments to perform differently: small growth stocks will wipe the floor with small value one year, and the next they'll both be flattened by large consumer companies. Such outperformance by one sector in your portfolio is going to upset the balance of styles you started with. Going back to those index funds, if smaller stocks do much better than large ones, your 70/30 allocation could easily become 50/50.

What should you do about the unbalancing? You have a choice: let your profits run or restore your original allocation. Intuition says run with it. After all, you risk throwing good money after bad if you move assets from a strong manager or market sector to a weak one—not to mention the taxes you must pay when you take your capital gains. But there are advantages to rebalancing. It keeps your portfolio diversified, and it exploits market cyclicity—the out-of-favor style or sector that lagged one year often takes off the next. If you rebalance rigorously, you'll be buying low and selling high, just like a good contrarian.

◆ If you're a rebalancer, sit down at least once a year with your fund statement or statements; figure out what percentage of your portfolio each sector or style represents. Then compare those figures with your ideal distribution.
If they're different, sell some shares in the funds that have grown beyond their allocations and buy more in the ones that have shrunk below theirs. In the indexing example above, you could restore the 70/30 distribution by selling part of your Extended Market Index investment and using the proceeds to buy more of the Index 500 fund.

But my advice to a pure indexer is, don't lose sleep over this. Indexing isn't supposed to exercise your gray cells. If you don't need to draw on your investments for several years, leave your portfolio alone. As the goals you're saving for near, start moving money from small stocks into larger stocks and bonds. This isn't science, but by reducing your small-cap exposure—and stock exposure in general—you increase the odds that the cash to pay for fast-approaching expenses will be there when you need it.

STRESS TESTS

"As far as the laws of mathematics refer to reality, they are not certain, and as far as they are certain, they do not refer to reality."
—ALBERT EINSTEIN

INSTITUTIONAL INVESTORS LOVE to quantify things—for instance, how much money they'd lose if the market looped back to 1987 or Klingons invaded Earth. That's why they love stress testing. It allows them to make official-sounding statements like "I can be 73.2 percent certain that the maximum one-week loss my portfolio will sustain is 23.8 percent." Cool.

I don't know about you, but I don't really need to know my profit and loss in seventy-five different scenarios. I'd rather spend the time on stock research or—better still—with my family. (And, hey, the Long-Term Capital Management debacle demonstrated that a little common sense can be better protection than the rocket science of Nobel-winning propeller heads.) However, there is a quick and dirty version of the stress test that I do find useful: You just estimate what would happen under a worst-case scenario if all your fund managers decided to max-out their allowable sector bets.

The first thing to look at is how exposed your entire stock allocation could leave you. Take out your latest statement and a calculator. Write down the dollar value of all your stock funds and add them together to get the total you have invested in equities. Now, what's the worst that could happen? We probably can't beat the 50 percent drop in the market between 1973 and 1974. To see how much you'd lose in a similar meltdown, multiply your total stock figure by 0.5. Could you absorb a loss of that size while you wait for stocks to recover? Your answer will depend on your other investments and how soon the bills you're saving for, like college tuition, will need to be paid. If you couldn't tough out the waiting period, consider allocating more of your savings to principal-conserving investments such as bonds.

Next, take a look at your managers' sector bets. This requires a little more work. For each fund in your portfolio, determine from the prospectus the maximum percentage of assets the manager can allocate to any one sector, then multiply the dollar amount of your position in the fund by that percentage. For instance, if the manager of a fund in which you've invested $100,000 is allowed 20 percent concentrations, your maximum sector exposure for that fund would be $20,000. Add together the figures you get, and the result is your dollar exposure if all your funds' managers decide to take their maximum allowable stakes in the same sector.

Again, what's the worst that could happen to you in, say, four months? Well, that's how long it took computer stocks to drop 30 percent in 1995. So to determine the dollar loss you'd suffer in a worst-case scenario, multiply your sector dollar exposure by 0.3. In my example, that one fund investment would lose $6,000.

If right about now your palms are sweaty and you're short of breath, calm down. Just because your fund managers can take maximum sector stakes doesn't mean they will, or that they'll all max-out the same sector at the same time (although you might consider the fallout should other sectors tank in sympathy). Second, big sector bets pose more of a danger in funds that have large asset pools and portfolios, and so can't move in and out of stocks as quickly as nimble smaller funds can. Third, at certain times in the business cycle, you might actually want a fund to be concentrated in very defensive industries, such as food and drugs.

Still, as I've said earlier, you shouldn't own more than one or two funds whose managers are allowed to take outsize stakes in one sector. The bottom line is that you don't want to get badly hurt. And though trading and sector bets can score big in the short run, which determines most portfolio managers' salaries, they don't pay off over the long term—*your* horizon.

For most of your small-cap investments, you should be looking at a twenty-year time frame. Over periods like that, three things seem to generate the best returns, and none of them is trading. The first is the earnings performance of individual companies; with a horizon of twenty years, I'd put my money on a fundamentals guy over a trader. The second element is diversification—not excessive, just owning a broad-enough cross-section of the market to reduce risk and to benefit from whichever area of the economy is prospering. The third and last is minimizing expenses: the fewer unnecessary trades a fund manager makes, the better your returns will be.

SOME SUGGESTIONS

WHEN THE SMALL-AND MICROCAP SECTORS are hot, funds pop up to take advantage of investor enthusiasm. In the boxes on the following two pages, I've listed a few funds that have reasonable track records or whose managers have proved themselves with similar styles elsewhere. To help you choose which ones to fill which slots in your portfolio, I've broken them down by style and segment. But don't take my word for any of them. Do your own research: Look in *Morningstar Mutual Funds*, read the fund prospectuses, scan some of the newsletters and Web sites listed in the "Resources" section. Then, once you've committed your money, be sure to monitor your choices' performance in the newspaper, online, and in the funds' own reports.

THIS CHAPTER HAS PRESENTED the ground rules for investing in funds in general and in small-cap funds in particular. You might decide that this is the way to go

SMALL-CAP VALUE FUNDS

FUND NAME	5-YEAR RETURN AS OF 12/31/98*	PHONE
Berger Small Cap Value Inst	18.69	800-551-5849
Longleaf Partners Small-Cap	18.50	800-445-9469
Barr Rosenberg US Sm Cap Ins	18.26	800-447-3332
Van Kampen Amer Value A	17.38	800-341-2911
Wachovia Special Values A	17.01	800-922-9008

* AFTER EXPENSES; NOT INCLUDING LOADS

SMALL-CAP GROWTH FUNDS

FUND NAME	5-YEAR RETURN AS OF 12/31/98*	PHONE
Lord Abbett Developing Gr A	21.78	800-821-5129
Baron Asset	19.86	800-992-2766
BT Investment Small Cap	19.43	800-730-1313
BlackRock Small Cap Grth Is	19.24	800-227-7236
Value Line Spec Situations	19.11	800-223-0818

* AFTER EXPENSES; NOT INCLUDING LOADS

SMALL-CAP BLEND FUNDS

FUND NAME	5-YEAR RETURN AS OF 12/31/98*	PHONE
Weitz Hickory	23.81	800-232-4161
Safeco Growth No Load	19.00	800-426-6730
PIMCo Micro Cap Growth Insti	17.50	800-426-0107
Schroder U.S. Smaller Co Inv	17.00	212-641-3800
Oak Ridge Growth	17.00	800-407-7298

* AFTER EXPENSES; NOT INCLUDING LOADS

SOURCE: (TOP, MIDDLE, BOTTOM) MORNINGSTAR

INTERNATIONAL SMALL-CAP FUNDS

FUND NAME	5-YEAR RETURN AS OF 12/31/98*	PHONE
SoGen Overseas A	7.83	800-334-2143
ONE Fund International	6.60	800-480-4111
MSDW Insti Intl Small Cap A	5.52	800-843-3326
Templeton Foreign Sm Co	5.28	800-387-0830
Montgomery Intl Small Cap R	4.09	800-572-3863

* AFTER EXPENSES; NOT INCLUDING LOADS

SMALL-CAP INDEX FUNDS

FUND NAME (NOT RANKED)	PHONE
Vanguard Index Ext. Market (Wilshire 4500)	800-662-7447
Vanguard Index Small Cap (Russell 2000)	800-662-7447
Rydex OTC (NASDAQ Composite)	800-820-0888
DFA 6-10 (small and microcap)	310-395-8005
DFA 9-10 (microcap)	310-395-8005
Schwab Small Cap Index Fund	800-435-4000
Federated Mini-Cap (Russell 2000)	800-341-7400

with your entire small-company portfolio. Or you might want to do some of your own stock picking. Either way, you will find information to help you in the following chapters. For individual stock investors, there's advice on putting together a list of candidates, deciding which to buy when, and biting the bullet when it comes time to prune your portfolio. Those choosing to stick with funds can use the tips on assembling and tending to an individual small-stock portfolio to understand how fund managers operate.

CHAPTER

BUYING
Individual
Stocks

LL RIGHT. YOU NOW know that to boost your portfolio's long-term performance and stabilize returns you should mix in small-cap companies. The previous chapter discussed using mutual funds for that purpose. Here, the focus shifts to individual stocks—which to buy when, and how long to hold them. These are crucial considerations for people ready to assemble their own small-cap stock portfolios. But the information is important even for fund-only investors. Don't forget—when you buy a fund, you are authorizing someone else to buy and sell individual stocks for you. Knowing how that's done makes you a smarter consumer.

This chapter outlines a general plan for creating a portfolio of small-cap stocks and maintaining it through rebalancing and disciplined selling. Chapter 4 takes the process one step further, describing strategies for ensuring that you buy at fair prices and at the right times.

INVEST, DON'T SPECULATE

"I like to tell a story about a man who wants to walk his dog across the park. He should have the sense to stay on the walkway, but the dog is going to wander off to one side of the path to chase a butterfly or to the other to get a sniff of something. The path is the shortest route from point A to point B, but if he assumes that the dog knows a better way, he'll wear himself out . . . . The path, of course, is earnings, and the dog is all of the things you hear in the press that make you want to be a trader."

—BILL BERGER, *retired manager of the Berger Funds*

SMALL STOCKS BRING OUT the speculator in people. Mention them at a cocktail party, and someone's sure to start talking up a miracle company: It's working on a process to turn swamp water into clean, edible fuel and is about to go public. It has no product or earnings yet, but it could dominate the $1 trillion energy market.

Yeah, and you could hit the lottery. Still, I wouldn't call filling out the "Pick 6" every week a savings plan.

This book isn't about taking a one-in-a-million chance to hit it big. It's about maximizing investment returns while minimizing risks. That means putting together a small portfolio of stocks in small, stable companies whose prospects you like and that you feel comfortable living with for a while. For that you need strategy, not speculation.

THE STRATEGY: BUY TO HOLD

"It's our experience over the years that really the best strategy is to remain fully invested and ride the cycle up and ride the cycle down. Hopefully, over a long period of time, you wind up with average returns higher than the Dow indexes. And that's really what we're looking to do, not to try and pick exactly when it's going to go up and go down."
—JIM OBERWEIS JR., *portfolio manager of the Oberweis funds*

WHY INVEST FOR THE LONG HAUL? Wouldn't you be better off jumping in and out, buying at the lows, selling off at the peaks?

Nope.

First, most of us would probably jump when we shouldn't—a very expensive misstep. Peter Lynch—celebrated former manager of the Fidelity, now in the front office as vice chairman of Fidelity Management and Research—recently told a group of journalists that if you had invested $1,000 in 1978 and just sat back, your money would have grown to $21,750 by the end of 1997. But if you had missed the best fifteen months during that period, your investment would be worth only $6,010. And chances are, if you'd done a lot of trading in and out of the market, at least some of those optimal months would have found you sitting on the sidelines.

Market timing is a tough trick even for pros like Jim Oberweis Jr. "Although sometimes we may guess what the markets are going to do, it is only that," he says. "And we wouldn't act on that, and we wouldn't invest on that. We think market timing over any substantial period of time is virtually impossible. I know of no one who has done it over any long period of time successfully. And we would urge investors against doing that."

The second reason to buy and stay put is that high turnover is highly expensive. *Turnover* refers to the percentage of your portfolio that changes over a particular period; for instance, if you swap around half of your holdings in a year, your annual turnover is 50 percent. This can present a problem, since large chunks of any profits made from those swaps are eaten up by capital-gains taxes— unless you're investing in a tax-advantaged account like a 401(k)—and in commissions and spreads. This is especially true when you're dealing with small-cap and micro-cap stocks. Those markets are relatively illiquid, and the volume of trading is small. As a result, spreads are wide and trading quickly in and out of a company almost impossible. Sellers of lesser-known microcaps can wait days to find buyers, and then they may have to dole out their shares over long stretches of time to keep from wrecking the price.

"One of the problems of a small-stock portfolio is that trading costs are very high—not only commissions but your effect on the price when you try to buy or sell 5 percent of a company," Ralph Wanger, manager of Acorn Fund, says in a February 1995 interview with *Kiplinger's* magazine.

The problems of accumulating or unloading large stakes in small stocks are important considerations for funds, even relatively small ones. Consider the case of Pulaski Furniture Corp., described by Preston Athey, manager of the T. Rowe Price Small Cap Value Fund, in a February 1995 *U.S. News & World Report* article. At the beginning of 1995, Athey's position in Pulaski, a Virginia furniture maker, was worth about $2 million. That represented a 17 percent gain since 1991, when the manager started buying the shares. If Athey had decided to realize his profit, could he have just dumped the company and counted his cash? Hardly. The fund's 100,000 shares represented more than three weeks of the stock's average trading volume. Athey would have had to parcel them out over a month or more. Because of such problems, and to control costs, he keeps his fund's turnover to a low annual rate of about 20 percent.

That should be your goal, too. You'll probably never have to worry, as Athey does, about moving the market with your purchases and sales. Still, the low liquidity of small caps can cramp your trading style, widening spreads and perhaps preventing you from buying or selling when you wish at the price you want.

The buy-and-hold approach avoids the pitfalls of trading costs, illiquid stocks, and mistimed leaps. "The whole point of investing is to buy good stocks, lock them up for ten years, and wind up with more money than you started with," says Bill Berger.

But that entails living with your picks for a long time. Along the way, you're sure to encounter some rocky periods. Stocks are volatile, and investors in the smallest companies suffer through the most extreme price moves. To weather the ups and downs, you must have faith in your selections.

"Acorn has a 20 to 25 percent turnover rate, which means that we hold stocks four to five years," Wanger says in the *Kiplinger's* interview. "If you are going to hold a stock that long, you need a reason to think that the stock will do better than average over a very long period of time."

And your reason had better be a lot more solid than assurances from your drinking buddies that a company is going to be the next Microsoft. Finding true distance runners involves research, which takes time and patience. You might wind up passing on a long shot that goes on to win big, but you'll also avoid the ones that throw their riders on the turn or fade in the stretch.

"Invest in haste, repent at leisure," says Robert Rodriguez, manager of First Pacific Advisors' Capital and New

Income funds, adding, "There's always another streetcar coming along."

Rodriguez is a good man to listen to: FPA Capital has been one of the highest-ranking funds over the past ten years, and, according to mutual fund rating company Morningstar, New Income has some of the best returns of any bond fund, along with very low risk.

WHAT TO DO

"I like [Warren] Buffett's theory: When you're born, you get a card with twenty investment decisions, and each time you make one, you get a punch, so you'd better make them count."
—ROBERT RODRIGUEZ

HERE'S THE BASIC PLAN (details come later). First, decide what portion of your small-cap holdings you want to be individual stocks, as opposed to mutual funds. Remember what I said at the end of Chapter 1: If you can't afford to buy shares in at least twenty small companies, do the lion's share—say, 70 percent—of your investing in this sector through funds. Once you've decided how many stocks you're going to look for, create a list of companies that have solid fundamentals and for which you have an edge. By edge, I mean that you understand their businesses and their prospects better than the average investor does. Then, using information from sources such as financial statements (which you can download from the Internet), winnow this collection down to twenty-plus names you really like. If that seems too few, remember that the best analysts in the world focus on a small number of companies, usually in a single industry. Chances are you can't efficiently follow more—or more diverse—stocks than they can. Rodriguez, for one, prefers to hold between twenty-five and thirty companies and adds only one to five new ones a year to his portfolio. "I don't see how anybody can follow fifty to one hundred companies," he says.

"What's more conservative?" asks Robert Sanborn, manager of the aggressive-growth Oakmark fund, whose long-term record Morningstar says is among the best out there. "Owning twenty stocks in businesses you understand that are priced right and have good management? Or owning five hundred stocks in many businesses that you don't understand, many of which are run by rotten people and many of which are priced insanely?"

A few very successful stocks are all you need, anyway. In a 1993 letter to shareholders, Acorn Fund's Ralph Wanger observed that just three great picks had made the difference for him between mediocre and outstanding results: Houston Oil & Minerals, an obscure exploration company that was added to Acorn's portfolio in 1973 and rose by a factor of 24, seeing Wanger through the ruinous 1973–74 bear market; Cray Research, in which he purchased a $1.5 million stake in 1978 that he ultimately sold for $20 million; and International Game Technology, a block of whose shares, picked up in 1988 for $5 million, was worth $80 million by mid-1995. Concluded Wanger: "It's a little bit like baseball. Babe Ruth hit a lot of home runs, even though he struck out a lot. The big winners can really carry the team to victory."

Once you have your own twenty-plus potential sluggers, your next step is to find out as much as possible about them. That means calling the companies, visiting, getting on mailing lists, and trolling the Internet. The information you gather during this research will help you determine which of your prospects are fully valued or overpriced and which are cheap.

Cheap is what you're looking for. Remember, not every good company is a good stock. The business can be sound and the management solid, but if the market has already factored in all those pluses, the share price has nowhere to go. Your job is to hunt for good companies that haven't yet been fully recognized as such. The efficient-market gang would say they don't exist, or at least are very rare. But even those guys would admit that you have a better chance of finding unmined lodes among companies like Javelin Systems, which designs and sells touch-screen computers for retail and restaurants and is followed by just one analyst, than among the market's Intels, which are scrutinized by more than fifty analysts each.

Finally, for every stock you decide to put money into, you should create a dossier, including a statement explaining why you bought it and what would make you sell. You'll review these notes periodically to see whether you need to rebalance your portfolio.

That's the general project. Now for some specific tips on how to implement it.

LOOKING FOR IDEAS

"I take an eclectic approach to finding new ideas. I go to lots of trade shows and read scads of trade journals. For instance, I spent three days last week at InterOp, the [computer] networking show in Las Vegas. Elvis and I were walking the floor. I also cull lots of IPO prospectuses and sometimes go to several road shows a day."

—From an April 1995 interview in Barron's *with* GARRETT VAN WAGONER, *who at the time managed the Govett Smaller Companies fund and now runs his own group of funds*

INVESTMENT IDEAS ARE all around you: in the industrial park across town, at the trade show you visit for business, in your local newspaper and the industry newsletters and journals your company subscribes to, even at the hardware store where you shop. Once you start looking, you can't miss them. If those sources don't inspire you, here are some other ways to work up a list of possible purchases:

◆ **Study the semiannual reports of some small-cap mutual funds with good performance records to find out what they hold.** Good places to search are top value and growth funds like Long-Leaf Partners Small Cap and Acorn—

though both are closed to new investors, you can still profit from the managers' expertise. *(For other places to prospect, see Chapter 2, page 84.)*

◆ **Call regional brokerages for leads.** Many of these firms specialize in small companies that operate in their parts of the country and often escape Wall Street's radar screens. The brokers will be happy to earn a commission on any purchase they help you identify. A list of regional brokers and their phone numbers appears in Resources.

◆ **Quiz people working at firms in fields in which you have an interest.** That's what Garrett Van Wagoner does, according to Peter Kris, managing director of the Van Wagoner funds: "[Garrett] wants to know what the new ideas are, who is starting up new firms, if they are capable managers, and who their competitors are likely to be."

◆ **Subscribe to *The Red Chip Review* and scan the *Value Line Investment Survey* at your library.** The *Review* is a weekly newsletter that covers the small- and microcap markets and profiles individual companies. The *Survey* is a compendium of one-page company reports published by Value Line, an investment advisory service that ranks stocks according to safety and their projected performance over the next six to twelve months *(see Resources)*.

◆ **Put your money where your expertise is.** Peter Lynch told me that he questions why people who know restaurants insist on buying options on biotechnology stocks. Lynch points out that investors working in the food industry have in recent years been perfectly placed to pick the 100- and 50-baggers—stocks, like Kentucky Fried Chicken and Brinker International's Chili's, that appreciate to 100 or 50 times their purchase price—out of the mass of failures. "You would have been able to tell the difference," he says, "between the real deal and some other restaurant that's a piece of junk: Its rents are too high. The menu's too complicated. It has bad locations. Forget it, there's no one in the stores."

SORTING AND SIFTING:
THE S&P PLAN

"You want to own tennis balls, not eggs, because tennis balls bounce."
—BILL BERGER

TO TURN YOUR INVESTMENT ideas into that list of twenty-plus solid small-cap prospects you need to find out about the companies behind the ideas. Stint the research at this point, and you risk disaster.

What if you don't have the time, skill, or patience for financial analysis? Get pros to do some of the legwork for you. That doesn't mean laying out $100 an hour. By limiting your field to stocks covered by Standard & Poor's Corp., you're essentially hiring a stable of well-trained researchers and analysts at far less than minimum wage. Since the S&P companies are all closely followed, you'll miss out on the truly buried treasure, but if your analytical skills aren't well honed, those stocks aren't for you, anyway.

To enlist S&P's help, all you need to do is shell out about $25 for the annual *Standard & Poor's SmallCap 600 Guide*. The S&P 600 is an index of 600 small companies, in the 50th to 83rd percentile in terms of market value. The stocks must be listed on one of the exchanges or Nasdaq; be priced above $1; and meet various ownership, seasoning, spread, volume, and financial criteria—the companies can't be in bankruptcy, for example.

Many small stocks are eliminated from the index by the screening process. Microcaps in the lowest 17 percent in terms of market cap ($0 to around $150 million, in 1998) are omitted as well. For stocks that aren't included, you might be able to find information at the *Bloomberg Personal Finance* Web site (www.Bloomberg.com) or in America Online's personal finance section. For all the companies that *are* in the index, the guide contains two-page research reports that provide overviews of their strengths and weaknesses, including up to ten years of financial data. The info may be slightly out-of-date by the time the guide is published. If you need more-current data, you can download an updated report from its Internet site (www.stockinfo.-standardpoor.com) or from Multex Investor Network (www.multexinvestor.com). Your broker might also be able to get you reports for free.

The reports are in alphabetical order, so looking up a prospect by name is a cinch. Or you might want to use the book for bedtime reading, boning up on a different company each night before you go to sleep (I bought a copy for a friend, and he keeps it in his bathroom).

It's a little harder to troll the guide for small companies in a particular region or business, as you might want to do if you're using it as a source of ideas. To help you out, we've broken down the six hundred companies by industry and state and presented the lists in the Appendix, providing Internet addresses for companies with sites as of May 6, 1999.

BESIDES PRICE, RATIO, AND financial-statement data and analysis, the S&P guide provides summaries of a company's business, operation, and past stock performance, as well as quantitative evaluations of the stock's prospects and attractiveness as an investment. A helpful introduction explains what the various numbers, letters, and symbols in the reports mean and gives useful definitions of financial terms and ratios.

The S&P pros have read and analyzed the raw financial documents for you and packaged the essentials into easy-to-digest bites. This doesn't absolve you from doing your own research, though, even if all your prospects meet the S&P criteria and are in the book. Your journal entries should include additional information that you must get off your duff to find. You'll need to go to primary sources, such as the financial reports and proxy statements described below, for more recent data, to cross-check conclusions, and to fill in the reports' outlines. That said, the guide gives you a good start, enabling you to pick out the companies on which you want to spend your research time.

How do you use the information in a guide report? If you want to do a thorough balance-sheet analysis, including evaluating the data and ratios relative to the norms for the company's industry, I'd suggest a little book called *The Guide to Understanding Financial Statements,* by Geza Szurovy and S. B. Costales, or the famous *Security Analysis,* by Benjamin Graham and David Dodd. In addition, any library should have several reference books. Even an old accounting text from a yard sale would probably give you the basics.

Meanwhile, here are some quick pointers, including what professionals such as Bill Berger, the Heartland funds' Bill Nasgovitz, and Jim Oberweis want to see. Remember, though, the criteria aren't foolproof. If they were, I'd have better things to do than write this book.

READING THE REPORTS

"Accounting's important, but people ought to learn how to play bridge or poker. The stock market is very similar to seven-card stud poker. You look around the table and decide, 'That guy has nothing. I have a straight.' Then out of nowhere come four eights. There were three in the hole. That's the preparation [you need for investing]."

—PETER LYNCH, *former manager of Fidelity Magellan fund in an interview with Christopher Graja*

HOW YOU READ A PARTICULAR company's report in the guide depends in part on what type of business you believe it is. You should be looking for two types: good businesses you can buy at great prices and great businesses you can pick up at good prices—in other words, fairly priced, quality growth and value stocks.

Some criteria are equally valid for both growth and value companies, though possibly more pertinent to one group than the other. For instance, professional investors and managers seem to agree that any prospect—small or large, growth or value—should show a history of earnings. "I simply refuse to buy a small stock unless it has earnings," says Doug Marx, a broker for investment advisory firm Warner Group in Sioux City, Iowa.

Most pros also seek a record of recurring increases. "We look for earnings acceleration—this quarter compared to the same quarter of the last year, and this quarter compared to the previous quarter. We like to see both of those," says Oberweis. "I also look at the revenues and then compare all of this to the price you're paying for the stock to make sure what you're doing is reasonable."

The pattern may not be as clear-cut for value stocks. Many of these are fallen growth stocks and could show a recent or current decline in income. You'll be hoping that the dip is just temporary and searching for signs of an earnings rebound.

Some more research tips that apply across the whole small-cap sector:

Check out the Quantitative Evaluations section, particularly the Outlook ranking, which represents a recommendation to buy, hold, or sell. You've gone to the S&P guide for the experts' help, and here is where they really deliver. Based on S&P's quantitative models and market data, the items in this section indicate the opinions about the stock held by the service's analysts, as well as by investors in general and by company insiders in particular. They're good guideposts. But always make up your own mind—it's your money that will go down the drain if the experts are wrong.

Take advantage of S&P's ratio analysis. These figures, found in the Per Share and Balance Sheet sections, are proportions that you can (and should) calculate yourself later from the financial data in a company's statements. Having pros do the work for you at this stage, though, is a convenient shortcut. All of the ratios are important, but none is essential. Remember, small and microcap companies almost have to have something wrong with them, particularly if they're value stocks. So a poor showing in one area shouldn't be a knockout blow but rather a warning, indicating a weakness to watch carefully.

◆ **ROE.** Bill Berger stresses the importance of strong *return on equity* (calculated by dividing average common equity into income net of preferred dividends). This indicates that management is getting a real bang out of the bucks stockholders like you give it.

Berger's emphasis is shared by Bob Barker, the head of investment firm Barker Lee & Co. "A stock sells essentially on its earnings," Barker said in a February 1996 episode of *Adam Smith's Money World*. "If you can find a company with a high rate of return—therefore, earnings on the capital it has—and a strong growth trend, you know that the stock is going to perform with the growth of the business."

Berger, a self-proclaimed chicken who doesn't "want to be up all night," likes to see an ROE of at least 20 percent. This is more than many small companies can deliver; you may want to set your sights a little lower—say, 15 percent.

◆ **ROA.** But you don't want attractive returns on equity that are generated by leveraging earnings. To guard against this, look at the company's *return on assets* (assets divided into net income). A low ROA (10 percent or less) might indicate that management has produced a high ROE by deriving a lion's share of earnings from assets funded with loans and bond issues rather than stock sales. That's not good news for investors. As Berger puts it, "Who needs a company that borrows a lot of money?" That's especially true of small companies, which must borrow at far higher rates of interest than big ones like Disney, which in 1993 issued 100-year bonds at an interest rate just slightly higher than that for 30-Year Treasuries.

◆ **Payout ratio.** A company's *payout ratio* is the percentage of its earnings that it distributes as dividends. Sixty to 80 percent should be the max. Anything above this would be too hard for a value company to sustain, and a real growth company should be able to make you a bigger profit by pouring its revenues back into its business than you could make yourself by investing its dividends.

Combining the payout ratio with the ROE produces another number that is incredibly important for buy-and-hold investors: the sustainable-earnings-growth rate. This is the rate at which a company can be expected to grow its profits over the long haul; since share price follows earnings, it gives you an idea of how much return your investment could generate. You calculate sustainable earnings growth by subtracting the payout ratio from one—to get the company's earnings-retention rate—then multiplying this figure by the ROE. The resulting percentage should be slightly higher than the long-term return you hope to earn on the stock, say, 15 to 20 percent. Value companies, because they have generally had operational problems, tend to have low sustainable earnings. This may be why Buffett, a committed buy-and-holder, avoids deep value plays.

◆ **Current ratio.** Will the company be able to pay its bills in the short term? The answer depends on its liquidity, which is measured by the *current ratio*. This is calculated by dividing *current liabilities* (the debts coming due within one year) into *current assets* (assets expected to be cashed in or used up producing revenue during the year). You'd like to see a ratio of around 1 or 1.5, indicating more than enough assets to cover obligations. This is particularly important for a value play, which might be in the process of clawing its way back to profitability.

On the other hand, too high a current ratio is not great. The company should be using its funds to grow, not just socking them away against expenses. One of Kirk Kerkorian's major beefs against Chrysler in his early-1996 stockholder campaign was the size of its cash holdings, which had risen from $1.5 billion in 1990 to $5.5 billion by 1995.

Under Balance Sheet Data, check *cash* and *cash flow*. The first is money in the bank—hard cash and government and other marketable securities. The second is net income plus depreciation, depletion, and amortization. Warren Buffett learned the value of both in high school, according to John Train's *The Money Masters.* The young Buffett bought a pinball machine for $25. At the end of the first day, there was $4 in the coin box. If you find businesses with cash flow like that, you'll be rich, too.

But until you discover your own money machine, look for cash and cash flow that are trending up. Value investor Bill Nasgovitz has a tougher requirement: He wants the cash number to be larger than the company's market cap (also shown in the report, under Key Stock Statistics). Stocks that measure up are available, he claims, although "not as much in a bull market . . . as [in] a big bear market."

Also in the Balance Sheet section of the report, review the past six years of liability and equity figures. "One of the classic mistakes [occurs when] people see a bunch of depressed stocks that have all gone from 50 to 6," Lynch told me. "Why don't they buy the one that has $150 million in cash and no debt? They're all losing money, but one has staying power for the next four years."

Benjamin Graham, the father of value investing, required that a company's current liabilities added to its long-term debt be less than its *book value*—its total assets net of liabilities and intangible assets, such as goodwill. (Multiply the figure under Per Share Data by shares outstanding to make the comparison.) That's still a good guideline. The point is, any company you invest in should be able to honor its obligations in hard times.

Small caps, in particular, have enough problems in slow economies without being burdened with a high level of debt. "Small companies can stub their toes," Nasgovitz explained on the February 1996 "Adam Smith's Money World." "One customer might account for 25 percent of their business. So if they get a downturn in orders, do they have the financial . . . capacity to withstand a downturn?"

William O'Neil, author of *How to Make Money in Stocks* and founder of the *Investor's Business Daily (IBD)* newspaper, adds that firms with a lot of debt can get clobbered during periods of high interest rates. He feels that the lower a company's ratio of debt to equity, the better and safer it is.

He also likes to see reductions in debt over a few years.

John Dorfman—an analyst with the Kemper-Dreman funds who is also a guest columnist for *Bloomberg Personal Finance* magazine—studied low-debt stocks from 1987 to 1997. He found that in a tough economic environment such as the 1990s, these stocks fell just 2.3 percent while shares of more leveraged companies were dropping 21.3 percent.

Another liability measure is debt as a percent of capital (found in the Ratio section). For companies held by Nasgovitz's Heartland funds, the average is 19 percent; those in Charles Royce's Premier, also a value fund, average 16.6 percent.

Look for a good story. The numbers and ratios tell you with certainty only where a company has been and is now, not where it will be in a year. For that, you want to see something in its Profile and Business Summary—a new product, new management, new market—that promises to fuel its growth or, in the case of a value stock, turn the business around. A catalyst is particularly important in the microcap sector. "Many companies that are very small deserve to be," says Daniel P. Coker, formerly a quantitative analyst with Schroder & Co. "They're often family-run and have only one good product." That's fine for the family, but investors need growth.

"For us, the payoff comes from finding small companies with earnings and then trying to identify a change that the company is making or responding to that will propel earnings further," says Warner Group's Marx. "Using this philosophy, we find a lot of good companies with great products."

One company that was catalyzed is Vans, Inc. The footwear maker rode high in the early '80s, as fans of *Fast Times at Ridgemont High* rushed out to buy the same Vans sneakers they'd seen Sean Penn slap himself in the head with in the film. But the company overexpanded. It declared Chapter 11 bankruptcy in 1984 and languished for a decade in the shadow of competitors such as Nike and Reebok. Then in 1995, former chief exec Walter Schoenfeld came out of retirement and oversaw a restructuring. The result: 35 percent growth in sales of Vans sneakers and snowboard boots in both 1996 and 1997. Just what the broker ordered. (Unfortunately, a catalytic effect lasts just so long. Vans shares suffered a 45 percent drop in 1998, precipitated, according to analysts, by the end of the skateboard craze, a slowdown in Asian sales because of the financial crisis there, and competition from "radder" shoes made by other manufacturers.)

Be on the lookout for market dominance or leading products in a growing market. Robert Rodriguez requires that any company he invests in be No. 1, 2, or 3 in its industry in terms of market share. Van Wagoner doesn't insist on top-three ranking, according to an April 1995 *Barron's* article, just a growing business. He'll go for an "up-and-comer that the big guys have just started to take seriously, [with a product or service] that's changing or influencing [the] industry."

Oberweis also stresses product. He looks for companies that have "a better hamburger, if they're producing hamburgers, or frozen yogurt, if it's frozen yogurt," he said on "Money World." "If [consumers are] buying 50 or 80 or 100 percent more each year [of] whatever [a company is] producing, that tells me it is doing something unique, something different, and something right that ought to catch our attention."

The business profile and summary in the S&P report should tell you about market share. You might also check your newspaper for stories about the business or call the company itself or one of its competitors. Other sources are industry trade journals, which you can find at the library, and *Hoover's Handbook of American Business* (which is available at www.hoovers.com).

A niche is nice. It's easier to dominate a market if the market is small. That's why Acorn's Ralph Wanger searches for companies in niche businesses. Harley-Davidson is one of his favorites. Harley is "the only motorcycle maker in the United States," Wanger says in the February 1995 *Kiplinger's* interview, "and the ones outside the U.S. aren't that exciting. What you've got in Harley is maybe the best brand name in the U.S. Coca-Cola is a good brand name, but people don't tattoo it on their bodies."

For an illustration of the growth potential in niche positioning, look at Guest Supply. You know those miniature shampoos, hair conditioners, lotions, and sewing kits you find in hotel bathrooms? Well, Guest Supply makes most of them. The company supplies fourteen of the fifteen largest chains in the United States, including the Motel 6, Marriott, Hyatt, and Hilton Hotels groups. But it has plenty of room to expand, according to Coker, who follows Guest. He estimates that it now reaches only about one-third of all hotel properties. And a large number of the company's existing customers purchase just a small percentage of the items it can provide: paper products, cleansing chemicals, and textiles, in addition to soaps, oils, and creams. With a stock like this, you should probably find out who its major customers are and when its contracts with them expire. You should also determine how sensitive its earnings are to the economy: Does it sell to hotels that would be hard hit by a slowdown, or is there steady demand?

Try to figure out just how safe your pet pick's franchise is. Does it have major competitors? Is its market wide open or protected by barriers, such as high start-up costs or government regulation? The quality of a company's competition can have a significant impact on what you'd be willing to pay for its stock. For example, the upside of turnaround star Vans was limited by the fact that it's sharing market space with Nike. If a company's report doesn't list its main market rivals, call the firm and ask for names of competitors; see if it will recommend a trade paper that will fill you in on industry issues. The ideal scenario is no competition in a growing industry that is difficult to get into, such as prescription drugs; the worst is a toehold in a slow-growing industry, such as printing, that is dominated by other companies that could squash your prospect like a bug.

Reap the downstream benefits of technology. One of Acorn's key investment techniques is searching out the secondary beneficiaries of new inventions. Wanger points to the television stations and cable companies that were spawned by TV and, more recently, to International Game Technology, which puts microprocessors into the video games and slot machines it manufacturers.

"IGT benefited marvelously from technology," he says in the *Kiplinger's* article. "It reinvented the humble mechanical slot machine, which inside looks like an old cash register, full of springs and cams and levers, . . . by replacing the works with a microprocessor . . . . It's a new device that offers more interesting games, eliminates maintenance, allows you to get progressive jackpots or add lottery components. All of a sudden, casinos are taking out craps tables to put in more slot machines. An IGT slot machine sells for $5,000. If the company tried to sell the same microprocessor for your kid to put inside a personal computer, it couldn't get $500 for it."

Apply the "quit test." This is Wanger's favorite criterion. As he explains in *Kiplinger's*, "You find a company that excites you so much that you say, 'This is so exciting and so much better than what I'm doing running a mutual fund that I'd like to quit this job, buy 100 percent of the company, and run it.' That's not practical, but sometimes people actually do it. One of the stocks we own is Systems & Computer Technology. It was followed by a nice young brokerage analyst we talked to frequently. One day he said, 'I'm not going to be talking to you again as an analyst.' I said, 'What happened? Did you get indicted again?' And he said, 'No, I'm going to work for Systems & Technology in its marketing department.' I sure as heck bought more of that stock."

Don't ignore what other investors think about the company. You can figure this out by looking at *relative strength,* the rate, relative to other stocks in a specified index or industry, at which a particular stock rises or falls in a rising or falling market. A high relative-strength ranking means that the company's shares have tended to climb higher and drop less precipitously than those of its peers—music to a buyer's ears. The Qualitative Evaluations section of the report contains a Relative Strength Rank figure, indicating how the stock has performed compared with all the others in the S&P universe on a rolling thirteen-week basis. The rankings range from a low of 1 to a high of 99. Oberweis requires a rank of at least 75 and prefers 90 or 95.

"I'm a believer that there are some other pretty smart people who invest in the market," he says. "If [my other requirements] are all [met] and the relative strength isn't, I better do some more homework and figure out why the stock isn't performing."

THE CRITERIA DISCUSSED SO FAR are valid for both growth and value stocks. The S&P reports also contain information that you may weigh and interpret differently for one group than for the other. Say you find a growth company with a good story and solid earnings that doesn't have an enormous amount of debt. You might next look at its price-to-earnings ratio. You'll find this under Per Share Data in the guide report (though you might also want to check the current value in the Wednesday *Investor's Business Daily* or on the *Bloomberg Personal Finance* Web site at www.bloomberg.com). The number will probably be much higher than the maximum 15 or so you'd want to see in a value stock. That's because you're expecting earnings to grow quickly, narrowing the gap with share price. The question is, is your expectation realistic?

For an answer, begin by reviewing past earnings growth. If there is an upward trend that seems to be steepening, you're on the right track.

Oberweis wants to see year-over-year increases of at least

30 percent in both earnings and revenues. "We never buy the biotechs or Netscapes of the world," whose revenue gains often don't translate into earnings growth, he says. He also requires a p/e no higher than one-half the growth rate—a ratio of 25, for instance, calls for 50 percent growth—and evidence that the company can sustain its earnings pace. The fastest-growing buggy-whip maker, he points out, wasn't much of a buy when the automobile was being introduced.

Oberweis, though, is unusually strict among growth investors. Van Wagoner will settle for year-over-year earnings growth equal to 20 percent and no lower than the p/e. Alexander Paris, president of Barrington Research, requires five-year profit growth greater than 10 percent and a p/e not more than twice this figure.

Check the company's profit margins, represented in the S&P report by the % Net Income of Revenues, under Balance Sheet Data.
You'd like to see the margins increasing, a sign that the company is either cutting costs or selling its product at higher prices, or both. At the same time, be on the lookout for quick nonoperational fixes—such as layoffs—which produce boosts in profits the company might not be able to repeat. Be wary of spikes in earnings that are not paralleled in revenues.

WITH A VALUE STOCK, YOUR FOCUS is different. Primarily, you want to see low p/e and price-to-book ratios. (Price to book isn't given in the report, but you can calculate it easily by dividing the listed book value into the share price.) It's as though you were buying the whole company: The higher its earnings and asset value in relation to its purchase price, the sooner you get back your outlay and start making a profit. "We look at the balance sheet as much as we look at the earnings statement," says Bill Nasgovitz. "What's the book value? What's going to hold this stock up if the plane crashes and things turn out to be fairly negative?"

Investment adviser Tweedy, Browne Co., in a booklet it sends to new and prospective clients, cites several studies showing that stocks with low p/e's have consistently delivered higher annual and cumulative returns than those with higher ratios and that among low-p/e stocks, small-caps outperform large ones. Other research has found that small stocks with low p/e's not only post higher returns than the market but do so with less risk. (Remember, though, that these statistics assume a "black-box" style of investing, blindly buying all the stocks in a particular p/e range without any other screening mechanism.)

◆ FPA's Robert Rodriguez requires that a value stock's p/e be less than 15.

This is a good guide, but you may want to be less absolute. Look for ratios that are 25 percent lower than the industry norm. You can calculate your own industry averages from the p/e's for similar companies listed in the newspaper, or ask your broker to look them up on the firm's Bloomberg terminal.

◆ Look for companies whose earnings yields are comparable to the yield on triple-A-rated corporate bonds.

Earnings yield—the reciprocal of p/e—is what the return on your investment would be if the company paid out all its earnings as dividends. Benjamin Graham required an earnings yield equal to twice the bond yield, but parity is a more realistic goal today. So, if corporate yields are 8 percent, you'd look for a p/e no higher than around 12.

◆ Remember: A low-p/e company whose earnings are expected to grow is better than one having the same p/e but no growth prospects.

As Warren Buffett has said, growth and value are "joined at the hip."

PRICE TO BOOK TAKES precedence over p/e for Charles Royce, president of the Royce Funds. "We do not buy stocks from a p/e standpoint," he says in an October 1992 interview with *Institutional Investor.* "As value investors, we're often buying companies that have taken the past year off, [so] their last-four-quarter p/e might be 48." You have to look beyond current earnings, he feels, to past performance and to other factors indicating a low valuation. One of the most important of these for Royce is the price-to-book ratio: "Our average there is about 1.5, compared with a range of about 3.5 to 4 in a growth portfolio."

Stressing price to book obviously works well for Royce—his Micro-Cap fund is praised by Morningstar for its "distinctive style and limited downside volatility." The statistical evidence is less clear. Academics Kenneth R. French and Eugene L. Fama have determined that for price-to-book ratio, as for p/e, lower is indeed better, and the lowest ratio combined with the smallest cap is best. Other studies, however, have been inconclusive. At Prudential Securities, for instance, director of small-cap research Claudia Mott, together with Coker (who was then with Pru) and Kevin Condon (now at Warburg Dillon Read), found the benefits of low price to book significantly "less robust" than those of other valuation measures.

One problem is that "low" is relative when talking about price to book. Manufacturing and capital-intensive businesses have more tangible assets and therefore higher book values than creative, knowledge-based ones. As a result, the price-to-book ratios of utilities in general are lower (averaging about 1.5) than those of software companies (about 9.5). But that doesn't make utilities necessarily better values. Another problem stems from accounting conventions. Assets such as real estate are carried at historical cost, the price paid to acquire them. This could be quite different from their current market value. Accordingly, price to book can paint an overly optimistic or pessimistic picture of a company's financial health.

For a company to be truly cheap on a price-to-book basis, its ratio should be lower than its industry's norm.
Look at the reports for other companies in the same business

and compare ratios. The S&P and Bloomberg Internet pages (listed in Resources) sometimes show industry averages. Or ask your broker to use the Relative Value (RV) function on his or her Bloomberg terminal.

Stocks with the lowest price to book seem to weather downturns better than highfliers do.

P/E AND PRICE-TO-BOOK RATIOS are the primary value indicators. But they aren't the only ones. Two other signals to look for in the reports:

1 A pattern of buying by a company's officers and directors. This could indicate that its stock is underpriced. The Tweedy Browne booklet points out that insiders often have "insight information" about operational changes or hidden assets, such as excess real estate, that could boost earnings. It cites several studies showing that stocks bought shortly after significant insider purchases became public outperformed the market index by large margins. For the inside track, check the Insider Activity section under Quantitative Evaluations. You can get additional information from newsletters such as the *Vickers Weekly Insider Report* and *Insiders' Chronicle* or at the associated Web sites: www.quote.com/info/vickers.html and www. cda.com *(see Resources).*

2 A company whose market cap equals 66 percent or less of its net net current asset value. NNCAV is not listed, but you can compute it by subtracting current liabilities and long-term debt from current assets. According to the Tweedy Browne booklet, Ben Graham earned 20 percent a year from the 1930s to 1956 by buying shares in companies that met this criterion. The booklet also cites modern studies showing that such stocks, if held at least two years, outperform even the ones in the lowest price/book category. One reason these companies are attractive is that they are often takeover targets. But the holding period is important—you may have to wait awhile before the stocks actually move.

You won't find a lot of companies today that meet Graham's 66 percent mark. As a compromise, many value investors will buy stocks at slightly above their NNCAVs. But bear in mind that such stocks are often in trouble—especially the smallest ones. "These companies can be very fragile," says Charles Royce.

A high NNCAV relative to market cap may mean the company has a large backlog of products (included in its current assets) that nobody wants and that it will have to discount to unload. Or its current assets may be swelled by accounts receivable that it will never collect, or perhaps the owners are liquidating the business. Read the company's profile to see what sent your value prospect down the tubes and if there's any reason to foresee a turnaround. Then check Balance Sheet Data to make sure that the company is solid enough to stay afloat while you're waiting.

To see both the up- and downsides of high net net current asset value, consider Deb Shops and Crown Books. In November 1996, both were trading below or close to their NNCAVs: Deb (a women's apparel retailer) had a market value of $57.7 million and an NNCAV of $52.5 million; the stats for Crown (a small book retailer) were $52.8 million and $53.2 million, respectively. But the book dealer's current assets consisted mainly of inventory, while the apparel retailer's included hefty amounts of cash and marketable securities. In 1997, Deb began making a profit; Crown continued to lose money. In May 1998, Deb's fourth-quarter earnings were more than double those of a year earlier and its stock had returned 51 percent since January. Crown eventually filed for bankruptcy.

This illustrates the importance of digging deeper into the numbers. Tweedy Browne analysts, for example, look at a value prospect as though they were underwriting an insurance policy on it. "We want married couples with a clean driving record who drive Volvos and walk to work," Tweedy partner John Spears told me one day at lunch.

You may have to put off this kind of examination until you've sorted your prospects using the S&P guide and are collecting and analyzing your own research materials *(see "Find Out About Fundamentals")*. At that point, for example, you can determine the balance-sheet health of a low-NNCAV prospect by checking what percent of its current assets are in inventory and accounts receivable: If the proportions are out of line with industry norms, you might want to steer clear. On the other hand, a large percentage of cash (including marketable securities) is generally a good sign.

Even before the data-collecting stage, though, you can search for survival signs in the S&P reports. Low debt is important. So is a high current ratio. Also examine the price chart on the first page of the report, as well as more-recent prices, in the newspapers or on Nasdaq's Internet page, at www.nasdaq.com; if the stock is still dropping, consider putting your buy on hold until it stabilizes.

GOOD GROWTH, FINE VALUE

IF YOU'D LIKE to take a cue from Philip A. Fisher and Benjamin Graham, venerable growth and value investors, respectively, here are a few of their key criteria. Some you'll be able to check on in the S&P guide; for others, you'll have to read the companies' reports and proxy statements, scan news and industry articles, and talk to management or other company representatives.

Philip Fisher—whose book *Common Stocks and Uncommon Profits and Other Writings* reportedly influenced Warren Buffet as much as Graham's *The Intelligent Investor* did—suggests that the following indicate a good growth stock:

◆ products whose sales have the potential to increase significantly for several years
◆ a management determined to develop new products when the potential of currently successful ones has been fully exploited
◆ effective research and development in relation to sales
◆ a successful sales organization
◆ strong profit margins

INFORMATION, PLEASE

"The first and foremost rule is to really get to know your company. And this entails getting all the financial information on the company that you possibly can and getting on the phone and talking to the people who run the company, talking to the people who are buying products from the company, talking to anyone you can think of that would have some sort of insight into this company's prospects."
—GORDON ANDERSON, *managing editor of* Individual Investor *magazine*, on Adam Smith's Money World

AFTER USING THE S&P GUIDE to pan your list of prospects, you'll be left with fifteen to twenty that could turn out to be golden. But before taking a stake in any of them,

- efforts to improve profit margins
- no outstanding labor or personnel problems
- a backup team of managers capable of running the show if something should happen to the CEO
- good cost analysis and profit controls
- a long-range profit strategy, including plans to cut costs, raise prices, develop new products
- a management that keeps shareholders apprised of the company's affairs in good times and bad

For a value stock, look for these criteria, from Ben Graham via Janet Lowe's *Value Investing Made Easy*:
- price amply supported by underlying value—that is, lower than its breakup value, or what its individual parts would be worth if they operated independently and had their own stock prices
- if possible, share price below net net current assets
- quality. "Investors do not make mistakes, or bad mistakes, in buying good stocks at fair prices," said Graham.

do more research, to find out as much as possible about their operations and finances, as well as about any developments, reorganizations, or projects that could propel them to a higher plane.

 Try the product.

This is a Peter Lynch classic. If you like what a company produces, others probably will, too. That means increasing sales, which should translate into good earnings and so higher share prices. It's simple advice, but even the pros follow it when they can. Steve Shapiro, when he was at Founders Asset Management in Denver, told me that he and a couple of the fund's managers happened to drive past a Rainforest Cafe around the time the chain was planning its initial public offering. Shapiro's passengers yelled at him to stop, and the whole group piled out of the car, credit cards drawn, to sample as many menu items as possible and quiz other patrons.

One caution: A quick customer-satisfaction survey can't be your only criterion. In late 1996 Rainforest, with about $460 million in market capitalization, had only a few operating outlets—not exactly a dream purchase, no matter how good the service. Since then the company's market cap has fallen to $134 million even as it has opened its thirtieth store and sales and earnings have risen.

 Keep a journal.

Here's another tip direct from Lynch. "Let's say you decide to research a retailer. Say to yourself, 'Okay, this is the size of the store; this is how many [stock-keeping units] the company has; this is its product line; these are its competitors.' Write everything down. Then keep watching. Say it has five stores open, and it costs X amount to open a store and so much for inventory. You know the company has enough cash to open six more stores. It opens stores in current markets; that's easy to do, because the company knows its products. Now it jumps to a whole new state. How are those new stores doing? This is the kind of stuff you monitor. After years, you'll learn something. You can probably become an expert on three or four companies that are either local or in your field. And you ought to know them cold. You have a file, and as things happen, you keep writing the notes down.

"There's the earnings of the company and the future of the company, and there's what you pay for [the stock]. If it's selling for $400 a share, guess what? It's [already priced] at a pretty impressive rate for the next eight years. But if you can look at the story you've put together in your journal and say, 'I think this has a very high likelihood of happening, and I'm not overpaying for it,' that's how you make money."

You can also use your journal to grade yourself, Lynch says: "What did I do wrong there? How did I miss the big picture? . . . Why did that not work?"

LOOK LOCAL

"All our companies are just a car ride away."
—JOSEPH BESECKLER, *founder, Homestate Pennsylvania Growth fund, in the May 1996 issue of* Individual Investor

WHEN YOU INVEST NEAR HOME, you have access to legal inside information. (I won't go into what constitutes the illegal kind, but as long as you aren't buying or selling a company's shares based on what you know as a director or heard from one, you're probably safe.) You can find out more about a hometown firm in your local newspaper than any out-of-town investor will read in the national press. And it's easy to see for yourself what's going on. All you have to do is drive by. Is the plant dark most of the time? Or is it running extra shifts, a sure sign that business is booming? Is the company hiring or laying off staff?

For more information, talk to people who work there. Have employees received competitive raises? And visit on days the community is invited inside. Is the working environment clean and safe, showing concern for employees? Can workers communicate easily with managers, or are the two separated by several floors and forbidding receptionists?

I like to walk into a company and see nice but not opulent digs filled with busy people. I don't want to be able to tell the difference between management and staff. When managers are mixing with workers, sporting the same frayed sleeves and dirty hands, it's a sign that, like my boss, Mike Bloomberg, they know "every damn thing that's going on."

Joseph Beseckler is a local man. The charter of Homestate Pennsylvania Growth, which he founded (and which is now managed by Ken Mertz II), requires that at least 65 percent of its assets be invested in companies that are headquartered in Pennsylvania or have substantial operations there. That gives it an edge, Beseckler says in *Individual Investor* magazine. The fund's analysts can easily visit all of the companies they cover, which, moreover, are generally underfollowed by Wall Street.

Local connections can also be leveraged for leads on businesses outside the area. Warner Group's Marx, for example, takes advantage of having personal-computer maker Gateway 2000 as a neighbor. "I get a lot of good information about computers and tech stocks just being here and talking to people in town," he says.

Tweedy Browne's John Spears enlisted family help while researching Fleming Cos. The company wholesales groceries, produce, and dairy products to supermarkets, so Spears talked to his family grocer, who generously answered questions about Fleming and its competitors. These insights helped Spears make a more informed investment decision.

Spears, who also quizzed his pharmacist about two drug distributors he was deciding between, cautions that a company's customers, suppliers, and rivals aren't always willing to dish the dirt. Even the big guys have trouble getting this information. On the plus side, that means if you succeed, you've got a real scoop.

Frequent travelers can cultivate personal connections in several localities. One money manager I know who specializes in the retail industry has the knack of getting out of companies before bad news hits. Her secret, she reveals, is to visit malls whenever she's on the road, checking up on her companies' outlets. She schmoozes with the managers over coffee and snacks, getting good gossip in return.

FIND OUT ABOUT FUNDAMENTALS

"The best way to get to know a company is to get the annual report and read it cover to cover."
—BILL BERGER

OF COURSE, UNLESS YOU LIVE in a very unusual town, not all your small-cap prospects are going to be local. You can't get the same insider's insight into companies that don't field a float in your local Memorial Day parade. But you can still find out more about how they work.

The companies themselves are great sources of information. The Securities and Exchange Commission requires them to publish financial and business data in their quarterly and annual reports and proxy statements. These contain updated versions of the raw material—the fundamentals—that the S&P experts massage and condense in the fundamental analyses in the guide.

Although Berger recommends a more thorough study, you can probably concentrate on the areas mentioned in the tips below: the president's letter, balance sheet, statement of cash flows, and income statement (in the reports), and the executive compensation section of the proxy statement. For companies not in the S&P guide, those documents are where you'll find the data you need to do your own analyses. For companies that are covered, these primary sources provide a sort of reality check on the reports' figures and opinions.

 The company's balance sheet should be "strong."
Many of the figures and ratios that contribute to this strength were discussed above, in connection with the S&P reports— low debt relative to equity and book value, increasing cash, a current ratio greater than one, to name a few. Again, if you

want to do a thorough balance-sheet analysis, refer to *The Guide to Understanding Financial Statements* or an accounting text. Meanwhile, here are a few other numbers you might want to crunch.

 Feel the burn.

The burn rate, that is. This is the speed at which the company is going through its cash reserves. Compare the figures for cash and marketable securities on the balance sheet with those for the previous quarter. If the current sum is smaller, divide it by the difference between the two quarters. That will give you a pretty good estimate of how many quarters the company can last without resorting to either equity or debt financing—neither of which is good for current shareholders. On the other hand, if the current sum is larger, your candidate is bringing in more cash than it can spend, a condition that will be confirmed at the bottom of the cash-flow statement. When you see that, you know you are getting warmer.

 On the income statement, study the sales figure.

Ideally, it should be equal to or greater than the company's market cap. "We look for a low price-to-sales ratio," says Oberweis. "Typically, someone who goes out to buy an entire company says, 'Okay, what am I paying for a company with revenues of such and such?' We'll also look at that, because we're buying pieces of the company."

Some investors substitute *price/sales* (calculated by dividing sales into market cap) for price/earnings in their financial analyses. There are two reasons for this: One, earnings can be heavily influenced by accounting decisions concerning inventory, depreciation of assets, and extraordinary charges; sales can't. Two, p/s is a better indicator than p/e for companies whose earnings are temporarily low or negative. One word of caution: A Prudential Securities study by Claudia Mott and Daniel Coker found that although p/s differentiated winners from losers, it didn't do so better than p/e, nor did it produce consistent results. Probably the best bet is to use both measures to cross-check each other.

Yet another caveat: You won't find many low price to sales ratios among companies that are dominant players in their industries. For dominance, expect to pay up.

◆ Dip into both the income statement and balance sheet to determine inventory turnover.

This indicates how many times in one year a company is able to sell its average inventory. To determine the turnover rate, first calculate average inventory by adding the figure on last year's balance sheet to the current one and dividing by two. Then divide the result into the cost of goods sold on the income statement.

Turnover will vary with the industry. Look for a rate that's higher than the competition's and speeding up, year over year. You definitely don't want to see a sharp increase in inventory. That's always a danger signal and can spell real disaster in the technology business. What do you think a warehouse of computers with 386 processors is worth? How about software that doesn't run on Windows 95? Microsoft has no inventory. Dell Computer isn't quite at that point, but it has come close by shifting its production system to build-to-order. In 1993, Dell was turning over its inventory every fifty days; by November 1998, it had pushed that down to every seven days, which compares with around once a month at Compaq.

Turnover in accounts receivable is significant, too. How quickly do customers pay their bills? The faster, the better—not just because a buck in the hand is worth two in the bush, but also because it shows that buyers want or need to do business with the company badly enough to pay up in record time. To get a speed measure, divide net sales (from the income statement) by average accounts receivable (the figure on last year's balance sheet plus the current one, divided by two). The optimal turnover rate will vary with industry and even season, but six times a year is a good benchmark. Of course, Microsoft pushes the envelope: In 1998, it turned over its receivables twelve times, meaning customers were paying their bills in about thirty days.

On the cash-flow statement, Robert Rodriguez likes to see something left over when he subtracts capital expenditures from cash from operations.

The remainder is called *free cash flow*, and it is essentially a measure of the company's ability to generate enough money to fund its own growth and still have a cushion for unforeseen costs or opportunities.

 Consider the source.

The statement lists cash from operations, from investing, and from financing. Positive cash from operations is essential. The company should be generating money, not just borrowing it—otherwise, it may be working on borrowed time.

 If the company distributes earnings, look for an above-average dividend yield, calculated by dividing the share price into the dividend per share.

A high yield (around 3 percent) is attractive, as long as it's not paired with a high payout ratio *(see above)*. Tweedy Browne cites studies showing that the companies with the highest dividend yields have also produced the highest investment returns. Bear in mind, though, that this measure is more significant for small value than for small growth stocks, which seldom pay much of a dividend, and it may be meaningless for microcaps. And, remember that dividends are taxed at a higher rate than long-term capital gains.

 Buy the formula.

Here are three equations, courtesy of Peter Lynch, Benjamin Graham, and Michael Berry, intended to help investors decide if they're putting their money in the right place.

1 Earnings growth + dividend yield / p/e > 1.5. In English, the sum of the company's expected annual earnings growth rate and its dividend yield should be more than half again as great as its price-earnings ratio; Lynch adds that twice as great is excellent. This is essentially the inverse of Oberweis's requirement that a company's p/e be no more than half its rate of earnings growth, but Lynch has made it less stringent by including dividends in the calculation. You'll find expected earnings growth rates—composites of analyst predictions based primarily on estimates provided by the companies' investor relations groups—in the S&P reports on the Internet or at the Web site for Zacks Investment Research. Or call the companies themselves for these numbers.

2 The intrinsic value of a stock = eps x [(2 x earnings growth) + 0.085] x 4.4/(AAA-bond yield). According to Ben Graham's formula, a stock should be selling for the company's annual earnings per share times twice the expected earnings growth rate plus the appropriate p/e for stocks with static growth (8.5 percent), times 4.4 divided by the yield on triple-A-rated corporate bonds. To see how this works, imagine that crockery maker Feet of Clay, which has 10 million shares outstanding, earned $20 million this year, or $2 per share, and has an expected growth rate of 5 percent. Assuming that triple-A corporates are trading at 7.33 percent, the intrinsic value of the stock is $2(2 x 0.05 + 0.085) x 4.4/0.0733 = $2(0.185) x 60 = $22.20. If Feet of Clay is selling for less than $22.20, it's cheap; above this figure, it's overpriced.

3 The rule of 2-2-2. Mike Berry, a former manager of the Dreman small-cap value fund who now handles the midcap portfolio at Heartland, looks for stocks characterized by three "2s": First, they should be trading at **half** the market multiple— that is, half the average p/e for the appropriate index. Second, the companies should be growing their earnings at **twice** the market rate. Third, their price to book must be less than **two**. Berry's rule is basically a summary of value criteria, spiced with growth. (You'll find market multiples and growth rates in *Barron's* and on the Bloomberg Web page; *IBD* also carries multiples.)

But don't sweat the math.

These are rules of thumb distilling the insights of market experts, not precise recipes to follow mechanically in arriving at your investment decisions. Stating them as formulae is misleading—it makes them appear more scientific and less biased than they are.

One place bias can appear is in the expected growth rate. Growth is notoriously difficult to forecast, and estimates are often influenced by considerations not strictly financial. In the past, companies and the analysts following them may have overemphasized good news to stir investor enthusiasm. Lately, though, they seem to be taking the opposite tack. Management has learned that bad things happen when announcements of actual earnings fail to live up to earlier predictions: At worst, angry shareholders sue; at best, the stock takes a nosedive. When the expectations prove too conservative, on the other hand, share price usually soars. So managements "tend to work with analysts to keep estimates low" says Jim Oberweis in his September 1996 *Oberweis Report,* a newsletter for shareholders.

 Earnings can lie in other ways as well.

John Dorfman, writing in the July/August 1998 issue of *Bloomberg Personal Finance* magazine, points out that not all earnings are created equal. He suggests ten quality-control checks. The first two concern inventory and receivables. You should be wary when either of these balloons—you don't want to see customers reluctant either to buy a company's products or to pay for them. The third caution regards "extraordinary expenses": Be skeptical when a company touts what its profits would be without some huge charge, which it claims was unforeseen and never to be repeated. "More often than not," says Dorfman, "it's a sudden recognition of a problem that has festered for years," and the company should have been shouldering the expense of fixing it all along.

His fourth point is to "place a smaller value on earnings derived from asset sales," which are not only non-recurring but may also signal reduced diversification of profit sources. Fifth, beware earnings growth accompanied by a cut in investment in research and development or (sixth) capital spending. Seventh, try to check out the company's revenue-recognition policies—it's very misleading, for example, if a book publisher counts every penny of profit from an initial shipment, since book retailers are allowed to return (and be credited for) unsold volumes.

Eighth and ninth, check out how much of the reported earnings are due to favorable foreign-exchange rates or fiddling with pension contributions. Finally, check sales against earnings—both should be rising roughly in tandem. If sales growth is higher, margins are slipping; if lower, the earnings growth may be the result of cost-cutting and so unsustainable.

 Ask companies' investor relations offices for their reports or search the Internet.

Reports filed electronically with the SEC are available through Edgar—short for Electronic Data Gathering, Analysis, and Retrieval—which you can access at www.sec.gov/edgarhp.htm. Company addresses and phone numbers are included at the bottom of the S&P reports and are listed in the Appendix. This information is also available in *Nelson's Directory of Investment Research*, an annual publication found in most libraries and bookstores *(see Resources)*. Or call 800-555-1212 for directory assistance—almost every company has a toll-free number these days.

Look into obtaining press releases.

Ask the investor relations office about getting on a mailing list or go back to the Internet. Some companies have sites that receive their releases; others send them to free services on the Net. One caution: There can be too much of a good thing. Bill Nasgovitz says he once received eight positive press releases from one company on the same day. He got nervous and sold. Sure enough, bad news lurked behind the spin—the stock dropped like a split-finger fastball soon after.

As you're gathering your data, remain skeptical of corporate figures.

That's another of Benjamin Graham's rules. Management puts its own spin on the facts, and even experienced analysts can have a tough time determining if the company's accountants are playing hocus-pocus with the numbers. A 1990s corollary: Be even more skeptical of anything you see on the Internet.

⬥ **Avoid companies whose financial statements aren't audited by one of the Big Five firms: Arthur Andersen & Co., Deloitte & Touche, Ernst & Young, KPMG Peat Marwick, and Price Waterhouse Coopers.**

"We've had a number of frauds over the last ten years," says Bill Nasgovitz. "And in each case, they were non-Big Five auditing firms." A reputable accountant's approval doesn't mean that the company is a good investment. It does mean that the report pre-parers have followed generally accepted accounting principles. That should make it easier for you to see what's going on and to compare the company's figures with those of others in the same industry.

But a good auditor doesn't override the previous point: Remain skeptical. One reader of the first edition wrote to point that even the big guys can be hoodwinked if management is intent on lying to them. Moreover, only the annual reports are audited; with the quarterlies, you're on your own.

Oberweis searches the reports for "hidden footnotes" and any other indications that "the company is doing something a little bit unusual."

VIEW FROM THE TOP

"The smaller the firm, the better the management needs to be."

—ALEXANDER PARIS *of Barrington Research*

NO MATTER HOW GOOD a company's balance sheet looks or how strong its brand name is, a group of bad managers can ruin it in a heartbeat. In a small company, the people at the top are particularly important. Often the business is their baby, and it lives or dies on their business smarts. Unfortunately, say some analysts, many entrepreneurs are not just crazy about their companies—they're just plain crazy. So before investing, get to know the people in charge.

Rodriguez prefers it if managers have been in place for at least two years, giving him material on which to judge them. He wants to see that they have developed a definable image for their company. Here are three ways to develop your own image of the management and its goals:

1 Read the letter to shareholders in the annual report. This will give you a sense of how the company officers think they're doing and where they want to go from here. Value companies, which are often fallen angels trying to fly again, should discuss their problems openly and be specific about solutions. Look for how a company intends to increase earnings. Peter Lynch lists five ways—cutting costs, raising prices, expanding into new markets, selling more in old markets, and disposing of losing operations.

"I . . . want to see a management that can articulate how they're going to grow the company, what they're doing to develop products and expand distribution," Garrett Van Wagoner says in an April 1995 *Barron's* interview. "I've also got to make the judgment that management is good enough to complete their plan."

Michael Murphy, of *The California Technology Stock Letter*, suggests going back several years to check management's promises against its actions. If it hasn't delivered in the past, don't have high hopes for the future.

2 Read the compensation and insider holdings sections in the proxy statement sent out before the shareholders meeting. Of all the documents, the proxy statement can be the most fun. This is where management is forced to tell you everything it would rather not—how much it compensates itself and lower-level employees, for example, and how much of a stake executives have in the company.

For Van Wagoner, the more stock insiders own, the better. "I want to see that management has enough financial incentive to be rewarded if [its] plan works," he says in the *Barron's* interview. "Professional managers are well and good, but that's not who I want running my company."

Nasgovitz agrees, adding that when "insiders—officers and directors—have a large percentage of stock ownership, . . . their interests are aligned with the public shareholders'." What percentage is "large"? Genesee Corp. is considered closely held with 12 percent insider ownership.

But Marc Robins, editor-in-chief of *The Red Chip Review* newsletter, demands even greater commitment. "Stock ownership of 20 percent [is] a good base level," Robins writes in the May/June 1997 issue of *Bloomberg Personal Finance* magazine. "To me, if insiders own this size position, they must have the kind of commitment that, over time, will pay me the kind of return I desire."

You might also take a look at the bios of the board of directors, if these are included. Outside members often ensure that insiders keep shareholders' interests in mind.

3 Try to meet managers face-to-face or talk to them on the phone. Nasgovitz, whose team visits more than 500 companies a year, says that value investors "love to go out and kick the tires, check if the bricks are in place and if management's there working full time, part time, what their incentives are, how eager they are to show up at work every day. In the value camp, we're generally buying distressed merchandise or wallflowers—things that, perhaps, are not in favor. And management is a critical element in terms of our analysis." Mario Gabelli once quipped, "I don't just kick the tires, sometimes I need to kick the management, too."

This isn't everyone's point of view. Oberweis, for one, avoids direct contact. "Over a long period of time," he says, "it really doesn't add that much value to our investing process." Worse, getting to know the people who run a company makes it harder to be objective about its prospects and to sell the stock when these prospects seem dim.

"Judging management is extremely difficult," Lynch says. "So I'd [focus on the business.] I'd rather own a business any fool can run, because eventually one will."

Royce, too, doubts that "meeting eyeball-to-eyeball with the CEO is necessarily going to get you anywhere." He believes that contact with outsiders connected in various ways with a company is just as important, and possibly more enlightening.

"You want to talk with suppliers and other people who have known management for a long time," he says in the

October 1992 interview with *Institutional Investor* magazine. "There are subtle things you want to find out, such as the culture of managements, their integrity, whether they change their minds too frequently. You want to know other ingredients besides just the facts."

Most analysts probably belong to the Nasgovitz camp. Lisa Gray, a Memphis stockbroker, for instance, feels that by visiting the managements of small companies in the neighborhood, a firm's research team can give its clients access to the best information possible.

David Schafer, of the Strong Schafer Value fund, also favors close-up looks at companies and their managers. He tells of visiting Jaguar in the early 1980s, when neither the car nor the stock had many fans. Schafer was the only analyst who bothered to visit the beleaguered British automaker, and he got an exclusive on its new manager and how he was handling problems with the company's quality-control program. The biggest obstacle to maintaining quality was posed by frequent defective shipments from outside suppliers. So the manager ordered that any broken part be dumped on his desk. He then personally delivered it to the CEO of the offending supplier. Impressed, Schafer bought a block of Jaguar stock for his fund, which he sold for a huge profit when Ford Motor Co. bought the company in 1989.

If you also prefer the Nasgovitz approach, there are several ways you can get a more personal feel for management. It's easiest, of course, when the company is local. You may be able to go to an open house there or get invited to a local Chamber of Commerce meeting. You might even attend the annual shareholders meeting, if you can get a ticket as a nonshareholder. Nasgovitz has been known to drive by a company's parking lot at 6 A.M., looking for managers' cars, and then again at 7 P.M., to make sure they're still there. Long hours, he feels, are a clue that management regards this as more than just a job; when that's no longer true, he says, the company's best days are over. If he sees a luxury car in the lot, he'll often ask whose it is. He'd rather hear that it belongs to an intern's parents than to a fat-cat executive.

If you're really lucky, one of the officers of a company will be teaching a class at a local night school or community college. Enroll—you'll learn something about business and hear good stories about life in the trenches.

For companies not in your neighborhood, you can always fall back on the telephone. Don't worry that managers will refuse a call from a small investor. As *Individual Investor*'s Gordon Anderson explained on *Money World*, "Most of these small companies are entrepreneurial. And an entrepreneur—I know this from the way we do business—it's your pride and joy. It's your baby. You want to talk about it because someone's interested."

Moreover, points out Michael Murphy, executives in general prefer small investors, who buy and hold, over trigger-happy Wall Street types, whose quick trades can destabilize stock price. So they should be happy to keep you happy by answering your questions.

If management is rude or evasive, stop right there.
Any company that doesn't treat its shareholders, present or prospective, with respect is not a good investment.

When you get an officer of the company on the phone, take a few interrogatory tips from Ron Ognar, manager of the Strong Growth fund.
According to the May 1996 issue of *Mutual Funds* magazine, Ognar asks "about company goals, earnings projections, operating margins, growth rates. How long will it take you to reach your targets? Can you go higher? Get there faster? Do you have enough cash and borrowing to make an acquisition? Who's the competition? Do you confine your service to the United States? How do you put a five-year plan together?"

Ognar also quizzes executives about how much stock they own and how far down the corporate ladder stock options are distributed. He wants to know about a CEO's personality and management style, how top managers are recruited, and if they have frivolous plans, like buying jets for executive travel. One last question: How would the company hold together if the CEO "went to the Fiji islands for six months?"

Find out when the company plans to make its next earnings announcement.

Then ask whether the figures are expected to meet, exceed, or fall below Wall Street predictions, and the reason for any difference. This is very important. Analysts deduce future quarterly and annual earnings from statements by the company, combined with their own readings of industry and larger economic trends. Based on their deductions, they issue buy, sell, or hold recommendations that may affect the stock's price. When analysts' expectations collide with reality, the market reaction can be violent. That's good news if they've guessed too low, bad news if they were overly optimistic. So be on the lookout for surprises—and for no surprise, as well: Because of the estimate conservatism noted above, an announcement that merely meets expectations often depresses share price. As Oberweis points out in his September '96 newsletter, "We investors aren't stupid. After a while, we figure out that a $0.15 estimate from an analyst really means that they are expecting $0.17 or $0.18 per share for the quarter." So actual earnings of 15 cents are disappointing. Estimates and report dates are available on the Bloomberg Web site.

If you're told that the company is going to miss its target, take heart. According to Bob Kern, president of Kern Capital Management and manager of the Fremont U.S. Micro-Cap fund, it's at least encouraging when management of a very small company has a good enough grasp of its finances to know its earnings are going to fall short. Far worse is when executives are just as surprised as everyone else by subpar performance.

Try to discover how the company treats its employees and the community.

"Look for companies that educate their employees and treat their customers and shareholders well and are good corporate citizens," says Bill Berger. "It isn't about capital anymore. It is about brainpower. It's a people world. Service is the key."

Berger cites the example of check printer Deluxe Corp. "A company that really educates its employees can dominate a market. Deluxe became a leader because its employees didn't make mistakes, so every bank gave them business."

Everything in moderation, though. You don't want to see companies robbing the bottom line to be good corporate citizens. Job number one is still to make money for shareholders.

NOW, WHAT ABOUT THOSE PENNY STOCKS?

"Penny-wise is pound-foolish."
—BENJAMIN FRANKLIN

AFTER READING ALL THIS about how crucial careful research is, you're sure to hear about a couple of guys who played a hunch and turned a penny stock into a 10-bagger. In 1996 two friends of mine did just that with a company called Advanced Viral Research Corp.: They paid a dime per share, and in a few days, the stock was selling for more than a buck.

I know what you're saying: A few stocks like that, and you can retire twenty years before you'd planned to. The trouble is that for every 10-bagger, there are scores that will take your money and just bag it. And telling the first type from the second is difficult, because penny-stock companies usually don't list on a major exchange and so don't have to report to the SEC. It's even harder to tell if this week's winner will become next week's impossible-to-unload turkey. Investors in Comparator Systems, a maker of fingerprint-ID software, learned that firsthand: During three days in May 1996, they saw their share price balloon thirty-fold, to $1\frac{7}{8}$ from $\frac{1}{16}$, then watched it deflate just as dramatically, to six cents in September.

One thing I can tell: Advanced Viral Research Corp. wouldn't have passed my battery of tests, starting with the

Crayon Criterion. Peter Lynch has often said that if you can't draw a company's product with a crayon, you don't understand its business. That means you don't have an edge and should stay away. AVRC produces and markets an antiviral peptide-nucleic acid complex under the name Reticulose. I'm out of the game right away. I studied biology and chemistry in college, but now I couldn't tell the difference between a peptide and a riptide.

How about fundamentals? In 1996 the company's income statement showed that its sales had been minuscule and that most of its expenses were administrative. It had been losing money every year. No analysts cover AVRC, so you can't check with them on its prospects for profitability.

The company does have shareholder equity. Must have been a lot of insiders buying, right? Wrong. From 1994 to 1996 officers of the company bought exactly zilch, while selling off more than 2 million shares.

So what made this stock move? The company claims its product can counteract a number of viruses that stimulate interferon production, such as those that cause influenza and hepatitis—maybe even AIDS. AIDS is a hot topic right now, and hot topics sell stock. In the 1960s, during the outer-space craze, the joke on Wall Street was that National Cowbell had just changed its name to International Bovi-sonics and the stock was going wild. The same goes for AVRC: We don't understand the business, but, hey, the cure for AIDS, that could be huge.

Another thing that put this company on the map was a report in the June 1995 issue of *Hot Stock Whispers*, by George Chilekis, saying the company was about to announce that an eminent medical doctor from a highly respected U.S. hospital had signed on as a scientific consultant. Chilekis also hinted at the possibility of a joint venture with a well-known pharmaceutical firm and predicted that the shares should soar upward (can you soar downward?) on the release of this oft-whispered rumor.

Let's count it up: whispers, rumors, and unconfirmed reports. Why would most people rather buy a stock on evidence like that than on a rock-solid set of financial statements? Just human nature, I guess.

What can we conclude? First, two people a lot less cynical than I am made a boatload of money. Second, the public loves to build castles in the air. Third, and most important, betting on penny stocks—even those that are managed by noble, honest people who may succeed someday—isn't investing. It's speculating or gambling. You can make a lot of money with companies that promise to cure AIDS or match fingerprints, but you can lose a lot, too. Those stocks are manipulated easily and often. Many of the people investing in them are unsophisticated. They're easy marks for shady dealers like the ones rounded up in 1996 by the FBI for bribing brokers to tout penny stocks to their clients.

My advice: Over the long run, you will get killed if you put money in penny stocks. One in a thousand may make you a bundle. But the whole thesis of this book is reaping rewards while reducing risk. If a company has no assets, no earnings, and no product, you're running lots of risk. And you don't need to rush in—should management prove capable and the stock turn out to be a keeper, you can still make a fortune by buying it after the product is actually developed and generating revenues.

If you can't resist the lure of the "pink sheets," which list penny-stock bid and ask prices, buy _Walker's Manual of Unlisted Stocks_ (see Resources).
The manual contains four years of financial info on 500 of these companies. But that's only a beginning. Be prepared to dig a lot harder than you would for a listed stock, even a microcap. As Jack Norberg, a pink-sheet specialist and president of Standard Investment in Tursint, California, told _Business Week_, "You have to take a hobby approach to investing in this area. This is not for the passive person."

ANTI-ANXIETY INVESTING

"The key to this whole game is winning by not losing."
—CHARLES ROYCE, *in the 1992* Institutional Investor *interview*

AFTER YOU'VE FINISHED YOUR digging and gathering, your sifting and sorting, you should be left with about twenty solid prospects. Some of these you'll buy; others you'll keep an eye on for the future. The next chapter describes strategies you can use to decide which investments to make, when. But before choosing your purchases or even a strategy, you should decide on an overall investment philosophy—particularly, how much risk you're willing to take for the possibility of higher returns.

I know, I've been pushing prudence. But even prudence allows for different degrees of risk tolerance. Your job is to figure out where you fit on that scale.

"When I first meet a client, we write out an investment philosophy for their portfolio," says Warner Group's Doug Marx. "I try to find out what my customer's risk tolerance is. [My firm] has a series of questions we ask, and then I add my own, like what would bother you more, to be in cash with the stock market going up or to be invested with the market going down?"

So do some soul-searching. The results will help you determine what risk controls to build into your portfolio and where to set your sell signals. It will also give you a measure for evaluating your holdings' performance, which you should do every quarter to see if you need to rebalance or otherwise restructure your portfolio.

When pros like Nasgovitz and Oberweis talk to brokers, they make clear what kind of stocks they're interested in and how they approach investing and risk.
That way, any stock suggestions they receive have a better chance of meeting their criteria. Try it. You'll save yourself and your broker a lot of time.

THE DEAN OF INVESTING FOR high risk-adjusted returns is
Quest Advisory's Charles Royce. His Royce Premier fund
has often had the lowest risk in the small-cap field, according to Morningstar. Royce himself was named in a 1995
poll of professional money managers, published in *USA
Today,* as one of three colleagues to whom they'd entrust
their own money. So he's a good man to turn to for tips
on how to build an ulcer-free portfolio.

Royce points out that every portfolio is subject to four
types of risk—valuation, financial, portfolio, and market—
each of which requires a different management technique.
Essentially, the portfolio-building tips given so far have
addressed the first three risks: Investing in companies with
low p/e and price-to-book ratios reduces *valuation risk,* the
tendency of a stock price not adequately supported by business fundamentals to collapse when the market mood turns
pessimistic. Strong balance sheets and adequate cash flows
provide companies with a margin of safety against *financial
risk,* which arises from unforeseen external changes. Diversification prevents concentrations in particular industries
or sectors that might boost returns but could just as quickly drag them down: *portfolio risk.* To manage the last type—
market risk—you need to look at a measure called *beta.* Market risk refers to the "rising tide lifts all ships"
phenomenon: The prices of all securities in a particular
class tend to move up and down more or less together. Beta
measures the sensitivity of the price movement of an individual stock to that of the equity market as a whole (usually represented by the S&P 500). A beta of 1 indicates that
the stock has moved 1 percent when the market moved 1
percent; 1.5 means that the stock's price will rise or fall half
again as much as the index; 0.5, that it will move only half
as far. Certain rare securities, such as gold stocks, have negative betas, indicating that they go against the current, rising as the market falls and vice versa.

Royce keeps his Premier fund's market risk low by
investing in nonmainstream companies—those with minimal institutional ownership—whose betas mostly fall

between 0 and 0.65. His reasoning: "If you don't want to get hit by a bus, stay out of the middle of Sixth Avenue." By avoiding the high-traffic zones of the market, Royce achieves stability: Premier will not soar with the hottest small-cap funds in a bull market, but it will drop less drastically when the bears take over.

Royce's style is not for everyone. Some Premier investors were unhappy with returns in the booming 1995–96 market that lagged those of more aggressive growth-oriented funds, such as Gary Pilgrim's PBHG Growth. However, if you lack the resources to recover gracefully from the rough landings that such highfliers make from time to time, you should probably aim for Royce's steady rather than for Pilgrim's spectacular results. Learn from 1995. According to the *Chicago Tribune,* the average stock fund returned 31 percent during the first nine months of that year, but only 3 percent in its fourth quarter. Funds with risk-control procedures did considerably better in the last quarter, posting double-digit returns by getting out of tech stocks and into new groups of companies that were rotating into favor.

You can check out your stocks' betas in the Key Stock Statistics section of the S&P reports; for companies not in the index, check with a broker.

To get an idea of your downside risk, and if you can stomach it, determine the floor under the share price.
John Dorfman, in the April 1998 issue of *Bloomberg Personal Finance* magazine, suggests calculating a stock's downside by averaging three factors. The first is the book value per share—approximately what a trustee could get for the company in a bankruptcy. The second is sales per share times 0.3, for cyclicals, or 0.5, for companies with steadier earnings. The third is the lowest per-share earnings figure in the past five years multiplied by 10 or, if you're a little more aggressive, 14 (the historical average p/e for the broad market). Dorfman applied this formula to Disney, which at the time was selling for $97.38. The floor he came up with: $15.87. Pretty scary. Losses of that magnitude do

happen, he notes, though usually to less celebrated stocks. Leah Zell, international fund manager at Wanger Asset Management in Chicago, adds a further caution: "In very bad markets, you will have overshooting," she warns. "Extrapolation or momentum will always take stocks beyond their fair value at both ends."

On the other hand, just because Disney is priced way above its floor doesn't mean you shouldn't buy it. Just be aware that, as Dorfman puts it, "your safety net is a long way down."

If you're investing in a highly volatile sector like technology, protecting your downside is particularly important. Michael Murphy suggests determining tech stocks' downside-risk value by using a somewhat more liberal variant of Dorfman's formula, averaging over (1 x sales) + (1.5 x book) + (earnings per share x 1/3 expected long-term growth). Again, there's no guarantee that share price won't fall through this floor. "But," notes Murphy, "if things don't work out, there may be a corporate buyer at or near our cost." Moreover, you can reduce your risk of a flame-out if you use the fundamental analysis discussed earlier to make sure you're buying fairly or under-priced companies with strong balance sheets and good niche products. For more on tech stocks see "Tech Stocks—Rule Breakers."

CARE AND FEEDING
OF A PORTFOLIO

"Reviewing a company when earnings come out and when new balance sheets come out is not a time-consuming process, especially if things are tracking. . . . Unlike other businesses, though, prices in this business change all the time, so you have to keep yourself in a ready position to take action. You must be organized in some disciplined way to buy and sell your securities on shifts in prices, which can happen very suddenly, or you will miss opportunities. We plan what we'll do with a stock at different price levels—add or subtract to our positions, or sell."

—CHARLES ROYCE, *in the 1992* Institutional Investor *interview*

ONCE YOU'VE SETTLED ON YOUR investment philosophy and risk tolerance and made your stock purchases with these in mind, you'll have some cleaning up and organizing to do. In the course of your research, you will probably have accumulated a huge pile of paper, which the twenty mailing lists you're now on are going to make even huger. To be able to access all the information contained in that pile, you have to put it in some order. You could flow it into a spreadsheet on your computer or stuff it in a file cabinet you pick up at a yard sale. At the very least, you should fill out an index card for each company, listing key telephone numbers and reference sources, as well as what it does and what your edge is. (A sample of the worksheet Nasgovitz fills out for each of his purchases is shown on the following two pages.)

Make up a card even for the companies you've decided to pass on for now. Their time may come—when the economic climate changes or you have more money to invest. The vetting you've already done will reduce the amount of research you'll need to do in the future. As new candidates come to your attention, create files and fill out cards containing the information you dig up on them and noting why you like their prospects.

For each stock you do invest in, write down your reason. Briefly state a goal toward which you can objectively measure the company's progress. "If you can't summarize your argument in three sentences, you don't really understand it," says Acorn portfolio manager Terry Hogan, who gives as an example: "This company will turn around in two or three years." In addition, describe the catalyst that you expect to transform the business, either turning it around or accelerating its growth.

Your reason for buying can be a brief statement, but it should be specific. Peter Lynch has told me he determines if someone he is mentoring is going to make it as a manager by asking why he or she owns a particular stock. If the answer is a "bunch of clichés—it's cheap, good management'," he says, "forget it."

WILLIAM NASGOVITZ'S TEN POINTS

Security: ABC Corporation   **Date:**   1/1/97

Location: Milwaukee, WI   **Analyst:** JK

Ticker: ABCD   **Desc:**   Manufactures widgets

                                     Phone: (555) 555-5555

1 **Low P/E Ratio:**	Earnings:	'96	$1.86	A	
	P/E:		12.9 x		

2 **Low Price/Cash Flow Ratio:**	Cash Flow:	'96	$3.21	A	
	P/CF Ratio:		7.5 x		

3 **Book Value:**		'96	$11.91	A
	Tangible:	'96	$11.25	A

4 **Financial Soundness:**

Debt: 25.0%

5 Positive Earnings Dynamics:	Q1	Q2	Q3	Q4
Fiscal Year: Dec		'96	0.26 A	
		'97	0.55 E	
Earnings Notes:		'98	0.60 E	

6 **Ownership:**   Insider: 25%

Buyback: Y

Authorized to repurchase

7 **Management:** Smith has over 20 years' experience in the
business. New vice president has 15 years'

8 **Hidden Assets:** ABC owns 30% of XYZ Forging Corp. (private
company). Carried on books at cost. Fair

9 **Catalyst:** Recent acquisition will double revenue and

10 **Chart:** Off recent highs—consolidating gains.

Price:	$24.00		Contact:	Joe Smith
# Shares:	5.0 m		Broker:	HAI
Rating:	BUY		Industry:	Manufacturing

'97	$2.55	E	'98	$2.90	E	Yes
	9.4 x			8.3 x		

'97	$3.65	E	'98	$4.20	E	Yes
	6.6 x			5.7 x		

'97	$14.45	E	'98	$17.35	E	No
'97	$13.50	E	'98	$16.65	E	

Net Net Working	Price-to-sell	Dvd/Sh.:	
Capital: $2.5	Ratio: 50%	$0.20 Dvd Yld:	Yes
			Yes

0.45	A	0.52	A	0.63	A
0.60	E	0.70	E	0.70	E
0.75	E	0.80	E	0.75	E

Institution: 30%	Insider Activity:	Yes
	Smith (president) bought	
	2,000 shares @ $15 on 6/96.	
Poison Pill: Y	Pct: 20%	
500,000 shares.		

experience and a reputation as a shrewd manager.	Yes
market value significantly higher.	Yes
will be accretive to earnings.	Yes
	Yes

SCORE | 9/10

Understanding why you bought a stock is crucial, because this will help you decide later whether to sell it. And knowing when to sell can be more important than knowing when to buy. As Bill Berger says, "You've got to weed the garden."

Strategies for when and why to unload your hard-won shares are discussed in the next section. Right now, you just need to know that there are basically two reasons to sell: success and failure.

It may be the company itself that succeeds or fails with a product. "One of the things we have in our database is the reason we own the stock," says Hogan. "It will say something like, 'I own this stock because these guys have a new drug for multiple sclerosis that's going to make the company grow very rapidly.' Now, one of two things can happen: Either some hamster in the lab gets diarrhea and the drug goes into the ash can—at that point you should sell the stock, because the reason you bought it doesn't exist anymore—or the drug succeeds. The stock goes from $10 to $50, and then its run is over. If a stock looks like it's getting really overpriced relative to our model, we have to take a look at it."

Alternatively, it may be the company's stock whose performance meets or falls short of your goals for it. To be able to judge this when the time comes, you should make two other notes on your index cards: a target price, at which you think the shares will be fully valued, and a stop-loss figure, indicating how far you will allow the price to fall before you bail out. When a stock reaches your target or stop-loss price, search for signs either that it will continue to grow or that its decline is just a temporary setback in an otherwise steady ascent. If you don't find any reasons to hold, you should probably sell.

The point, says Lynch, giving a twist to Berger's gardening advice, is "to be careful that you don't dig up the flowers and water the weeds." That's why you have all this information in one accessible place—to make it easier to reevaluate your portfolio and see what changes you need to make. You should go through this process roughly every three months, when the quarterly reports start rolling in: Check fundamentals for improvement or deterioration. And see if your reason for buying a company is still valid, becoming a reason to hold it. For instance, if your rationale for purchasing Microsoft Corp. in the 1980s was "It's the leader in building the software that runs personal computers," you're probably still a holder. On the other hand, if you bought Kmart Corp. because "It is and will remain the dominant retailer in the United States," you should have given up on it a while ago.

To set a target price, first use the company's expected growth rate to come up with what analysts feel its earnings per share will be three or five years down the road. Then, based on the current average p/e for the sector and how dominant you think the company will be in its market, figure out what its future p/e will be. From this you can calculate the target price.

Say you're considering Up 'N' Coming, priced at $10, which earns $1 a share and has a projected earnings growth rate of 30 percent and a current p/e of 10 in an industry whose average is 20. You believe that in five years, Up 'N' will be a major player in its market. So you figure its future p/e as 22. To calculate what the stock will be worth then, add 30 percent to the $1 per share earnings, raise the result to the 5th power, then multiply by 22. The answer: your $10.00 stock will be worth $81. That's the power of multiple expansion and earnings growth.

When a stock reaches your target, reexamine the company to see if something has happened since you set your price objective that would lead you to adjust it upward.

Your mailing lists and local contacts may have told you about a new product or management scheme that the general investing public hasn't glommed onto yet. If you believe the share price will soar when this information becomes common knowledge, set another target and sit on your hands for the moment. If you can't find a compelling reason to raise your objective, though, and you see other investments that promise significantly more growth, you should probably make a trade. Marc Robins, of *The Red Chip Review*, calls this "swapping up in quality."

Set your stop-loss on a small stock at 15 to 20 percent. But you may want to give a few special stocks more leeway. The more lenient stop-loss for superior companies was suggested by a study my colleague, Bloomberg senior markets editor Bill Hester, and I did on additions to the S&P 500. Our thesis was that these companies would outperform. What we actually found was that they did about the same as the index as a whole, maybe slightly better. As a sidelight, though, the study turned up an interesting pattern: Many of the stocks that later produced big gains first took huge hits, dropping more than 15 percent before rallying. That's a large stock swinging widely over the course of one year; you can expect small caps to be much more volatile. The bottom line: For most stocks, consider cutting your losses at 15 or 20 percent. With superior businesses that you're sure are solid, let your money ride a bit longer. But be disciplined. No stock should be on probation indefinitely.

For a value stock, look to see if that catalyst—a new product, a reorganization—you'd hoped would turn the company around is on the horizon or is having the effect you'd hoped for. Heartland's Nasgovitz says he generally gives a company two years to prove it isn't "permacheap." He may decide to hang on longer, though, if he finds a reason to keep the faith: a high-powered management or balance sheet or a significant competitive edge in its industry. Nasgovitz cites a company the fund bought recently at less than cash per share. "Things are not going to change that dramatically in the short run," he says. "We think it's a great opportunity, based on its balance sheet, so we'll hold on and hang in there."

DUH BEARS—WHEN
THE MARKET FALLS

"The man that once did sell the lion's skin while the beast lived, was kill'd with hunting him."
—WILLIAM SHAKESPEARE, *Henry V*

MANAGING YOUR PORTFOLIO in a down market can be scary, particularly if you've never suffered through one before. Chances are pretty good you haven't: According to Bill Nasgovitz, more than $4 out of every $5 invested in the stock market today has never seen a 10 percent correction, let alone a real bear attack.

Well, fasten your seat belts, it's going to be a bumpy ride. "Stocks, over the long term, might go down one out of three years," Nasgovitz says. "We haven't had that kind of market for a long, long time. We had the crash back in 1987, but it was very quick and over in a period of months. And then it was up, up, and away again. So I think the stock market probably is due for much rougher years ahead. The S&P 500, I think, should have a lot more down years than it's had over the past fifteen."

The good news: He also thinks that small caps, which have lagged a bit since the mid 1980s, may be ready to outpace the pack. But Nasgovitz himself, tongue firmly in cheek, admits to "eternal hope." So make sure you're prepared for the worst.

 Review your investment goals, taking into account your stage of life and long- and short-term financial needs.
If you're going to need to cash in some securities to meet obligations in the near future, you're better off doing it now than after the market has corrected.

 Think through your game plan thoroughly. Then stick to it.
Investors who panicked during the 1987 crash sold into a declining market. Those who held were buoyed as the market reached

unprecedented heights. "Make fewer investments, and know what you own," advises Rodriguez. "That takes out a lot of the uncertainty and fear."

 Don't try to time the market.
"If you start investing in equity funds, yet we have a down year, probably the worst thing [to] do is yank that money out, stick it somewhere else, hopefully catch when the market turns around again and get it back in," says Prudential's Mott. "You're better off to try and sit it out, even though you may get your quarterly statement and not be too happy with the numbers that are on there."

SELLING

"There's no black box for when to sell, like sell your winners when they are up 50 percent, and sell your losers when they are down 20 percent. It sounds seductive, because your upside is 2.5 times your downside, but it isn't that cut-and-dried."
—ROBERT RODRIGUEZ

WHEN DO YOU SELL A STOCK? The answer most people would like to give is never, but that isn't realistic. Most of us aren't good enough at stock picking to find companies that will continuously outperform the market. At some point, almost every purchase you make will have to be sold, either because you screwed up and it's an abject failure or because you were brilliant and it met your objectives and now has nowhere to go. You aren't divorcing your spouse or selling a friend down the river. Just Do It.

One of the biggest mistakes small-cap investors make is falling "in love with a company," *Individual Investor's* Anderson said on "Adam Smith's Money World." "They come up with a scenario by which this little company, this tree, grows to the sky. And they lose sight of the fact that not every tree grows to the sky. And they don't sell when all rational indicators say, Get out of this stock."

It is because so many of us tend to let emotions into our

investing that stop-loss and target prices are important: They make us deal with hard facts. Say a stock you bought at $10 goes to $13 a share. Emotionally, you'd be tempted to let it ride. Realistically, though, you should ask yourself if the share price has anywhere to go after a 30 percent rise, which is huge. Setting a target price at a reasonable level will force you to pose that question.

Selling the losers is relatively easy. It's also vital to your survival as a stock picker. In his book, *IBD*'s Bill O'Neil quotes the famous investor Bernard Baruch: "Even being right three or four times out of ten should yield a person a fortune if he has the sense to cut his losses quickly in ventures where he has been wrong."

One signal that you might have been wrong about a company is a drop in its share price below the stop-loss you set for it—for most small stocks, about 15 or 20 percent below the level at which you bought it. Having said that, the decision to sell at this point is not mechanical. If what you've learned about the company and its business leads you to believe that this drop is a just a detour on an upward road, you might decide to hold.

"If you know why you bought a company and can ask what's wrong and if anything has changed, you can be a lot more rational when the stock price is down," says Rodriguez. "Sometimes when a stock is down 50 percent, you don't want to be selling; you want to be buying more."

Another thing to watch is earnings. They are what drive stock prices. So a negative surprise—when a company's actual earnings come in below analysts' expectations—should have you looking for the door.

"What tends to happen," Oberweis says, "is when a company has one bad quarter, things are actually happening behind the scenes that may not be obvious, but they tend to have a second or a third bad quarter down the line, as well."

It's the old cockroach theory: If you see one, you know plenty more are around. The same goes for bad quarters.

"One of the traps that people get into," says Prudential's

Claudia Mott, "is not believing when a company has its first negative earnings surprise. For example, the company misses a quarter, [and you tell yourself] it's only a one-time thing—next quarter is going to be fine. Lo and behold, come the next reporting season, you get hit with another negative surprise. . . . All too often, especially in small caps, it's the beginning of the end."

Oberweis doesn't believe in second chances. "My father always uses the analogy that he's been married to his wife for twenty-nine years now, and when she makes a mistake, it's all right, he can learn to live with it," he says. "However,

PETER LYNCH ON HOLDING A STOCK

I ASKED PETER LYNCH how you get the courage to hold a stock when it gets pricey or falls out of favor. His answer: "You have to know where you are in the ball game." Lynch illustrates his point with Wal-Mart stores, which ten years after going public, had done very nicely for investors. They might have been tempted to take their profits and run. But the company still had only 15 percent of the United States, and it hadn't saturated that share—it was only in the second inning of a nine-inning game. Investors who realized this and so held on to their shares saw their investment go on to triple in value.

On the other hand, if a company you own stumbles, producing a negative earnings surprise or an unexpectedly bad quarter, Lynch advises you to determine if it's a temporary setback or a sign of something essentially wrong. You could judge this in part by the company's official explanation: "Is it 'Listen, we went to a new state and we opened the wrong stores'? Or is it just a bunch of rationalizations?" he asks. "Frankly, if the story has deteriorated, you're better off to just take your losses and stay with the [stocks] that are right. You're better off having a portfolio of companies where the stories are valid than one with twenty cheapos. Out of those twenty, maybe one will work. Out of the twenty good stories, probably five or six will work."

it's not true with the companies we invest in. One bad quarter, and we're headed for divorce court. And we're going to make very little exception to that. . . . This discipline's a major part to our investment philosophy."

That's the main reason Oberweis doesn't want to get to know the people who run the companies his funds own. After you spend time with management, he says, it changes "from company ABC to Bob's company. Whenever a report comes out and they show a negative quarter, Bob's immediately on the phone telling me, 'Look, Jim, it was a bad quarter. . . . A few orders came in late, but they're going to get booked in the coming weeks. Next quarter we'll be fine.'"

Shelby Davis, former manager of the New York Venture Fund, now retired, is more lenient. "A company is a collection of people," he says. "I don't throw my son out of the house when he has a bad report card, and I don't throw a company [out of a portfolio] because they miss one quarter's earnings."

Schroder's Dan Coker also weighs in on the side of leniency. His point is that with small companies, you need to regard both expected and announced earnings with a certain skepticism. Revenues and profits in this size segment are volatile, reducing the accuracy of predictions. Figures, moreover, are rounded: Actual earnings of 24.49 cents would be reported as $0.24, appearing to fall one full cent short of an estimate of 24.51, which is rounded to $0.25.

Both Davis, whose sons have taken up the family business, and Oberweis have been successful with their opposite approaches. Most of us, though, would do best to follow a middle course, basing decisions to sell on a combination of factors. One of these is valuation. A single negative surprise could well torpedo a company whose p/e is high, either absolutely or relative to those of similar companies, but it might leave unscathed a company with a very low ratio.

Check the stock's relative strength.

Relative strength, as discussed above, is a measure of how your stock's market performance stacks up against that of other companies in its industry or an appropriate index. This is crucial when you're considering breaching your stop-loss. If your stock has previously risen higher and has now fallen less sharply than its sector or the broader market, it may be a leader worth hanging on to. During the big plunge in tech stocks in 1995, for example, Intel Corp. dropped significantly, but by far less than its peers. The people who held on to the semiconductor maker are now happily counting their cash.

You can calculate relative strength by dividing the percent change in the index into the percent change in the share price. Your stock is outperforming if the result is greater than one in a rising market, or less than one in a falling market. For a more complete description, take a look at Tom Dorsey's book, *Point & Figure Charting (see Resources)*. Dorsey is a master at explaining technical analysis in clear terms.

DUMP THE WINNERS?

"We do take a long view, and we tend to buy cheaply, so usually price is not the problem. Opportunity cost is the problem. You can own something for ten years and make 20 percent. So you have to be vigilant about what you own, and you have to draw lines in the sand about the limits of your patience. But frankly, the wind blows over the lines all the time."
—CHARLES ROYCE, *in the 1992* Institutional Investor *interview*

THE STOCKS THAT HAVE MADE you money are tougher to let go. You know them, and when you sell you'll have to pay hefty capital-gains taxes. Paul Nadler, one of the most dedicated finance professors around and a former Rothschild Co. chief economist, teaches students a good rule of thumb: Before selling a decent stock that has given you a good run, find a replacement whose prospects are 50 percent better. That's how much extra return is needed to off-set the commissions and taxes you'll have to pay on a trade.

A friend of mine says the small-cap mutual fund he manages will sell a stock that's been a winner in three situations:

1 The stock meets the price objective set for it, and the fund's analysts can't find a reason to raise their target.

2 A major brokerage issues a sell recommendation on it. Brokers don't say the 'S' word often. When they do, the company CEO may call to raise hell and promise never to do another lick of business with the firm. So if these guys do pull the emergency brake, something's really wrong. A second reason to heed their warnings is that other investors will. When mutual funds start unloading their huge stakes in a company, its share price will go down the tubes.

3 Fundamentals shift significantly. This change can be anything that affects earnings power or assets, such as a major law suit, a failed product, the death of a dynamic manager, or the emergence of a serious competitor. Oberweis, who follows this rule as well, defines the fatal blow as anything that compromises the special advantage over competitors that first attracted him to the company.

 Oberweis will also look closely at a stock whose relative strength weakens or whose earnings growth slows.
The first, because it indicates investor disenchantment, which he takes seriously; the second, because it may mean the company has lost its competitive edge.

 Keep an eye on the p/e.
As a strict value investor, Bill Nasgovitz buys out-of-favor stocks priced at, say, 6 or 8 times earnings and sells them when their p/e's reach 20 or more and they are becoming Wall Street sweethearts. That may be a little rigid for you, but you should start getting antsy when a stock's p/e approaches parity with the company's expected five-year earnings growth rate. As Oberweis says in his July 1996 *Oberweis Report,* when ratios get

high, investors may be "discounting bright prospects so far into the future that the price of the stock no longer makes rational investment sense." (He begins to worry at around 70 times earnings.)

"Some of the research we've done has shown that you can probably go to almost 1.5 times growth before you start to see the stocks begin to underperform," says Claudia Mott. "But that is obviously still a very high valuation point, if you look just on an absolute basis. And, unfortunately, in times when the market's not just going up, those are the kinds of stocks that usually are going to get hurt more. So you do leave yourself open to a little bit more downside risk, if the market starts to correct."

SOME INVESTMENT PROFESSIONALS practice a defensive discipline of selling off portions of winning holdings. Warner Group's Marx will often sell a third of a position that has appreciated 30 percent, another third when it is up 50 percent, and the final third when the stock has risen 100 percent. "It won't get you any 10-baggers," he says. "But you protect your wealth and make sure you keep your profits."

Robert Rodriguez makes what he calls "keep myself honest" sales, unloading around 10 percent of his position in a stock whose price has risen significantly. But the FPA manager believes in adjusting his discipline to fit the company. As illustrations, he cites retailers Ross Stores and Claire's Stores. Rodriguez bought the two stocks at roughly the same time and watched them appreciate about the same amount. In August 1996, however, he decided to sell Claire's and keep Ross. The reason: He considered Claire's share price reflective of the company's current value; on the other hand, he had invested in Ross as a play on California's recovery, which he believed was still in progress.

Sell if the company's p/e seems out of line with its market and market dominance.
That's why Rodriguez decided to unload Nike, the oldest position in his fund. He bought the stock in 1984 for a split-

adjusted price of less than $1 and sold it at $80 during the second quarter of 1996. At that level, he explains, the sneaker maker had "the valuation of Coke and McDonald's. Although Phil Knight, Nike's chairman, thinks they deserve it, there is a key difference: Coke and McDonald's have been successful in selling to several generations of people, and until Nike proves they can do that, I don't think they deserve the same valuation."

ONCE AGAIN YOU MIGHT NOT want to play strictly by the numbers. Any emerging-growth company will have periods when its valuation is horrendous—as much as several hundred times earnings. Smart, persuasive people will start saying how overvalued the stock is. Eventually it will fall from the sky, and for a time nobody will want to own it. But the guys who get the 100-baggers are those who hang on through thick and thin. I wish I could teach you how to tell a keeper from a flash in the pan. One piece of advice I can offer is that you're most likely to go the distance and possibly score big if you build your portfolio around a diversified group of relatively conservative picks while devoting a small portion to the flashy ones. A football analogy: A big-play offense is successful only if you also have running backs who can pound out short yardage and a defense that can hold the other team after an interception.

TECH STOCKS—RULE BREAKERS

THE TECHNOLOGY SECTOR can provide big-play stocks. Just ask Alberto Vilar. Benjamin Graham passed up IBM's initial public offering because it didn't fit his emphasis on earnings and assets. Vilar would never make that mistake. Vilar, a tech-stock fan, is the antithesis of a value investor. The stance has brought him great success—the Amerindo Fund he comanages earned investors a 174 percent return for the year ending January 31, 1999—and great hostility.

"Other fund managers tell me that I'm worse than a drug dealer, that I belong in jail, and that God should punish me," says Vilar, who has a $1 cost basis for the 1.2 million shares of America Online his firm, Amerindo Investment Advisors, owns. Amerindo is the sixth-largest holder of Yahoo! and has a cost basis of less than $12 for 3 million of those shares. "They tell me I should invest in real companies, and they use phrases like hype, mania, and tulip craze

RULES FOR RULE-BREAKERS

FOR THE FIVE YEARS ENDING January 31, 1999, the Alliance Technology Fund has earned an annualized return of 32.49 percent through patience, good stock picking, and the strength of the technology sector. Peter Anastos, who comanages the New York–based fund with Gerald Malone, says their strategy is to own about fifty high-quality companies. He and Malone have kept their annual turnover at 51 percent, compared with the 300 percent achieved by some of their competitors. Still, Anastos says, "low turnover isn't so much a goal of our strategy as it is a result. It is impossible for us to come up with two or three names a week."

How does he find these names? He talks with management. And he applies the following eight criteria:

1 Companies should have open-ended opportunity—if they're small or mid-sized, all the better. That's one reason Anastos likes Internet stocks.

2 The CEOs should have good business sense. "That would seem obvious, but it isn't in technology," Anastos says. "Some CEOs love technology for technology's sake. The biggest challenge that venture capitalists have is getting rid of the original management and replacing them with more seasoned managers." The rare exceptions are tech whizzes who can manage, like John Chambers of Cisco Systems; Michael Dell, who founded his namesake computer company when he was in college; Bill Gates of Microsoft Corp.; and Andrew Grove, recently retired from Intel Corp., who wrote a book about the tech industry called *Only the Paranoid Survive*.

3 Companies must be populated with youth but still have parental supervision. Timothy Koogle, for example, fills the parental role at Yahoo!

to explain why I'm beating my bogey and they can't. But you know what? I think AOL is a damn good company, with 14 million customers who pay them a fee every month."

Vilar believes we are at the start of the third computing and communications revolution in a generation and has positioned the assets of his firm to take advantage of it.

4 The granting of stock options must go deep into the organization. "The more employees whose interests are aligned with ours, the better," Anastos says.

5 Good marketing is crucial. "Many of these companies think that if they have good technology, the world will beat a path to their door," says Anastos. "It doesn't work that way. If I could have great technology and mediocre marketing or good technology and great marketing, I'd take great marketing."

6 Brand image is also vital. "[It] is expensive to get, but it is even tougher to take away," Anastos says.

7 A little insecurity and a lot of resilience are useful. "I like companies that run scared," Anastos says. "Heaven forbid they become meek or humble. You have to love Andy Grove's paranoia. And people with great character bounce back from adversity. That's the measure of great companies as well."

8 A leading competitive position is key. "We love to have a large market share," says Anastos. "We don't think much of the we-try-harder approach. We like to own companies that are number one."

Anastos will unload companies if the fundamentals are deteriorating or the valuation is excessive. "I have tremendous impatience for fundamental deterioration, but more patience for quality companies that get overvalued," he says. Some factors that cause the Alliance managers to reevaluate a stock: falling gross margin (sales minus cost of goods sold divided by sales); high employee turnover; a pattern of stock sales by company insiders that substantially reduces their ownership; a delayed product introduction.

C.G.

The first cycle started in the 1960s. "You sat at a dumb terminal and talked to a mainframe," Vilar says. "If you had identified that IBM was going to be the leader and bought the shares, you could buy 10 percent of Manhattan right now." The second revolution started in about 1985 and created $1 trillion in wealth through sales of Cisco's routers, Microsoft Corp.'s operating system, and Intel Corp.-powered computers from Compaq Computer Corp. and Dell Computer Corp., as well as desktop publishing software and relational databases. "But we've hit the wall there," he continues. "Now we're in the Internet generation, and the leading technologies will give you access to everyone else's computer." Players here include Amazon.com, AOL, At Home Corp., Inktomi Corp., and Yahoo!.

Once Vilar has a list of potential winners, he builds a portfolio of twenty stocks. Next he eliminates "the guys who aren't going to make it. If three of us go to college together and I make A's, you make B's, and the third guy makes C's, we all graduate. Not true with tech investing. Technology stocks either get A's or they flunk. All I need in a twenty-stock portfolio are three out of twenty that are going to become 10-baggers. They will carry the day. The quicker I realize [a stock isn't] going to be Phi Beta Kappa, the better."

Weeding out the B students takes the most skill. It requires knowing which rules of growth-stock investing do not apply—such as dumping stocks that post negative earnings surprises or get downgraded by analysts.

"When a company misses a number, we've got to have a coming-to-religion discussion with the management," Vilar says. "Fifty to 60 percent of the time, we dump it. Regardless, we're going to give you a punch right between the eyes. When you're looking at a sector that is going to reinvent the wheel, you ask, What is the size of the market that this company is in and what share do they have? You've got to sit on the edge of your seat, bite your nails, and pray, but you don't just sell a stock because an analyst doesn't like it."

What about high valuation? Can AOL and Yahoo! really get the 8 zillion customers that would justify current valuations? Vilar says he heard all of the same questions with Cisco.

"Technology is the only area I know that generates increasing returns to scale," he says. "When the price point of the microprocessor comes down every year, it is going to be a component in more products, like telephones and cameras. On day one, you have no idea how big the market is going to be. . . . Every tech stock I ever owned that was any good ran way ahead of the fundamentals, but that's how I made my nut. They never look cheap and they aren't cheap now, but when the institutions have to start owning these stocks, their prices are going to explode."

AN S&P ALTERNATIVE: *IBD*

"We're looking for a company that is making a product that you and I are buying 50 or 100 percent more [of] every year, and are likely to continue doing so for some time."
—JIM OBERWEIS JR.

FOR A SMALL PORTION OF your portfolio, consider following a strategy similar to the one the folks at Oberweis use. You can either shell out the money for *The Oberweis Report* or try to do what Jim Jr. does, yourself.

First, go through the list of companies in *Investor's Business Daily, The New York Times,* or *The Wall Street Journal* and pick out the ones whose earnings and revenues are increasing at rates greater than 30 percent a year. Then, check this list against the tables in the most recent Wednesday *IBD,* and discard any stock whose p/e is higher than half its growth rate.

Next, test the stocks' relative strength—keep only those ranked 70 or better. (Oberweis performs this step later, but doing it here will cut your research time.) Just for the heck of it, take a look at the companies' earnings-per-share rankings, too; you'll vet their financials before you put any money down, but at this point the EPS ranks provide you with a good basis for comparison. You are probably looking for 70 or better here, as well.

By now your list should be considerably smaller. For companies in the S&P 600, check the guide to make sure their earnings have been growing and to see what the analysts say about their business prospects; insider activity isn't an Oberweis criterion, but it wouldn't hurt to look at that, too. If a company isn't in the 600, you'll have to check the financials on your own, the quicker the better—a few weeks, and you've probably missed the boat. Ask your broker to fax you some data. But remember that many of these companies are not closely followed.

Now buy the stocks that pass all the tests. To monitor the companies, do what Oberweis does: Find out when they're going to announce their earnings, and ask their investor-relations people what they told Wall Street to expect and what the Street estimates are. If the figures are negative, sell right away: You don't want to see companies like this go from making 50 percent more each quarter to losing money.

Finally, wait for the earnings reports to come out. If a company continues to grow rapidly, you can probably count on another quarter of decent gains. If earnings are weak, you're outta there.

As a shortcut, you can let your fingers do the walking: The Friday *IBD* contains a list of all the stocks on the exchanges and Nasdaq that are priced above $7 and within 15 percent of their twelve-month highs and whose earnings-per-share and relative-strength rankings are better than 85 percent.

There's your candidate roster. Just research the businesses and place your bets. For each stock, the paper also shows the highest-performing mutual fund with a large stake in it. You can invest in the funds holding most of your favorites, or just use this information to see where the smart money is going.

COST CUTTERS

ON A BUSINESS'S INCOME STATEMENT, you don't want to see all the revenues being eaten up by expenses. In investing, too, you want to prevent costs from cutting too deeply into your profits. One way to accomplish this, as I hammered home in Chapter 1, is to keep your trading at a minimum by buying to hold.

You'll still have to buy and sell sometimes, though. When you do, try to keep it cheap. Among the expenses you can control are your broker fees. If you feel comfortable forgoing some of the advice and other services offered by full-service brokerages, you can reduce transaction costs by using their discount colleagues *(see "Picking a Small-Cap Broker" on the following two pages)*.

Another cost-cutter is to place limit, rather than market, orders. A market order gives your broker permission to buy or sell shares at the best ask or bid available when the trade is executed. Since execution is rarely immediate, the price you actually get may be considerably different from the one in effect when you placed your trade. Moreover, since market makers' quotes are good only for specified numbers of shares—by law, at least 100, though dealers will often go higher—a large order or one involving an illiquid stock could be filled at two different prices.

A limit order, on the other hand, can only be filled at the price you specify or better. So when you place one, you know what you'll get. Except that you may get nothing if you are trying for a better price than the market makers are currently offering. To get immediate execution, put your sell or buy order in at the current bid or ask price; even then, if the market moves against you, the order won't fill and you'll have to decide whether to lower your sights or wait for another move—this time, you hope, in your favor.

A limit order can be either *day* (in effect until the end of that day's trading) or *GTC* (Good Till you Cancel it). By tacking on an *AON* (All Or None), you can require

PICKING A SMALL-CAP BROKER

YOU'LL DO MOST OF YOUR STOCK TRADES, and possibly your mutual-fund transactions as well, through brokers. These come in three varieties, distinguished by the types of services they offer and the size of the commissions they charge to execute trades.

1 Full-service brokers, such as Merrill Lynch & Co. and Salomon Smith Barney, offer the largest palette of services: advice on money management, for instance, and recommendations on financial instruments based on their own staff research and analysis, as well as a certain amount of hand-holding. They also have the highest commissions: anywhere from $80 to $150 for a 100-share trade, though some firms offer special deals in which a client pays a relatively low flat fee to do a certain number of trades a year (and commissions generally are being pushed down). If you're an experienced investor, you may not want to pay the full brokerage fees for your normal transactions. On the other hand, regional brokers, like Raymond James in St. Petersburg, Florida, can provide you with research on small local stocks that you might miss on your own *(see Resources for more names)*. And full-service brokers that specialize in microcaps may be the best sources for the detailed information you must have to invest in this lucrative, but very volatile, segment. They not only can give you research on their favorite microcap stocks but are also the best sources for microcap initial and secondary public offerings. *(See Chapter 4 for more on IPOs.)*

2 Discount brokers, such as Charles Schwab, Fidelity Investments, and Jack White, are considerably cheaper. These charge from $30 to $40 for a 100-share trade, often much less if it's done by computer. They won't give you advice, but they do provide other services, such as asset accounting and research reports from outside sources like S&P. If you feel comfortable finding your own candidates and digging to get the real dirt on them, you might use a discount broker, possibly in addition to a full-service one for the more esoteric IPO and secondary-offering markets. Each spring *SmartMoney* magazine publishes surveys of discount brokers, rating them on various criteria, such as service, costs, and customer satisfaction. Check out the most recent survey before opening an account.

3 Deep-discount brokers, such as National Discount and Brown & Co., often have minimum commissions of $35 or less for big trades that involve money in one of their money market funds. Many also offer flat rates. Datek Online, for example, charges $10.00 a trade for an unlimited number of shares of Nasdaq stock. (Remember, though—you still pay the spread.) This is a real advantage when you're investing in very low-priced microcap companies: Even a deeply discounted per-share commission on a trade involving a few thousand dollars worth of a $0.25 stock could come to hundreds of dollars.

If you're new to investing, it might be a good idea to start with a full service or discount broker until you get more familiar with the market. Once you know what you're doing, you can try out a deep discount broker.

A few tips:

◆ **Look small.** Doug Marx, a broker in Sioux City, Iowa, suggests that a broker from a smaller, local firm has a better handle on small companies because it will take the time to get to know their operations and to build relationships with management: "This is a relationship business, and you tend to do business with people most like you. As a small midwestern firm, we focus on small companies with a very good work ethic."

◆ **"Ask where [brokers] get their ideas and what their sell discipline is," says Marx.**

◆ **Be prepared.** Lisa Gray, a broker in Memphis, suggests "you find a broker who has a plan for all market conditions."

that your entire order fill at one time or not at all. This avoids the multiple commissions you pay if a dealer fills your order in several installments over several days. The problem with an AON is that the market makers might not take it if it is "too large." AON orders they do take are put at the end of the queue and will therefore be filled last. So, to be sure of execution, place one early in the day.

NOW YOU'VE GOT DOWN THE BASICS of small-cap investing and have learned two ways to build and maintain a portfolio of individual stocks. In the following chapter, you'll find more strategies for searching out and selecting investments and for deciding when to commit your hard-earned cash. But the first lesson is the most important: Do your research and find the best stocks available; then be ready to split when better ones come along.

CHAPTER 4

TRADING
Strategies

ORE IN-
vestment ideas than money—institutions generally
don't have this problem; many individuals do. The
previous chapter set you on your way to a solution by
showing you how to screen for the stocks with the
highest ratio of reward to risk. But chances are you'll
still be left with more candidates than you have money
to buy or time to follow. So you need to make some
hard decisions: Do you spring for the growing
company that's capturing the market for satellite-dish
beanies? Or do you opt for the fallen angel whose ex-
CEO, now in the witness-protection program, has been
replaced with Warren Buffett's godson?

This chapter contains suggestions and strategies for
making those decisions. Sometimes it's a matter of
understanding which broad economic trends could
favor one group of companies over another. In other
cases, more localized signals will help you narrow your

stock searches or provide a finer mesh for sorting companies to buy from those to watch. None of the strategies is fail-safe. But knowing how to apply them could improve your investing odds. John Spears, a partner at investment advisers Tweedy, Browne Co., contends that even small tilts in your favor make huge differences in the returns of a portfolio held for twenty or thirty years. This book is about giving yourself the edge that will tip the scales.

THE BIG PICTURE

"My point of view has tended to be that when small does well versus large, that has mostly to do with what's going on with the U.S. economy. If you go back and look over the course of postwar history, small caps tend to do best when we're coming out of a recession. It tends to be their period of best return when we are coming out of a very weak economic cycle. I think the problem, though, is that not every recession has led to one of these fabled multiyear small-cap cycles."
—CLAUDIA MOTT, *director of small-cap research at Prudential Securities*

NATIONAL AND GLOBAL economic trends and events affect which groups and subgroups of investments do better than others. By diversifying your portfolio among the various groups, you achieve stable returns without constantly having to adjust your holdings to the current environment. Still, you shouldn't ignore the larger economic effects discussed in this and the following five sections: the business cycle, both domestic and international; fluctuations in interest rates and in spreads between different credit ratings; foreign exchange movements; and cycles of small-cap under and overperformance. Keeping track of these trends and understanding how they boost or batter which classes of securities will help you make successful investment decisions.

 Vote Democrat.

I don't mean to be partisan, but small-cap stocks do better under Democratic than Republican presidents, according to a Liberty Financial Cos. study reported on in the August 27, 1996, *Investor's Business Daily*. From the beginning of the Hoover administration to the present, the report says, small stocks have risen an average of 22.8 percent annually under Democrats, compared with 1.9 percent under Republicans.

ONE OF THE BIGGEST NATIONAL economic trends is the business cycle, discussed in Chapter 2, pages 72–73. It plays a major role in equity performance: At different points in the cycle, small or large stocks, growth or value, will outperform.

   The effect is illustrated in the chart at right, which graphs the relative returns of small growth and value funds against the business cycle, represented by one-year changes in expected earnings per share of the Standard & Poor's 500 companies, as reported by I/B/E/S. When a cycle is just beginning, value stocks tend to do best, according to studies performed by Merrill Lynch's Satya Pradhuman. During this phase, earnings (and expectations about them) rise in general, but those of turnaround stocks tend

SOURCE: MERRILL LYNCH QUANTITATIVE ANALYSIS, I/B/E/S, MORNINGSTAR

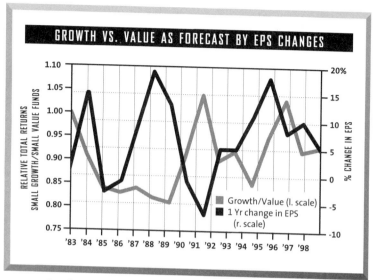

GROWTH VS. VALUE AS FORECAST BY EPS CHANGES

to snap back spectacularly, producing double-digit growth that attracts investors' attention.

Small caps as a group often outperform at the top of the cycle. Large caps have been played out, and investors seeking to prolong their roll must turn to smaller and smaller stocks, which haven't been bid up as high. The strong bull market of 1995 was a classic case. Big companies had notched up their best showing since 1987, and investors began to look beyond the Microsofts, Intels, and IBMs, which had seen huge gains in the first half of the year, to tinier, less well-known—and cheaper—tech stocks.

People "are always chasing returns," James Floyd, of the Leuthold Group, told *Investor's Business Daily* in August 1995. "And things have turned away from the bigger companies to the smaller ones."

After the cycle's peak, as a slowing economy puts a brake on corporate profits, value stocks fall behind. At this point, says Pradhuman, emerging-growth companies, which still have some earnings momentum, attract investors. During the "soft-landing" period of July 1994 to March 1996, for example, Merrill Lynch's index of small-cap value mutual funds returned 24.2 percent, compared with 50 percent for small-cap growth funds and 51 percent for the large-cap Standard & Poor's 500 index.

But when recession looms, investors flee small caps altogether for the relative safety and liquidity of large stocks. The best performers in this climate are consumer companies like Philip Morris Cos. and Johnson & Johnson, whose profits are very stable.

"[Small companies] can thrive in a soft-landing environment," John H. Laporte, who manages the $5 billion New Horizons Fund, says in a June 1995 *Washington Post* article. "They also can do fine in an environment where corporate earnings flatten out. If, on the other hand, we see a major recession, . . . they will not do well."

In a true bear market, small-cap stocks really suffer. Russell Creighton, senior vice president of Barnett Trust Co., points out in a 1994 *Pensions & Investments* article that when investors can't stand watching their principal erode any further, they start selling their holdings. And this drives down small stocks, which have fewer shares and fewer potential buyers, faster and farther than large ones.

"The liquidity problem is one of the key risks to small stocks," Pradhuman says. "All you need is the same amount of sellers for small as for large stocks, and small stocks go down more because of wider [bid-ask] spreads."

In the 1994 article Creighton cautioned that a recession could hit small caps even harder than in the past, because of the growing institutional interest. "Billions of dollars have been put into the markets in the last several years, primarily through mutual funds," he says. "A lot were small cap in the last three years. Mutual fund managers will be forced to sell. We have never had a period with this many small-cap funds trying to liquidate."

Though 1998's economic slowdown was hardly a recession, it demonstrated the accuracy of Creighton's scenario. Investors, spooked by stagnating earnings and international turmoil, fled from small-cap funds to the relative safety of the biggest and most bombproof companies, as well as to Treasuries. To raise the large amounts of cash necessary to honor the flood of redemptions, small-cap fund managers had to sell their most liquid holdings, sending the sector reeling.

On the plus side, the same factors—illiquidity and institutional participation—can drive small stocks to heady highs in a generally rising market. Stephen Lieber, chairman of Lieber/Evergreen Asset Management, notes in the *Pensions & Investments* article that "in a strong market, limited liquidity is an aid. There's less stock around, so if you want it, you have to chase it."

 Don't try to time the market.

After reading about the correlations between the business cycle and stock performance, you might be tempted to try to rebuild your portfolio every time you think you see a new phase starting. Don't do it. First, even the pros can get the signals wrong. Second, the signals point to trends, which are a property of groups and which the individual stocks you hold (or plan to buy) may or may not follow. Third, as Claudia Mott's quote at the beginning of the section points out, even the groups don't always follow the script. And fourth, when they do, the market generally anticipates, rather than follows, economic developments.

"In equity, you're worried about what will happen, not what has happened," Mark Riepe, at the time vice president of consulting firm Ibbotson Associates, told *Pensions & Investments*. "Stocks more often than not are predictors of business cycles." So by the time you see an economic trend forming, it's too late to act on it.

Your best course is to buy the best companies available, then review them when they hit your stop-loss or target prices *(see Chapter 3)*. However, if you're on the fence about a purchase or a sale, the current stage of the business cycle could be a factor that tips you one way or the other.

"We pick stocks because, individually, they are attractive," Charles Royce, president of the Royce Funds, says in a 1992 interview with *Institutional Investor* magazine. "And we can't rely on macro factors to be part of the decision process. Often, too, you get high performance in periods of overvaluation."

My advice: Handle the business cycle with care. That goes for the other big-picture trends, described below, as well. Your best course is to diversify. If she were constructing a portfolio, Claudia Mott says, she would "try to run both disciplines—valuation on the one side, earnings momentum on the other—and structure a portfolio that would look very much like the S&P 600 small-cap index."

A GLOBAL PERSPECTIVE

"More great companies, less coverage."
—The Miller Lite theory of international small-cap investing, propounded by Founders Passport Fund manager M I C H A E L
G E R D I N G

THE UNITED STATES, OF COURSE, is not the only country with a business cycle. Nor is the U.S. cycle the only one that an investor should consider. Even in our increasingly global economy, nations are rarely in sync—one region's growth will be peaking when another's is just beginning or falling off the edge. The United States, for example, lagged European Community countries in the early '90s only to jump ahead in the middle of the decade: From the end of 1996 through mid-December 1998, the S&P outperformed the Bloomberg Europe 500 index, 58 to 48 percent, for an annualized difference of 4 percent.

That doesn't mean you should move your money around the world, chasing the latest hot economy. Rather, you should exploit varying regional cycles as you exploit complementary sector performance: by diversifying.

Small companies are the best medium for global diversification. Most large companies draw at least some of their income from operations abroad. Because of their foreign affairs, they can't be pure domestic plays. On the other hand, their earnings and stock prices are still tied mainly to their home economies, so they don't provide true foreign diversification, either. To get the purest exposure to each country's cycle, you have to go down the scale, to small companies that do all their business within their own borders.

Another reason to invest in small foreign companies is that they present the greatest opportunities. Two-thirds of the world's market capitalization now lies outside the United States, points out Michael Gerding, of the Founders Passport Fund. And, adds Ralph Wanger, the small-cap part of that is generally less efficient.

"In many of the emerging markets abroad, it's like the 1960s were here," Leah Zell, the Acorn International fund manager, told *Kiplinger's* magazine in August 1995. "There are fewer analysts, and it's easier to find a good company that's not widely followed."

Put the emphasis on "good." "These aren't bamboo companies in Vietnam," says Gerding. "These are world-class companies, with some of the smartest managers in the world."

The easiest and safest way to internationalize your small-cap holdings is through mutual funds.

Foreign markets present challenges that even pros find daunting. Gathering information on the companies is difficult, as is interpreting what you manage to dig up. Paradoxically, investors often have fewer problems in emerging markets, many of which have adopted U.S. accounting standards; some companies in these countries even have Big Five accounting firms for their outside auditors. In contrast, Germany's and Switzerland's accounting rules—particularly those concerning cash reserves and earnings—are very different from their U.S. counterparts. This makes comparing Swiss and German companies' financial statements directly with those of U.S. companies very difficult, if not impossible.

Beyond those obstacles, most governments impose limits and taxes on foreign investors and their profits. You're better off letting a mutual fund manager worry about these headaches, as well as about whether and how to hedge against foreign-exchange risk. For specific tips on investing in international small-cap funds, see Chapter 2, pages 73–75.

INTEREST RATES

"Not surprisingly, when 90-day Treasury-bill rates are overlaid with growth and value cycles, the cycles tend to follow with a reasonable degree of closeness, after a time lag, the longer-term direction of interest rates."
—KENNETH FISHER and JOSEPH TOMS, *president and senior vice president, respectively, of Fisher Investments, in* Small Cap Stocks

THE ECONOMIC CYCLE IS closely allied to the level of interest rates. Money, after all, is the lifeblood of business, and many companies rely on loans for their transfusions. When interest rates are low, as they generally are during and just after a slump, companies can fund their projects more cheaply. As a result, their earnings tend to pick up. When rates start to rise again, in response to an expanding economy and fears of inflation, margins erode.

Since earnings drive share price, the equity market mirrors interest-rate levels, rising as they fall, falling as they rise. Research conducted by Daniel P. Coker, then an analyst at NatWest Securities, confirms this pattern. Among other subjects, Coker studied stock-market performance during the month following an initial Federal Reserve Board interest-rate change (one reversing the direction of the preceding moves). He found that since January 1948, initial rises in the *discount rate* (the rate the Fed charges member banks) have been followed by market declines averaging 2.1 percent; initial Fed easings produced average one-month rises of 2.8 percent.

The effect is exaggerated among small-cap stocks. These "are very [influenced] by interest rates in terms of valuations," Bill Keithler, who now manages a technology fund for Invesco, says in the 1995 *IBD* article. "When rates are going up, it's very tough sledding." According to Coker's study, the average one-month declines for large, small, and microcap stocks in response to a Fed tightening were 1.9, 2.5, and 2.6 percent, respectively; the same groups rose 2.2, 4.9, and 6.1 percent after an easing.

The reason for the difference in interest-rate sensitivity is suggested in a 1995 paper by Merrill's Pradhuman. Although large companies usually borrow in the bond market, he explains, many small companies, because of their lower credit ratings, must borrow from banks at prime. The prime rate is higher than interest rates for investment-grade debt; it also rises faster and falls more slowly. So small-cap earnings tend to respond more dramatically than large-cap earnings to changes in the Treasury rate (the benchmark for corporate bonds). In fact, Pradhuman found the spread between prime and the 10-year Treasury yield to be a very good predictor of whether large or small caps will do better: When declines in the prime rate (usually triggered by Fed easings) outpace those in the ten-year yield, narrowing the spread, small stocks generally outperform.

Kenneth Fisher and Joseph Toms, in the book *Small Cap Stocks*, report similar correlations for value versus growth stocks: "We found that when interest rates drop significantly, with a time lag, a value cycle ensues. Likewise, when rates rise significantly, again with a time lag, the result is a growth cycle."

Why? Because value companies generally carry much more debt, both short- and long-term, than growth companies, which can raise capital more cheaply by issuing stock. Fisher and Toms point out that high p/e ratios, a growth characteristic, translate into cheap capital: Selling stock at 30 times earnings is equivalent to borrowing at a yield of $1/30$, or 3.3 percent, which is well below the usual prime rate. In contrast, a p/e of 10, more characteristic of value stocks, translates into a capital cost of 10 percent, and that's seldom better than prime.

So rising interest rates will hit the profits and prices of value companies harder than those of more modestly leveraged growth firms. Conversely, value stocks should shoot up higher under the impetus of falling rates.

Merrill Lynch strategist Steve Kim has found that the slope of the current Treasury yield curve can also be used to forecast whether growth or value will be the better per-former. The curve is a graph plotting Treasury yields against various maturities, from three months to thirty years *(see the chart below)*. Its normal shape is gently "posi-tive," with yields rising gradually as maturities increase. This configuration reflects the fact that investors ordinar-ily require somewhat higher rewards for taking the greater risk of tying up their money for longer periods.

The yield curve may steepen if a Fed lowering of short-term rates, to stimulate economic growth, raises fears of inflation that keep long-term rates from falling propor-tionately. This signals a good environment for value stocks, which tend to outperform in a hot economy. Conversely, a flatter curve results from a tighter monetary policy, designed to cool the economy, and fewer long-term infla-tion fears. This configuration is better for growth stocks, which can post decent earnings even when growth is slow. The rare inverse curve, with the short end rising above the long, occurs when the Fed raises short-term rates sharply, showing it's serious about cooling the economy. Long-bond investors take heart and buy, pushing down long yields. An inverse curve gives a heads-up for recession—and tough going for both value and growth.

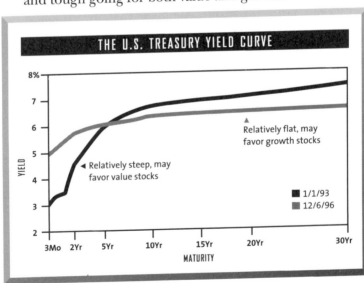

THE U.S. TREASURY YIELD CURVE

SOURCE: BLOOMBERG L.P.

How much faith should you put in these signals? "The yield curve never lies," says William Wilson, vice president and economist at Comerica Bank in Detroit. Moreover, its warnings come enough in advance to enable you to act before events overtake your equity strategy.

"The yield curve gives you pretty long leads, longer than the stock market," says Victor Zarnowitz, director of the Center for International Business Cycle Research at Columbia University in New York.

Don't fight the Fed. Rising interest rates mean tough going for stocks, especially small ones. You increase your odds of success tremendously if you take fewer risks and remain hard-nosed about your stock selection criteria when the Fed is tightening.

How can you tell in advance what the Fed intends? Look at the federal-funds futures contracts, which you can find in *The Wall Street Journal* or *Barron's*. They will tell you what yield the market expects to be in effect when they expire. Just subtract a contract's price (in the Settle column) from 100. If the result—the expected yield—is lower than the present funds rate, the market is betting on the Fed to loosen; if it is higher, a tightening is predicted.

On the other hand, expect equities to excel when the 30-year Treasury yield is lower than its 52-week moving average. Add up the reported bond yields of the past 52 weeks (you can find them at the Bloomberg Web site, www.bloomberg.com) and divide by 52. That gives you the *average*. To make it *moving*, recalculate each week by dropping the oldest data point and adding in the most recent one. The relationship between the moving average and the current yield is a gauge of interest-rate momentum. A current yield below the average indicates a trend toward lower rates, which, as discussed above, is good for stocks. Research covering the period from 1969 to 1996—and reported on by Salomon Smith Barney analysts John Manley Jr. and Jeffrey Wanrantz in October 1997—found that the S&P 500 always rose when the current yield was 10 percent below the average and failed to gain only once when the difference was 8 percent.

CREDIT SPREADS

"I'm a bottom-up stock picker. I can't forecast the market or the economy; my shareholders have empirical evidence of this."
—JAMES BARROW, *manager of the Vanguard Windsor II mutual fund*

THE ABSOLUTE LEVEL OF corporate bond rates is one indicator of what to expect in the small-cap sector. The gap between rates for companies having different credit ratings is another. Both Ibbotson Associates founder Roger Ibbotson and Merrill's Satya Pradhuman have shown that when the spread between the interest rates for lower and higher credit ratings tightens, small caps tend to outperform *(see the chart below)*.

One explanation for this relationship is that spreads narrow when the economy is strong, making lenders optimistic about the prospects of risky ventures and willing to give them money at attractive rates. So small companies, which generally fall into the high-risk group, find it easier at these times to get the money they need to feed their rapid growth.

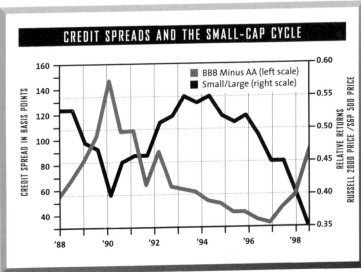

CREDIT SPREADS AND THE SMALL-CAP CYCLE

BBB Minus AA (left scale)
Small/Large (right scale)

CREDIT SPREAD IN BASIS POINTS

RELATIVE RETURNS
RUSSELL 2000 PRICE /S&P 500 PRICE

SOURCE: MERRILL LYNCH QUANTITATIVE ANALYSIS

This was certainly true in March and April 1996. From May 1994 to March 1996, investors had required an average of 40 basis points to switch from the security of AAA-rated (bombproof) bonds to shakier BBB-rated (water-repellent) bonds. Then the economic rally began. This panicked traders, who started smelling inflation, and encouraged low-grade-bond investors, who believed it would help riskier businesses. As a result, 10-year bonds backed by the U.S. Treasury lost 9 percent of their value while debt of lesser credits rose a few percent. Meanwhile, funds like Oberweis Microcap and Van Wagoner Emerging Growth jumped almost 50 percent.

The reverse is also true: When credit spreads widen, small stocks fall. Small-cap investors learned this to their sorrow in 1998. Between July 1 and November 16, the yield difference between Treasuries and BB2 corporates grew to 300 basis points from 200, and small stock indexes dropped 10 percent.

Investor's Business Daily carries information about the Treasury curve and credit spreads. This data is often provided by Bloomberg News (BN), so the Bloomberg Web page is another good place to look, as are the bond columns in *The New York Times* and *The Wall Street Journal.*
Again, don't use this information to try to time the market. However, if you are deciding between a large stock and an equally attractive small one, a tightening of spreads or a change in the shape of the curve could tip the balance one way or the other. For instance, if you see in *IBD* that the yield difference between AAA- and BBB-rated bonds has narrowed, you might opt for the small company over the large.

THE DOLLAR

"But then one is always excited by descriptions of money changing hands. It's much more fundamental than sex."

—NIGEL DENNIS, *English novelist and playwright*

HERE'S ANOTHER CONNECTION: The *dollar exchange rate* (how many dollars a unit of another currency will buy) is linked to companies' foreign earnings, which, in turn, are linked to their share prices. When the dollar weakens against foreign currencies, U.S. businesses with overseas sales benefit. Not only are their products now more competitive with foreign-made ones, but their yen or franc earnings translate into many more dollars. Eyeing these profits, investors pour money into the stocks of companies with foreign exposures, most of which are large. A strengthening dollar produces the opposite effect. The overseas profits of large companies are eroded, while homebound small-cap earnings, unaffected by currency fluctuations, draw investor interest *(see the chart below)*.

The first scenario was played out in 1995. From spring to year end, a weak dollar energized the earnings and share prices of large U.S. multinationals such as Coca-Cola Co., Gillette Co., and McDonald's Corp., which draw as much as 40 percent of their revenues from abroad. Meanwhile, small stocks were hit with a double whammy: higher interest rates, which made financing expensive, and a

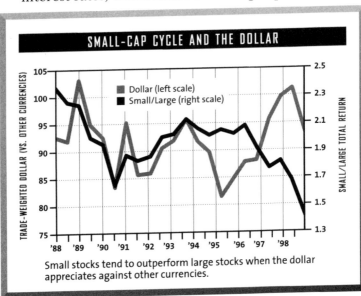

SMALL-CAP CYCLE AND THE DOLLAR

■ Dollar (left scale)
■ Small/Large (right scale)

TRADE-WEIGHTED DOLLAR (VS. OTHER CURRENCIES)

SMALL/LARGE TOTAL RETURN

Small stocks tend to outperform large stocks when the dollar appreciates against other currencies.

SOUCE: MERRILL LYNCH QUANTITATIVE ANALYSIS

dearth of the overseas business that equity investors were seeking. By mid-1996, though, the second scenario was materializing. Rates had eased, the dollar was strengthening, and profits from multinational operations abroad were becoming slimmer. Analysts saw an opportunity for small, domestic companies to shine. (Unfortunately, predictors are fallible, even the almighty dollar, and a rush to quality in the face of instability abroad derailed the analysts' high small-cap hopes through the end of 1998.)

Finding exchange rates and other currency data is easy—just look in the newspaper. Using this information is more problematic.

All it tells you is which sectors are likely to do better than others. But doing better is not the same as doing well. If you drop only 10 percent while the market drops 20, you've outperformed, but your family still starves. Moreover, individual small companies that sell principally to large ones could be slapped indirectly by a strengthening dollar that hurts their customers. And large enterprises generally have better mechanisms than smaller ones to handle currency risk. All in all, the dollar's relative strength should serve mainly as a warning signal. When it's very weak, as at the end of 1994 and the beginning of 1995, you'd better have rock-solid convictions about any small stock you choose over comparable large ones. A strengthening dollar, on the other hand, lowers the bar.

THE SMALL-CAP CYCLE

"People think small caps tend to outperform for seven years and then underperform for some period of time, [but] the relationship really isn't that perfect. . . . I think it is very hard to time."
—CLAUDIA MOTT *of Prudential Securities*

IN ADDITION TO ALTERNATING periods of earnings growth and stagnation, falling and rising rates, wide and tight spreads, and dollar weakness and strength, many analysts detect cycles of small-cap under- and overper-

SMALL-CAP "OVERPERFORMANCE" CYCLES

PERIOD	DURATION (IN YEARS)	CUMULATIVE SMALL-CAP RETURN	ANNUALIZED SMALL-CAP RETURN	EXCESS RETURN VS. S&P 500
1932–37	4.8	946.0	62.5	16.0
1940–45	6.0	534.1	36.0	13.0
1963–68	6.0	267.7	24.2	10.8
1975–83	8.5	1072.6	33.6	14.5
1991–94	3.3	142.8	30.8	11.3
Average	5.7	592.6	37.4	13.3

SOURCE: CRSP; THE UNIVERSITY OF CHICAGO; PRUDENTIAL SECURITIES, INC.

formance *(see the chart above)*. These cycles last from three to more than seven years, depending on who's counting.

The June 1995 *Washington Post* article cited earlier delineates two recent cycles based on the performance of the T. Rowe Price New Horizons Fund. New Horizons, founded in 1960 as the first small-cap fund, has been used ever since as a barometer for the sector. The *Post* points out that from June 1983 to October 1990, the fund lost 1 percent while the S&P 500 was gaining 138 percent. That seven-year period was one of the all-time worst for small-cap stocks. The tide turned in October 1990. From then until March 31, 1995, New Horizons climbed 167 percent—despite losses during parts of 1992, 1993, and 1994—compared with a rise of only 88 percent for the S&P 500. After those numbers were published, small caps again entered the depressed phase of their cycle, with New Horizons returning a mere 2.72 from October 31, 1996, through October 31, 1998, as the S&P was growing 61.15 percent.

Why do small stocks clobber or get clobbered by large stocks for years at a time? Probably for the same reason that last year's audience favorites will be next year's box-office poison: overexposure. When one group of stocks is in favor, their valuations become extreme. Investors looking for bargains suddenly rediscover the last phase's dar-lings, which have been snubbed and are now attractively cheap. Money flows into that sector, and the cycle starts all over again.

You can see this process at work by looking at two indi-cators. The first is the relationship between the average p/e of the New Horizons Fund and that of the S&P 500; the second, small-cap market share.

The theory behind the p/e indicator is this: Because New Horizons invests in fast-growing small companies, you expect its average p/e to be higher than that of the index, which contains slow growers such as Bethlehem Steel *(see the chart below)*. When the two averages are about equal, therefore, small-cap stocks should be cheap. They may have fallen far out of favor, or the market may not yet have caught on to a recent spurt in income growth. Either way, small stocks are a good buy. This can't last, though— investors will soon rediscover the sector and bid up prices. When New Horizons' average p/e reaches twice the S&P's, small stocks are considered overheated.

The second indicator, small-cap market share, is defined

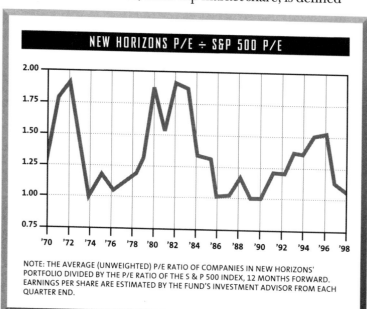

NEW HORIZONS P/E ÷ S&P 500 P/E

NOTE: THE AVERAGE (UNWEIGHTED) P/E RATIO OF COMPANIES IN NEW HORIZONS' PORTFOLIO DIVIDED BY THE P/E RATIO OF THE S & P 500 INDEX, 12 MONTHS FORWARD. EARNINGS PER SHARE ARE ESTIMATED BY THE FUND'S INVESTMENT ADVISOR FROM EACH QUARTER END.

by Fisher and Toms as "the percent of the aggregate value of the total stock market represented by small caps." This number, the authors say, indicates "faddishness."

"When a style has a large share of the market compared to history," they write, "[it] has become more popular. When a style has a low share of the market compared to history, it . . . has been losing popularity. Generally, styles that are too popular have already been bid up in price—all the buying has been done." The two authors note that small caps went from a market share of only 14 percent in 1974 to a peak of 22 percent in 1983. In hindsight, they say, 1974 was "the best opportunity to own small-cap stocks since the end of the Great Depression." By their measure, the end of 1998 looked like an even better opportunity: In mid-November, small caps, represented by the Russell 2000, accounted for *less* than 14 percent of the entire market, represented by the Russell 3000.

When the S&P 500's average p/e and inflation are both running high, the whole market may be due for a downturn. According to Gail Dudack, chief market strategist at UBS Securities, when the annual change in the Consumer Price Index added to the average p/e of the S&P 500 exceeds 20, trouble is brewing.

The chart at right shows that the average p/e of the stock market moves opposite to the direction of the inflation rate. This means that one of the most dangerous times for stocks is when p/e's are high and inflation starts to rise. That was the situation in the early 1970s. During the post-World War II, pre-Vietnam war nirvana of the early 1960s, low inflation had supported high stock prices. Then inflation heated up, making life in the '70s and early '80s miserable for investors.

The same could be said when the earnings yield is below the yield on 10-year Treasuries. As explained in Chapter 3, earnings yield—the reciprocal of p/e—is what the return on your investment would be if the company paid out all its earnings as dividends. Since equities are riskier than Treasuries, you'd expect the S&P 500 to have a higher yield than the 10-year

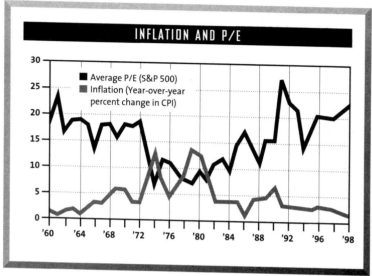

bond. But in 1998, the relationship was reversed, with the S&P yielding 4.7 percent, versus the 10-year Treasury's 5.57 percent. This implied that the market considered blue chips safer than government debt—an irrationally exuberant belief if there ever was one. A situation like that can be corrected in three ways, according to Deutsche Bank Securities chief economist Edward Yardeni: Expected earnings can rise, bond yields can decline, or stock prices can drop. At mid 1998, earnings seemed unlikely to grow fast enough, and rates would have had to fall by almost 90 basis points. That left a drop in stock prices. And, in fact, between July 17 and August 28, they did plummet 13 percent, pushing the earnings yield 10 percent above the 10-year yield and making equities look cheap. When the Fed cut interest rates in October to prop up the economy, stocks rallied and the relationship moved back to parity.

Watch out when the cash levels of small-cap mutual funds are low—a down cycle in small stocks is about to begin. Prudential's Claudia Mott points out that minimal cash reserves mean the funds are fully invested. So they won't be pouring a lot of new money into small-cap stocks, and growth will probably stall *(see the chart on the following page).*

SOURCE: INVESTMENT COMPANY INSTITUTE; PRUDENTIAL SECURITIES, INC.

CASH AND RETURN

Below-average cash levels tend to mean below-average returns.

CASH LEVEL OF AGGRESSIVE-GROWTH FUNDS	SUBSEQUENT RETURN (%)		
	3 MONTHS	6 MONTHS	12 MONTHS
<9.7%	2.6	4.6	8.0
Average of 9.7%	2.9	5.8	11.2
>9.7%	3.3	7.0	14.6

NOTE: DATA COVER THE PERIOD JANUARY 1971 THROUGH SEPTEMBER 1995. RETURNS ARE FOR THE NASDAQ COMPOSITE AND DO NOT INCLUDE DIVIDENDS.

Once again, though, don't restructure your portfolio according to where we are in a small-cap cycle. Sure, you'd like to jump in at a bottom and out again at a top. But it isn't that easy.

THE JANUARY EFFECT

"Or is it the January defect?"
—SATYA PRADHUMAN, *director of small-cap research at Merrill Lynch*

THAT DOES IT FOR BIG PICTURE trends. Here's a more modest cycle—one you can pretty much count on year by year. For the past couple of decades, stocks have generated the lion's share of their annual returns in one month: January. The best explanation for this "January effect" is taxes. Simply put, at the end of the calendar year, investors sell shares that have fallen in price so they can book losses and reduce their tax bills. Then, after the thirty-day waiting period required by law, they buy back the losers they still have faith in. The result is a market decline at year end and a rebound the following January.

This pattern, which has been confirmed by various researchers, is particularly marked among small caps. In fact, a large percentage of the returns that have made the smallest stocks the best long-term performers have come in January. Since 1926, according to small-cap expert Coker, microcaps have returned 8.7 percent on average during January, compared with 1.4 percent for all months. Merrill Lynch's Pradhuman adds that small value stocks have been the biggest gainers. Connected to this is the fact, also cited by Pradhuman, that the effect has been most pronounced in Januarys following years of poor small-cap performance.

How can you exploit the January effect in your investment strategy?

An easy way would be to buy a no-load small-cap mutual fund in December, after it distributes its capital gains (see Chapter 2, page 71), and then sell it again at the end of January. Or you could use fundamental analysis to define a subset of small caps that appear oversold and perform the same trades on them.

If you choose to follow either of these schemes, commit only a small portion of your investment funds, just enough to boost your annual returns. Your general plan should still be to buy excellent companies and hold them for a long time. In this context, the January effect might help you time your trades. For instance, if a small value stock is on your radar near the end of the year, you might wait until prices drop in December to pounce. Conversely, December is probably not a good time to sell shares, unless you want to take a tax loss.

Some small companies are better candidates for a January rebound than others. In an article in the December 1998 issue of *Bloomberg Personal Finance* magazine, Dan Coker gives the following pointers: Stocks priced under $10 produce the greatest excess return; those within 30 percent of their 52-week lows also do well, as do stocks with low price-to-book values; high and growing liquidity is another good sign and can serve as a hedge should the effect fail to materialize; growth characteristics seem to have no bearing on January performance; health care is a good January sector; financial and utility stocks are not.

One caveat: The January effect has been getting earlier. Coker notes that "since 1980 the average return for small caps in December has been 2.4 percent; since 1990 it has increased to 4.1 percent, while the average January return has decreased to 1.9 from 3.1 percent."

◆ **If you like the tax strategy behind the January effect, implement it early.**
That's the advice given by Bloomberg applications specialist Sanjiv Gupta in a November 15, 1995, Bloomberg News article. "Smart year-end tax sellers will do it [in November]," he says. "They will get a better price for their shares than they can a month [later]. And—if they are reluctant to part with their losers—they can buy them back at bargain prices in December, when others are dumping them. The wash rule says that when you take a tax loss, you cannot buy the stock [or fund] back for thirty days. Selling early means that you will be in a position to buy them back at the end of December." Coker points out that mutual funds, most of which have an effective tax year ending in October or November, often take their losses in those months and do their repurchasing in December, perhaps explaining the January effect's drift backward in time noted above.

TO MARKET, TO MARKET—IPOS

"When you're working your way toward all-time high levels of IPO activity, it usually means the market's getting a little overvalued. People are obviously trying to take advantage of a very favorable window to get their financing done."
—CLAUDIA MOTT *of Prudential Securities*

ANOTHER PLACE TO LOOK AT for smaller-scale signals and trends is the IPO market. An *initial public offering*, or *IPO*, is the first sale of a corporation's stock to the wider community. It's done to raise money and also, sometimes principally, to let existing investors reap big profits on their shares, which will be valued for the first time according to the company's perceived growth prospects. Since IPOs almost always have limited market capitalizations—80 percent are under $60 million, according to Mott—they serve as a litmus test for the small-cap market in general. The volume and quality of deals brought to market in a certain period can signal how hot the small sector is, and how long it's likely to stay that way.

Companies typically do IPOs when they think the market is riding high enough to bring them a good price for their shares. If many issuers start rushing to market, they may be exploiting a window of opportunity before it closes. In other words, small caps may be due for a correction.

In fact, corrections usually do follow an IPO surge, according to a study performed by Mott. Mott looked at the Nasdaq Composite stock index's performance after months during which a large number of offerings were made. She found that from 1979 through October 1995, IPO activity and small-cap prices have peaked at the same time. In addition, as the chart below shows, returns on the Nasdaq have been flat or negative three, six, and even twelve months after months in which more than fifty IPOs came to market.

Recent trends have presented no exception to this rule. In October and November 1997, respectively, 77 and 88 IPOs went to market; in the twelve months following October 31, 1997, the New Horizons fund lost 8.6 percent, even as large stocks were rallying 22 percent. Better small-cap days may lie ahead, however: In Sep-

SOURCE: SECURITIES DATA CORP.; PRUDENTIAL SECURITIES, INC.

AN ACTIVE IPO MARKET IS BAD FOR SMALL CAPS

NUMBER OF IPO'S	SUBSEQUENT RETURN (%)		
	3 MONTHS	6 MONTHS	12 MONTHS
<10	11.1	20.4	38.5
11–20	3.4	7.4	11.4
21–30	3.5	5.8	14.3
31–40	2.9	8.0	9.3
41–50	3.7	9.5	16.4
51–60	-0.8	-3.4	-1.2
61–70	-0.4	-1.8	0.0
>71	-1.6	-2.9	-2.7

NOTE: DATA COVER THE PERIOD JANUARY 1979 THROUGH OCTOBER 1995.
RETURNS ARE FOR THE NASDAQ COMPOSITE AND DO NOT INCLUDE DIVIDENDS

tember and October 1998, only 5 and 9 deals were done.

Just as important as the volume of IPOs are their price levels—specifically, where the actual prices lie within the "price talk," or presale range set by the offerings' underwriters. A large percentage of deals coming in at the high end of the talk, says Heartland's Bill Nasgovitz, "would indicate [a] tremendous amount of speculation and 'froth' in the marketplace." And froth signals the end of a rally.

The financial solidity of the companies doing the deals is another factor to watch. "When the portfolio managers I speak to start complaining about the quality of deals," says Mott, "I know we're getting into trouble."

Your broker can help you find out what's been going on in the IPO market.
Ask him or her to check the Equity New Issue Calendar on the shop's Bloomberg terminal. This will show the number and total dollar value of deals done every month this year and last. The brokerage should also be able to determine their position within the price talk.

IPOS SERVE AS A SMALL-CAP early-warning system: A lot of activity means that the small-cap market is overheated and you might want to put off purchases until it cools down a bit. (If you discover a really attractive, really cheap small company, though, don't wait.) Heeding the IPO warning could save you money. But can you use these offerings to make money, as well?

Yes, but not the way you're thinking. You're unlikely to rack up big profits by buying IPOs, unless you're a pension fund or some other big shot. My former Bloomberg sidekick Matt Wright, who covered the IPO market for Bloomberg News, says that underwriters allocate all the best deals—the ones that go up 40 or 50 percent the first day of trading—to institutional and large individual investors. These generally make big profits by flipping— buying stakes in the new offerings and then quickly selling them once trading opens.

Investment banks regard IPOs as "the payback to their best institutional or mutual fund clients, like us or Fidelity," John P. Kinnucan, fund manager at the Crabbe Huson Group in Portland, Oregon, told Bloomberg News in August 1995. "It is a game of mutual back-scratching."

Institutions place orders with a firm's trading desk, paying it tidy commissions, and are rewarded by being let into hot deals at their offering prices. When Netscape came public, for instance, Kinnucan was able to get in early and flip his shares for a profit.

That profit was made possible by us little investors. Like mullets, we listen to the sales hype and place market orders to buy pieces of deals at whatever price is available. As we bid the stock up higher and higher, the institutions unload their stakes. When that drives the price down, we're left holding the bag.

One of the Netscape bag-holders was Blaine Kubesh, who describes himself as just "another sucker." He explains, "I was unfortunate enough to have a pending order to buy Netscape at the market price. By the time I heard it was going to open at over $60, it was too late—I couldn't get my cancel order in quick enough." His order to buy 200 shares was executed at $71. He issued a sell order immediately. It was confirmed at $58.50, landing him a $2,500 loss.

The playing field has been leveled somewhat, with brokerages such as Charles Schwab and E*trade now offering clients shares in IPOs obtained through alliances with deal underwriters. But, as John Dorfman points out in the January/February 1998 issue of *Bloomberg Personal Finance,* "institutional investors will likely find ways to keep the lion's share of the truly hot deals." So the best way to profit from IPOs is still probably by following these tips:

 Be a pilot fish instead of a mullet.

Other companies in the same industry as a new offering often get caught up in the feeding frenzy surrounding it. So when a successful IPO surfaces, look for solid stocks in the same sector that you can scoop up at reasonable prices.

 **Catch 'em later.**

Charles Royce, president of Quest Advisory, points out that about a year after their initial offerings, many former highfliers are lying low: The underwriters have stopped touting them, insiders have cashed in their shares, and many will have had a quarter of weaker earnings. At this point, smart investors can pick up shares of good companies at attractive levels.

"There is opportunity in the literally 3,000 companies that went public in the last five years," says Peter Lynch, former manager of the Fidelity Magellan fund, who trounced the market during his tenure by 13 percentage points a year. "Over half . . . are below the offer price: They came public at 10, and the first trade was 18. At the time, [investors] got mad that they only got 100 shares and not 5,000. Now the stock's at 4, and no one cares. . . . These busted [initial public offerings] are amazing."

By waiting, you also avoid the many one-day wonders. According to Mott, the afterlife of the average IPO is dismal. The most successful—and long-lived—deals have solid fundamentals.

ECONOMIC TRENDS AND CYCLES tell you which sectors and industries should do better than others. To figure out which individual stocks are your best picks, you have to look at the particular, not the general. Cues include company earnings, share-price histories and patterns, and the trades of those in the know. These are the subject of the next six sections.

BEYOND YOUR WILDEST EXPECTATIONS

"Surprise is the great corrector."

—DAVID DREMAN, *founder and manager of the Kemper-Dreman High Return Fund*

EVERYONE LOVES A NICE surprise, and Wall Street is no exception. Investing in companies that report earnings above analysts' expectations produces market-beating returns. That's been the consistent conclusion of research dating back twenty-five years, and it was recently reiterated in a 1996 report by Mott and Melissa Brown, then director of quantitative research at Prudential (now at Goldman Sachs). The effect of positive surprises, moreover, is enhanced among small companies. These have less analyst coverage and more room to grow, so when one announces better-than-expected earnings, investors listen closely. Mott found that small-cap stocks posting positive surprises generated average three-month returns of 13.7 percent, 10.4 percent better than the S&P 500. By comparison, large-cap surprises, according to Brown, returned only 5.7 percent on average, or 3.1 percent more than the benchmark.

Mott and Brown also discovered that the positive-surprise effect lasts three months. So you don't have to buy shares the day of an earnings announcement to reap the benefits. That's good news for small investors, who usually get information later than the bigger players and can't act on it as quickly. (Be aware, however, that with more people wising up to the effect of earnings surprises and buying directly after positive ones, the window for action is likely to shrink in the future.)

You'll find a list of positive surprises at the Primark Investment Research Center Web site (www.pirc.com), published the day after they are announced or if you set-up a personal page on Yahoo.com.

STILL YOU'D OBVIOUSLY BE ahead of the game if you took your stakes before the stocks were bid up. And you'd really be sitting pretty if you could scoop the market by anticipating positive surprises. But how can you predict when Wall Street's best and brightest will be wrong? Easy. Remember the cockroach theory I mentioned in Chapter 3? Well, when you see one positive surprise, look for others. In 1993 Mott surveyed small companies that had beaten estimates one quarter and calculated they had a

34 percent better chance of doing so again the next quarter than companies that had merely met or fallen below expectations.

 Put your stockbroker on the case.
The firm's Bloomberg service can generate a list of all the companies that produced positive surprises in the current quarter. But bear in mind one drawback to the roach approach: Companies that have previously sprung positive surprises aren't just likely to repeat; they're also probably more expensive than those that produce surprises out of the blue.

Another, very valuable resource that you can put to work is I/B/E/S International.
I/B/E/S is a subscription-only service that tracks analysts' earnings expectations and publishes a list of the small-cap stocks it feels will beat them. In the past, three-quarters of the firm's picks have turned in positive surprises, and the list as a whole has regularly beaten the S&P 500. For $9.45 a month, you can screen stocks and download reports on up to fifteen companies at the service's Web site, www.ibes.com. Analyst information is also available under America Online's Personal Finance channel and on Bloomberg.com.

HOWEVER YOU FIND THEM, you should have plenty of surprising stocks to choose from. Expectation-beating earnings are becoming more common—and not necessarily because businesses are better run than in the past. In the indisputably lackluster third quarter of 1998, 49 percent of reporting companies posted positive surprises. The reason, analysts suggest, is that management has discovered the benefits of understatement. If a company is too conservative and actual earnings exceed forecasts, the market usually reacts favorably. In contrast, projections that later prove to be overly optimistic can prompt lawsuits from disappointed shareholders. So, again quoting Jim Oberweis's September 1996 *Oberweis Report,* managements "tend to work with analysts to keep estimates low."

The result is somewhat like "gradeflation" in academia. Just as grad schools today might give the same weight to an undergraduate's Bs that they used to accord to Cs, so investors increasingly react negatively to companies that merely meet expectations or whose overachievements aren't astounding. In October 1996, for example, both Intel and Sun Micro Systems announced third-quarter earnings above their average estimates. The next day Intel was up 5 percent, but Sun was down 9.8 percent. The difference? Unlike Intel, "Sun didn't beat expectations strongly enough," says analyst Martin Pyykkonen, who at the time was with Furman Selz and removed the stock from his "recommended" list. Investor skepticism may perhaps also explain the fact that the duration of the positive-surprise effect has shrunk from six months to three.

When you have a list of companies most likely to fool the wise guys, what do you do with it? You probably don't have enough money to buy shares in them all. Even if you did, it wouldn't be a good idea. Remember, you're looking for stocks to hold, not one-quarter wonders, and some surprises could reflect onetime gains, such as the sale of property by a company whose real business is computers.

"Understand where the new earnings growth came from, and then question whether it can be duplicated," recommends Christine Baxter of the PBHG family of funds. Did the surprise result from new sales or from one-time non-operational gains? And what effect will the recent outperformance have on future growth? Baxter says that sometimes a young company overworks employees or forces sales on customers before the end of the quarter so that it will meet or exceed its earnings estimate. This can strain resources and put the company in a hole the next quarter, making growth difficult to sustain.

Your best defense against unrepeatable surprises is good fundamental analysis, like that described in Chapter 3. You can incorporate earnings surprises into the buy-and-hold schema outlined there at either the beginning or the end of the stock-picking process. In the first case, your surprise list will give you ideas to research and analyze; pay special attention to relative strength, since Mott and Coker found that stocks scoring high on this measure were the best performers. In the second case, you'll cull the buy candidates you've already researched for those most likely to surprise analysts with their earnings strength. Either way, if the surprises you expect materialize, you'll be holding solid companies with momentum; if they don't, you're still left with good stocks. I'll take those odds anytime.

This strategy is particularly useful for picking value stocks. David Dreman, of Dreman Value Management, a manager known for producing high risk-adjusted returns, noted in a 1996 talk at the New York Society of Security Analysts that, though out-of-favor stocks carry less risk than highfliers, they don't add much to your returns if they stay out of favor. Earnings surprises, he said, provide the juice that boosts value returns above growth.

Dreman cited a study of the period between 1973 and 1993 in which he and Michael Berry (now with Heartland Advisors) looked at how companies' shares performed during both the quarter and the year following positive earnings surprises. All the surprising stocks outperformed,

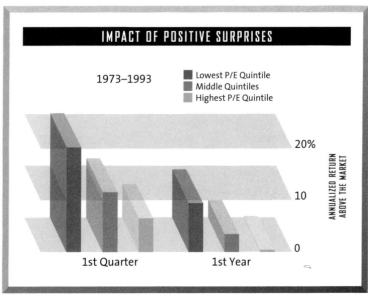

IMPACT OF POSITIVE SURPRISES

1973–1993

- Lowest P/E Quintile
- Middle Quintiles
- Highest P/E Quintile

ANNUALIZED RETURN ABOVE THE MARKET

20%

10

0

1st Quarter   1st Year

SOURCE: THE DREMAN FOUNDATION

but—as you can see from the chart at left—the stars were those with the lowest p/e's: They beat the market by 20 percent during the first quarter following an announcement and by 9.39 percent during the first year. The numbers for the stocks with the highest p/e's during the same periods were 6.63 percent and a mere 0.32 percent, respectively.

If you're worried about the effect of negative surprises on your portfolio, take heart—value will see you through. Dreman and Berry's study also found that one year after missing analysts' estimates, the stocks with the lowest p/e's still outperformed. Companies with low p/e's that failed to meet expectations underperformed the market during the first quarter by only about 4 percent, compared with 18.4 percent for high-p/e stocks *(see the chart below)*. And once they pass the one-year mark after a negative surprise, the lowest-p/e stocks generally go on to outperform the market by a slim margin.

Get insider insight into earnings—where the extra growth came from and where the numbers are likely to go from here.

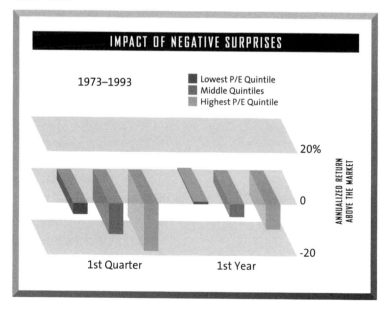

IMPACT OF NEGATIVE SURPRISES

1973–1993

■ Lowest P/E Quintile
■ Middle Quintiles
■ Highest P/E Quintile

ANNUALIZED RETURN ABOVE THE MARKET

20%

0

-20

1st Quarter   1st Year

SOURCE: THE DREMAN FOUNDATION

Bug the heck out of the investor relations people to be allowed to listen in on the conference calls in which management explains earnings. If that's not possible, at least see if you can get transcripts of the calls on the companies' Web sites *(or their Internet addresses, see Resources)*. You might also check out TheStreet.com. Hedge-fund manager James Cramer's online financial newsletter (available at www.thestreet.com) often discusses what goes on during these conference calls. Its focus is large caps, but Cramer's reports are always great to read. Another new source is Broadcast.com.

Earnings surprises may also indicate the general health of the market.

There hasn't been much research on this. On an anecdotal level, though, Bloomberg senior markets editor Bill Hester and I have found that in recent history the S&P 500 has posted stunning results when twice as many companies in the index produce positive surprises as produce negative ones. When the two groups run neck and neck, the market has returned a scanty 0.21 percent per quarter.

Check interest rates, too. Low rates enhance returns in strong earnings quarters and buoy them in weak ones. But beware of quarters where earnings are coming in weak and rates are rising.

ESTIMATE REVISIONS

"It is rare to find a factor that so consistently defines winners and losers."
—CLAUDIA MOTT *and* DANIEL P. COKER

ESTIMATE REVISIONS ARE LIKE earnings surprises with better timing. Say a dip in the cost of raw materials cuts a manufacturer's costs. If the analysts following the company see this and have time to recrunch their numbers before the earnings announcement, you've got a revision; if they don't, you've got a surprise. Either way, the effect is similar—the stock price rises. It's a matter of math: If a company earning $5 a share is trading at $50, investors must believe the stock is worth 10 times earnings; raise the earnings to $10 a share, and the stock value bounces up to $100.

According to Mott and Coker, buying companies whose estimates have been revised upward is a great small-cap strategy. It works for both growth and value stocks, in up and down markets, and across industries. Pradhuman agrees. He has found that stocks for which analysts keep raising their earnings estimates have, on average, produced annual returns of almost 25 percent. But be careful. He's also found that they generated those returns with a volatility of 20.5 percent—that is, their prices bounced around, with peaks and valleys that diverged 20.5 percent from the mean. My advice here is the same as it is for surprises: Use the revisions as a source of ideas to research or as a final filter for candidates you've already vetted.

You can put together a list of small stocks whose earnings estimates are being raised by checking the Bloomberg Internet page (www.bloomberg.com).
Or ask your broker; if the brokerage is one with a lot of clout, like Merrill Lynch, it should be able to get you the names. And Zacks Investment Research offers a service on the Internet (www.zacks.com) that will conduct searches like this for $150 a year.

IF THEY GO UP, BUY 'EM!

"The race may not be to the swift nor the victory to the strong, but that's how you bet."
—DAMON RUNYON

MOMENTUM IS A SUPER STRATEGY for a bull market. But at least one Bear has used it, too: Chicago Bear William "the Refrigerator" Perry. Mike Ditka, the Chicago coach at the time, made the 300-pound Perry a running back because he figured that bodies in motion tend to stay in motion, and if the body is home-appliance size, watch out! Momentum investors are betting that stocks with a recent history of steadily rising prices are 300-pound backs under a full head of steam.

The investors have a better record than Ditka. Jim O'Shaughnessy, author of *What Works on Wall Street*, has found that since from 1954 through 1998, portfolios composed of the fifty stocks posting the biggest price increases in the previous year have returned about 16.6 percent annually.

Reducing the cap raises the returns. Merrill's Pradhuman has found that small caps with momentum have returned more than 20 percent a year. There's a catch, though. These stocks have also demonstrated average annual volatility of about 24 percent.

Another caution: Share price may rise for reasons that have little or nothing to do with the quality of the underlying business—the stellar performance of other stocks in the same sector, for example, or rumors that the company is a takeover target. When price increases are not supported by financials, momentum isn't going to carry the stock very far.

A refinement of the strategy puts it on a sounder fundamental footing by shifting the focus from price to earnings. The father of earnings-momentum investing is Richard Driehaus, a Chicago broker who manages over $1 billion in assets. His reasoning is that since earnings drive stock prices, companies with accelerating earnings should outperform. American Century Investors fund managers, who use this approach, explain in a February 1996 *Kiplinger's* article that they apply Driehaus's insight by looking for companies whose profits and revenues are growing at least 30 percent, year over year and quarter over quarter. They then narrow their choices by talking to analysts and managements to determine if the companies' acceleration will continue. For instance, the funds pounced on computer chipmaker Burr-Brown after learning that the company was selling its new higher-margin analog chips as fast as it could produce them. American Century started acquiring the stock at 25 to 30 percent above the previous day's close and kept right on buying.

PBHG Growth manager Gary Pilgrim also looks for

accelerating earnings growth—of at least 20 percent—but he requires upward estimate revisions and positive surprises, as well. He told *Kiplinger's* in an October 1996 article that he uses a combination of revisions, surprises, and growth, weighted 35, 25, and 40 percent, respectively, to rank the stocks in the PBHG universe: 10 is perfect; 1 means forget it. (This strategy, which soared in the mid-'90s, when Morningstar ranked PBHG Growth among the top five of all funds in five- and ten-year performance, got hammered in the tougher markets of the late 1990s; with much of the data Pilgrim's model crunches now widely available for $9.95 a month, his edge may be blunted for some time to come.)

In contrast to the American Century managers, Pilgrim prefers not to know too much about the operations of the companies he owns. Instead, he uses statistical measures to calculate each one's underlying long-term growth rate. "My objective is to know how these companies are doing, as opposed to what they are doing," he told *Kiplinger's*. "It's much more important to know that analysts are raising earnings estimates, that competitors aren't gaining ground, that controversies over products are being resolved. In other words, I want my knowledge to be a mile wide and an inch deep."

Both American Century and PBHG agree, though, on pulling the plug when the acceleration that attracted their attention begins to slow. First Team Sports, a maker of in-line roller skates, for example, dropped out of the American Century universe when its annual revenue growth fell from 100 percent to 48 percent and management began painting a less rosy picture of its prospects.

Check historical earnings rates in the S&P 600 guide *(see Chapter 3)* **or the company financial reports.**
Again, use this research either to suggest ideas or to screen your finalists. But remember, one of the momentum managers' most important assets is discipline—they adhere strictly to their criteria for buying and, especially, for selling.

THE EARNING MOMENTUM STRATEGY can pay off big:
American Century Vista and PBHG Growth returned 47
and 50 percent, respectively, in 1995. But, like price
momentum, it can also bomb. Vista and PBHG dropped
about 41 and 50 percent at one point in 1987, and 15 and
9 percent in 1990. If you can't stomach this much volatility, try the Aurora approach.

AURORA

'If you want a Ferrari, you gotta pay for a Ferrari.'
—GARRETT VAN WAGONER

THE MAIN REASONS THE RETURNS of strict momentum
investors like Gary Pilgrim and the American Century
managers vary so widely is that their models have no value
component. "If we can find securities that have a year or
two of positive surprises ahead of them, the p/e today
doesn't matter," Glen Fogel, manager of the American
Century Giftrust fund, told *Kiplinger's*, "because growth
overwhelms the current valuation."

That may be true, and Giftrust did return 38.32 percent
in 1995. But value criteria can provide a useful safety
valve—one that might have helped Fogel in 1998, when
his fund was down 40 percent at one point. By looking at
p/e and price/book ratios, momentum managers might
avoid buying grossly overvalued stocks. Value criteria
might also help them discern when a theme has run its
course and it's time to jump ship.

Adding a value safety valve is fairly easy. It's also profitable. O'Shaughnessy found that when he pared his list of
stocks with good price momentum to just those with price-
sales ratios less than 1.5, average annual returns from 1954
through 1998 increased to more than 18 percent. You can
put O'Shaughnessy's research to work for you by screening
the "Bloomberg 100"—a list, compiled in January and published in *Bloomberg Personal Finance* magazine, of the previous year's 100 best performers—for companies with
price-sales ratios less than one.

Aurora is another, more mathematically rigorous, approach to tempering a fundamentally emerging-growth style with value. Its designer, Merrill's Satya Pradhuman, uses a model that ranks stocks—from a low of 1 to a high of 100—according to a weighted combination of three factors. The first is relative strength, a momentum indicator measured by a stock's percentage price increase over the past year; the second is the size of positive earnings-estimate revisions; and the third is a "valuation" component emphasizing low price to cash flow (a measure similar to p/e but less vulnerable to accounting manipulations) relative to the stock's industry sectors.

The Aurora portfolio is composed of the stocks scoring in the top percentile when the strength, earnings, and valuation components are assigned weights of 40, 30, and 30 percent, respectively. From February 1980 to March 1999, this approach returned a whopping 30 percent a year, with 200 basis points less volatility than pure momentum.

In a less bullish market, Pradhuman thought it would be wise to change emphasis, to a basic value style spiced with growth. So he also created the Enhanced Contrarian Portfolio, using fundamentally the same model but changing the weightings to 70 percent value, 15 percent strength, and 15 percent earnings. This approach generated returns of 25.5 percent per year from 1980 to March 1999, with volatility of 19.5 percent.

The Aurora and Contrarian portfolios share an Achilles heel: If the market really tanks—dropping, say, 8 percent in a month—both will get spanked, perhaps even slightly worse than stocks picked using other methods.

You can create a poor man's version of Pradhuman's portfolios using the Friday edition of *Investor's Business Daily*, which lists stocks' percentile scores for relative strength and earnings momentum.
Pick out the ones with the highest scores and lowest p/e's. Then apply one of Pradhuman's weighting systems. Finally, choose the high scorers with the best fundamentals.

INSIDER TRADING,
THE LEGAL WAY

"Executives have a good insight into an industry, where Wall Street sometimes has a myopic view."
—THOMAS FITZGERALD, *president of T.H. Fitzgerald & Co., which runs the Reserve Informed Investors Growth Fund*

INSIDERS — OFFICERS, MEMBERS OF THE BOARD—should have a better idea of a company's prospects than any outsider, no matter how talented. They have what Tweedy, Browne Co., in its customer booklet, terms "insight information": firsthand knowledge of new marketing programs, planned cost efficiencies, and price hikes, as well as industry conditions. You can trade on this information indirectly by watching when insiders buy company stock. This tells you that the people who really know the business have enough confidence in its future to stake their own money on it.

"We like to invest alongside the people that run the companies," says Praveen Gottipalli, a principal at Symphony Asset Management, which manages Bear, Stearns & Co.'s Insiders Select Fund.

Buying with the insiders certainly worked for purchasers of Guidant Corp. shares. In late September 1995, roughly a year after it was spun off by Eli Lilly & Co. at $14\frac{1}{2}$, the medical-device maker's chairman, president, and chief financial officer all bought large blocks of its stock. The share price at the time was 26; a year later it had more than doubled, to $55\frac{1}{2}$.

Nejat Seyhun, a professor of finance at the University of Michigan, conducted a study of the one-year performance of companies following a year in which insiders were either net buyers or net sellers of their stock. Seyhun found that companies associated with insider buying beat the market by almost 5 percent, while those associated with insider selling performed worse than the market.

When sorting through your investment ideas, check your prospects' insider-trading histories.

Anyone who owns more than 5 percent of a company's shares or holds a high position in its management must notify the Securities and Exchange Commission whenever he or she trades the stock. You can find out who's done what by checking form 4 (which must be filed by any insider trading a company's shares) and form 144 (filed by holders of restricted stock); both can be accessed on Edgar (www.sec.gov).

If purchases accounted for the greatest dollar volume of insider trades during the past year, that's definitely a plus. Selling is a much less perfect indicator: Though people generally buy stock for only one reason—because they think it will make them money—any number of reasons exist for selling. And some have nothing to do with the company's prospects. An executive may want to diversify his portfolio, for example, or need the cash to pay his daughter's college tuition. Also bear in mind that the absolute number of shares someone sells is less important than the percentage of his or her total stake this number represents. For example, the fact that Microsoft chairman Bill Gates sold 520,955 of his company's shares in August 1996 looks less significant when you realize that he still held 141 million.

Once you've made your purchases, keep an eye on insider activity. It could tip the balance if you're wavering between holding and selling a stock.

Insider buying's value as an indicator may be somewhat undercut by a trend discussed by Gretchen Morgenson in a November 15, 1998, *New York Times* article: Executives are increasingly making their purchases with loans from their companies, secured by the shares bought and sometimes forgivable. Such loans, Morgenson notes, though still rare, are not always as well publicized as the purchases, making the insider signals considerably harder to read.

A VARIATION ON INSIDER PURCHASING occurs when the company buys back its own shares on the open market. This is a good sign for several reasons. By reducing the number of shares outstanding, a buyback raises earnings per share and reduces the amount of money that must be paid out in dividends. Perhaps most important, though, it usually indicates that company officers feel the stock is cheap. So if you follow management's lead, you could be picking up a bargain.

Share price does tend to increase after a buyback. According to a 1994 study by Rice University professor David Ikenberry, stocks rise an average of 3 percent the day an announcement is made and then beat the market by 12 percent over the next four years.

With results like that, buybacks should definitely have a role in your stock selection, either as a source of ideas or as a screen. They're a particularly good signal when you're choosing value investments. In the Rice study, buyback stocks that were cheap according to value criteria "returned an average of 45 percent more over a four-year period than similar nonbuyback stocks."

Be a little skeptical, though. Ask yourself why a company is spending its money on its stock rather than on its business. Has it run out of growth opportunities and products to research? Or is the buyback just a quick way to boost share price? Often the announcement itself accomplishes that goal, and the companies never actually follow through. In fact, some analysts estimate that only a third of the shares slated for buybacks get repurchased. Empty talk won't sustain share price long.

If you buy a stock on the basis of an announced buyback, check the next quarterly statement to see if shares outstanding have decreased, indicating that the company is making good on its promise.

Another way to profit from other people's purchases is to jump into stocks just before the big guns discover them.

Many professional investors will look for stocks with very low institutional ownership and hope that new-product launches or earnings surprises will draw fund managers' attention. A tiny stake by institutional standards can be enough to drive a small company's shares sky-high.

You'll find the percentage of institutional ownership among the Key Stock Statistics in the S&P guide reports. If the company isn't in the guide, ask your broker to check Morningstar, Bloomberg, or the charts put out by *IBD* publisher O'Neil & Co. Make a low institutional stake one of your sorting criteria, but not a must-have.

TECHNICAL MARKS

"I use fundamentals and technicals closely. Fundamentals are first, and if you have them, you have a huge advantage. But market conditions change, and you need to have a plan for that. I often use technical analysis to determine how much downside a stock might have. The ideal situation is when our fundamental upside is three or more times greater than [the stock's technical support level]—for example, where we see the upside as being 50 percent, but the downside is only 10 percent."
—LISA GRAY, *a Memphis stockbroker*

PRETTY MUCH ALL THE STRATEGIES discussed to this point have involved fundamentals, such as the figures on a company's balance sheet and income statement. Fundamentals were also the focus of Chapter 3. The reason is that they give you a window on how a business is run and what management is thinking. Many analysts ignore fundamentals, though, and focus not on a company's business but on the stock itself. *Technical analysis,* as this approach is called, treats a company's shares as commodities subject to market forces that can be traced by charting trade-volume and price trends. Analysts use the patterns revealed in these charts to predict where a stock is headed.

If you want to find out how they do that, read Thomas

Dorsey's book, *Point & Figure Charting*. Listening to some tech guys, you'd think the waves and angles they graph were cabalistic symbols with mystic connections to the future. Dorsey brings it all down to earth, invoking the prosaic forces of supply and demand. The idea is to deduce from the patterns of volume and price moves whether sellers or buyers are dominating the market. You want to be holding a stock when buyers outnumber sellers.

To determine who has the upper hand, technicians may use bar and line graphs, which plot share price and trade volume against time, or point-and-figure charts. Dorsey favors the latter. These indicate the magnitude and direction of share-price moves, but not the time they occur: Each square represents a specified price unit; when a stock's price moves up a unit, an X is put in the square above the previous point; when it falls, an O is entered one square down. Whenever the direction changes, the marks are made one column over, so each column contains either all Xs or all Os. An example of a point-and-figure chart, for Veterinary Center of America, appears at right.

Charting—whether by bar, line, or point and figure— reveals patterns, which must be interpreted. Interpretation involves a combination of science and art. Some of the signals are pretty clear. When each rising trend reaches a summit higher than the previous one, the buyers (bulls) are riding high; seller (bear) domination is indicated by successively lower falls. When both rises and falls remain within a narrow horizontal band, the stock is said to have stabilized, or based; if this period of stasis was preceded by a rise, it will probably be followed by a further rise; a preceding drop foreshadows a future fall.

Often a chart will show a series of peaks or dips that reach but never pass a particular price. The ceiling to rises is termed a resistance level; the floor to drops, a support level. Similar to these are trend lines, which connect series of declining peaks or rising dips. When a stock's price breaks through a resistance level, it means that investors are willing to buy at higher levels than in the past; a fall

EXAMPLE OF POINT AND FIGURE CHARTING

Veterinary Center of America (VCAI)
(5/16/94 - 1/8/97)

```
35.0 ┬
34.0 │
33.0 │           *
32.0 │          X *
31.0 │          X O *
30.0 ┼·····X···X O··*·································
29.0 │       X O X O        *
28.0 │   X   X O X O          *
27.0 │   X O X O X O     X   *
26.0 │   X O X O   O X   X O  *
25.0 ┼··X O·····O X O X O····*························
24.0 │   X       O X O X O     *     *
23.0 │   X       O X O   O       *   X *
22.0 │   X       O       O     X *X O *
21.0 │   X               O     X O X O   *
20.0 ┼··X···············O X·····X O X O X··*··········
19.5 │   X             O X O X   X O  O X O   *
19.0 ┼··X·············O X O X O X····O X O X···*·······
18.5 │   X             O X O X O X     O X O X O    *
18.0 ┼··X·············O X O X O X··*·O··O X O···*······
17.5 │   X             O X O X O   *     O   O         *
17.0 ┼··X·············O X O X··*··················O·······*···
16.5 O   X             O X O X *                  O            *
16.0 ·O X··X··········*O X O *···················O············
15.5 O X O X       *   O X *                    O
15.0 ·O X O X·······*···O *·······················O·········
14.5 O X O           *       *                   O
14.0 ·O X·············*·····························O·········
13.5 O X         *                               O
13.0 ·O·········*·································O X·········
12.5 │       *                                  O X O
12.0 ·│····*·····································O X O········
11.5 │   *                                      O X O
11.0 ┼*·········································O X O········
10.5 *                                         O X O
10.0 ·········································O X O········
 9.5                                           O X
 9.0 ·········································O X·········
 8.5                                           O X
 8.0 ·········································O·········
 7.5
 7.0 ┼·························································
 6.5
 6.0 ┼·························································
 5.5
 5.0 ┴
```

through a support level signals willingness to sell at lower prices. Breaching a trend line may presage a change in the direction of price movements.

Opinions are divided on how great a role technical analysis should play in small-cap investing. Charts are most valuable, technicians say, in liquid markets, where information is freely available and which are too large to manipulate. For example, in the huge government bond market, crucial information—such as employment, GDP, and inflation rate—is kept quiet until it can be released to all players simultaneously. So T-bond price and volume movements are good indicators of where other players in the market are willing to buy and sell. In the small-cap sector, in contrast, the prices of the many thinly traded, low-priced stocks are easily manipulated. An unscrupulous investor with a lot of microcap shares to unload might pick up a large block of the stock at a higher price, hoping others notice the volume and assume the smart money is loading up. When duped investors rush to buy the stock, the manipulator can sell his stake at a tidy profit.

Ease of manipulation reduces the reliability of small-cap price and volume patterns. Accordingly, many investors in the sector use technicals merely to supplement their basic fundamental analysis. Dorsey, for example, infers from his charts how defensive or aggressive an investor should be. Other managers employ technicals to reduce their risk— to ensure, say, that an undervalued company isn't going to stay that way too long. Bill Nasgovitz is one of those. Though charts aren't a cornerstone of Heartland's stock-picking strategy, Nasgovitz does what technical types call base building. He looks for out-of-favor stocks whose charts resemble "a dead man's heartbeat"—in other words, flat-liners whose prices have based after a period of decline and, he hopes, are poised to take off.

Nasgovitz wants to be the first to discover a story. Jim Oberweis, in contrast, feels that other investors are too smart to get scooped too often. He becomes concerned if nobody else is excited about one of his picks. So he studies charts—like those published by O'Neil & Co.—that plot relative strength, searching for signs of an uptrend and market outperformance.

 Keep technicals in perspective.
Over the long run, fundamentals drive stock prices, period. But if you can check a chart, do it: You'll reduce your risk by looking for good value and growth companies that are emerging from a base.

 Some of Tom Dorsey's research appears on the Internet at www.dorseywright.com. Try the e-mail contacts at that address for help finding a local brokerage with good research on small stocks that can also chart your holdings.

UP TO NOW, I'VE TALKED ABOUT using economic, fundamental, and technical signals to decide what stocks to buy and sell when. The remaining sections discuss some more esoteric trading techniques, as well as cost-cutters.

GOING SHORT

"We've put together a relatively small short portfolio of about fifteen of Wall Street's most overvalued, most overloved securities, which we think are ripe for a fall."
—*Heartland funds'* BILL NASGOVITZ

RULE NUMBER ONE IN SMALL-CAP investing: Beware of froth. When companies become Wall Street sweethearts and institutions own a large percentage of their shares, not enough demand remains in the market to drive their prices higher. Worse, their high p/e's increase the risk that one disappointment will send them tumbling.

Such stocks are poor buys. But they may be good candidates for *shorting*—selling shares borrowed from a broker in hopes of replacing them with others bought later at a lower price. Bill Nasgovitz used this tactic in his Small Cap Contrarian fund, attempting to improve his odds by looking for frothy stocks being sold by company insiders *(see above)*.

"When we're buying shares, we like to see insiders expressing their confidence by buying, too," he says. "With shorts, it's just the opposite—we look for high-flying stocks where there's been strong and consistent insider selling, in size."

Short selling, however, is tricky, and the downside is unlimited. Some of those frothy sweethearts are going to keep going up on pure momentum, just because they are market darlings and everyone knows their names. When that happens, shorts have to pay dearly to replace their borrowed shares. The risk is particularly acute with small stocks. These are thinly traded, and shorts seeking to cover their positions are easily caught in a "squeeze," having to chase scarce shares and bidding their prices up in the process.

Shorting is not a technique for the general public. To make it work, you almost need to discover inaccuracies in a highflier's financial statements or business model, and that's not easy to do. Even Nasgovitz had to throw in the towel when a number of his short positions blew up, costing his Contrarian fund about 17 percentage points in 1998, by his reckoning. In fact, in the fall of that year, shareholders voted to fold the fund into Heartland Value.

Here's a less stomach-churning way, also used by Heartland, to make money on short sales. Start with your group of thoroughly researched, solid companies, and buy those with high short interest—your broker can check the stock screens for you, or you can look yourself at the back of *Barron's*.
The key to this strategy is that all the shorts will ultimately need to buy shares to cover their positions. Of course, they could know some deep, dark secret about a company that will keep its price in the dumps despite their purchases. So check what insiders are doing. If the corporate execs, who really know the company, are buying, you can be more confident that the shorts are wrong and that their covering will drive the share price up.

PAIRED TRADING

"[Trading stocks in pairs] is a way to contain risk but still play with some of the juicier, riskier types of securities."
—ERIC KOBREN, *money manager and publisher of* Funds-Net Insight, *in an interview with Scott Schnipper of Bloomberg News*

A VARIATION ON SHORT SELLING that Nasgovitz also used in his Contrarian fund is *paired trading.* It's like betting the spread in football: What counts is not who beats who, but by how much. A paired trade is a bet that the best company in an industry will thump the worst. The bigger the spread, the more you earn.

It works like this: You take a long position on your pick to win while shorting your designated loser. Then if the two companies perform as you expect, you pocket profits from both ends.

Paired trading also provides protection against bad bounces. Say you hold complementary positions in an industry that tanks, as the semiconductor group did in fall 1995. Your profits from the shorted stock will offset your losses on your long bet. As Kemper-Dreman analyst and Bloomberg columnist John Dorfman writes in the September 1998 issue of *Bloomberg Personal Finance,* "The effect is to nullify, or at least muffle, the effect of overall equity-market movements. You stand or fall on your stock-selection skill alone."

In 1996 Nasgovitz pulled off a successful paired trade in the videoconferencing industry. The laggard of the group, Boca Research, was an ideal value buy. Despite the fact that its earnings had soared 50 percent the previous year and it had recently announced plans to bring videoconferencing to personal computers, the company was trading at only about 13 times estimated earnings. In contrast, Picturetel Corp., whose book value of $6.09 a share was comparable to Boca's $6.50, was selling at 37 times earnings, topping the sector.

Nasgovitz bought the first and shorted the second in early spring. By April, Boca had moved little, but Picturetel shares had tumbled to 29¾ from a February peak of almost 45, allowing Contra to cover its position and realize a profit.

Paired trading works best when equities are neither roaring ahead nor going down the chute. "In a raging bull market," Dorfman points out, "short selling [is] a drag on performance. What's more, in this bubbly environment, the speculative frothy stocks that pairs traders often short [do] well." On the other hand, a bear market can sink the best-run companies. A stagnant market is also exactly the environment in which you need ingenious ploys like this to spice up bland returns.

In any environment, however, this technique, like straight shorting, is probably best left to the pros. Even they make miscalls. Dallas-based money manager David Tice, for instance, paired Sullivan Dental Products and Patterson Dental, two comparable companies whose market valuations seemed out of line with their fundamentals: Sullivan's too low, at 1.6 times book value, and Patterson's too high, at almost 6 times book. Tice bought the first and shorted the second. Patterson proceeded to rise almost 5 percent, while Sullivan advanced a mere 1 percent.

If you decide to try this at home, start by sorting through your list of researched candidates for the best value prospect. Then enlist your broker's help to find its evil twin—a company in the same business whose fundamentals don't seem to support its share price.

Next check insider activity. You want to see the companies' officers on your side of the trades, buying your long pick and selling your short. Finally, to be certain you're not walking into a squeeze, have your broker pull up your short candidate's *short-interest ratio*. This tells you what percentage of the stock's daily trade volume the total outstanding short positions in it represent. If the percentage is too high, you'll have a lot of competition when you go to cover, which will drive up the price .

A PENNY SAVED

NO MATTER HOW GOOD your stock picks are and how disciplined you are about selling, you'll always do better if you can keep your transaction costs down. I already outlined a few ways to do this in Chapter 3. Here are a couple of other, more sophisticated, tricks of the trade:

◆ **When you buy a stock, place a limit order between its bid and ask.** Occasionally, your order will fill and you'll end up with a price that's better than the one market makers are offering.

◆ **See if your broker will allow you to match trades within the brokerage or its market maker.** Charles Schwab, through its Assurance Trading program, is one of the few firms offering this service. If you're allowed to do it, matching can get you a better price than the bid or ask. It may not work too well, though, with small stocks that don't trade heavily, because there won't be many people willing to take the other side.

Small-Cap
RECAP

THIS IS THE END. NOW I've given you every technique and tactic I know for making money in small stocks. The danger is that in all the details, you can lose sight of the fundamental investing process. So here, in summary, are the basic precepts.

Be an investor, not a speculator. This book is about achieving superior returns over a long term with reasonable risk. Small-cap stocks play an integral role in that process, but only as part of a balanced portfolio whose makeup reflects your long- and short-term savings goals.

So, diversify. Invest in both small and large stocks—in domestic and foreign companies—that reflect both growth and value styles. Put enough money in cash and bonds to take care of expenses looming in the near future. Then, with the rest, you can ride the equity market's ups and downs, ultimately reaping its superior long-term returns.

Look for great companies at good prices and good companies at great prices. As Warren Buffett says, growth and value are joined at the hip. A crummy business that can't make money is no bargain, no matter how cheap it is. Even a wonderful business won't make you much money if its market value is hyperinflated.

Exploit your edge. The markets, by and large, are very efficient. Few good companies stay undervalued for long. The guys who make real money are the ones who find out first about whatever it is that drives a stock's price up. Your chance of scooping Wall Street on one of the big companies are almost nil. The odds get better as you go down the scale in size. With small companies, which are not well followed on the Street, special knowledge of a business or acquaintance with management can give you a real edge to exploit.

Tip the odds in your favor. You're searching for companies with great products, whose management you trust and whose financial house is in order. But not every good business is a good buy—you need some indication that the share price is going to increase. Success is more likely if the stock meets the following criteria:
1 earnings yield is higher than corporate bond yields.
2 Its price-to-sales ratio is less than 1.5.
3 It is priced below book value.
4 Its ROE is greater than 20.
5 It is being bought by insiders or by the company itself.
6 Analysts are raising the company's earnings estimates.
7 Earnings consistently exceed expectations.
8 Sales and earnings are growing faster than 30 percent annually, or quarter over quarter, or both.
9 The company has a strong brand name or dominates an industry or niche.
10 The stock has been outperforming the S&P 600.

Buy to hold. Invest only in companies you feel comfortable living with for a long time. Jumping in and out of stocks costs too much in fees, spreads, and taxes to be profitable, even assuming you could time your trades successfully.

But don't be sentimental about your investments. You'd better have a good reason for holding a stock in the following situations:
1 The company's p/e is greater than 1.5 times a conservative estimate of its long-term earnings growth rate.
2 Insider selling of its shares exceeds insider buying.
3 The company carries more debt than equity.
4 Its management or investor relations officer sidesteps your questions.

5 Growth in earnings, revenues, or profit margins has declined in several consecutive quarters.

6 The company posts earnings significantly below analyst expectations.

7 Analysts lower their earnings estimates.

8 Analysts rate the stock a sell.

9 The stock has consistently underperformed the S&P 600, and management has not enunciated a clear plan for turning things around.

10 Everyone loves it.

Enjoy yourself. Some people get a kick out of doing research and playing with numbers; others leave that to the pros by investing in well-managed mutual funds. Whatever your style, you should get a warm feeling watching your savings grow.

RESOURCES

HERE ARE SOME SOURCES you can use to delve more deeply into the topics touched on in the book, as well as to implement the strategies discussed. They're divided into three sections: **READING MATTER**, which lists the books, newsletters, and magazines mentioned in the text, together with some additional ones you might find helpful; **WEB SITES**, containing useful Internet addresses; and **REGIONAL BROKERS**, which provides the names and phone numbers of some brokerages that specialize in companies located in particular areas of the country.

READING MATTER

ENTRIES PROVIDE PUBLISHING or subscription information, but before you shell out a lot of money, you may want to check your local library's holdings.

BOOKS

BOOKS ARE SOME OF THE GREATEST tools for an investor. By spending about 10 to 50 bucks and a few days studying, you can absorb knowledge that it has taken some smart person years to acquire. Though I mostly advocate bottom-up, buy-and-hold investing, I've included in the list below books on other disciplines and trading, which will give you a broader understanding of how the stock market really works.

The Art of Short Selling, by Kathryn F. Staley [John Wiley & Sons, 1997; $34.95, hardcover].
 Well written and thoroughly researched, this book will open your eyes to the perils of investing without doing thorough research, and it will teach you how to be a better analyst.

The Art of Speculation, by Philip L. Carret [John Wiley & Sons, 1997; $19.95, pap.].
 A great lesson on the difference between investing and speculating.

Bloomberg by Bloomberg, by Michael Bloomberg and Matthew Winkler [John Wiley & Sons, 1998; $16.95, pap].
If you really want to invest in small growth companies, you should read Mike's book. It will teach you what goes on behind the numbers.

Classics: An Investor's Anthology [Business One Irwin, 1988, hardcover] and **Classics II: Another Investor's Anthology** [Irwin Professional Publishing, 1991; $50.00, hardcover], by Charles D. Ellis and James R. Vertin.
Though *Classics* is out of print and may be hard to find, it and its sequel, *Classics II*, include some of the finest articles ever written about investing. Reading these books will make you a seasoned veteran.

Common Stocks and Uncommon Profits and Other Writings, by Philip A. Fisher [John Wiley & Sons, 1996; $19.95, pap.].
According to press sources, this book had a huge influence on Warren Buffett. Enough said.

Contrarian Investment Strategies: The Next Generation—Beat the Market by Going Against the Crowd, by David N. Dreman [Simon & Schuster, 1998; $25.00, hardcover].
Dreman is one of the great students of investing. I got a copy of this book to review. I dropped everything and read it cover to cover.

Every Investor's Guide to High-Tech Stocks & Mutual Funds: Proven Strategies for Picking High-Growth Winners, by Michael Murphy [Broadway Books, 1999; $27.50, hardcover].
One of the best books I've read on investing. Presents a very logical approach to picking tech stocks.

The Gorilla Game: An Investor's Guide to Picking Winners in High Technology, by Geoffrey A. Moore, Paul

Johnson, and Tom Kippola [HarperBusiness, 1998; $26.00, hardcover].

This is a fantastic book. It is anti-small cap in the tech sector, but nevertheless provides great advice and strategies for tech investing.

The Guide to Understanding Financial Statements, by Geza Szurovy and S.B. Costales [McGraw-Hill, 1993; $14.95, pap.].

About as easy to read as accounting books get. It is short, to the point, and has great instructions for creating a spreadsheet to calculate important ratios.

Hoover's Handbook of American Business 1999, by various authors [Hoover's Inc., 1999; $129.95, serial, two-volume set, hardcover].

Hoover's provides great descriptions and history on a large number of companies. It should be available in most public libraries.

How to Buy Technology Stocks, by Michael Gianturco [Little Brown & Co., 1996; $13.95, pap.].

Gianturco does an excellent job explaining how investors can make profits in tech stocks without betting the farm.

How to Make Money in Stocks: A Winning System in Good Times or Bad, by William J. O'Neil [McGraw-Hill, 1994; $10.95, pap.].

I've told you that *Investor's Business Daily* is one of the best sources for learning about small stocks. O'Neil's book will teach you how to use all of the tables of information in *IBD* to improve your investing.

The Intelligent Investor, by Benjamin Graham [Harper-Collins, 1997; $30.00, hardcover].

One of the greatest investing books of all time. You should read it every five years.

Investment Intelligence from Insider Trading, by Hasan Nejat Seyhun [MIT Press, 1998; $29.95, hardcover].
John Spears of Tweedy, Browne said, "We have used several of the strategies suggested by Seyhun, and they work! Don't buy this wonderful book. We don't need the competition!"

Market Timing for the Nineties: The Five Key Signals for When to Buy, Hold, and Sell, by Roger S. Conrad and Stephen Leeb [HarperBusiness, 1994; out of print].
Offers some commonsense market indicators.

The Market Wizards [HarperBusiness, 1993; $15.00, pap.] and **The New Market Wizards** [John Wiley & Sons, 1995; $34.95, hardcover], by Jack D. Schwager.
Even if you never intend to be an active trader, you will become a better and more confident investor by reading these books.

Mastering Microcaps: Strategies, Trends, and Stock Selection, by Daniel P. Coker [Bloomberg Press, 1999; $55.00, hardcover].
If you like Chapter 4 of my book, you will love Coker's book. He tells you everything you'll want to know about microcaps and provides great, original research on how this asset class performs.

Midas Investing, by Jonathan Steinberg [Times Books, 1998; $15.00, pap.].
This book from the editor of *Individual Investor* magazine is a good handbook on investing in momentum stocks.

Mind Over Money: Match Your Personality to a Winning Financial Strategy, by John W. Schott and Jean S. Arbeiter [Little Brown & Co., 1998; $23.95, hardcover].
Schott is a psychiatrist who teaches at Harvard Medical School and manages money. This is a great book that teaches investors how to manage their emotions.

The Money Masters [HarperBusiness, 1994; $15.00, pap.] and **The New Money Masters** [HarperBusiness, 1994; $16.00, pap.], by John Train.
Interviews with some of the best money managers.

The Mutual Fund Business, by Robert C. Pozen and Sandra D. Crane [MIT Press, 1998; $37.50, pap.].
This is a comprehensive guide to the mutual fund biz by Fidelity's CEO. If you really want to know how the business works or if you aspire to work for a fund company this is the one book you need to read.

Nelson's Directory of Investment Research [Nelson Information, 1997; $535.00, pap.].

The New Commonsense Guide to Mutual Funds, by Mary Rowland [Bloomberg Press, 1998; $15.95, pap.].
Mary Rowland is one of the few people writing about mutual funds today who has been doing it for more than ten years. Her guide contains much of the wisdom she's gleaned from meeting hundreds of great and not-so-great investors. It's a quick read that will probably improve your investment results.

One Up on Wall Street: How to Use What You Already Know to Make Money in the Market, by Peter Lynch and John Rothchild [Penguin USA, 1990; $13.95, pap.].
I recommend this and anything else Lynch writes or has written. The guy is a genius.

Options As a Strategic Investment, by Lawrence G. McMillan [Prentice Hall, 1992; $49.95, hardcover].
If you really want to invest in options, you better read this book first.

Point & Figure Charting, by Thomas J. Dorsey [John Wiley & Sons, 1995; $59.95, hardcover].
If you think technical analysis is a bunch of baloney, you

should read Dorsey's book. Dorsey believes that picking the most solid businesses won't necessarily make you money, since about three-quarters of a stock's risk comes from the market and the industry. He reduces his risk by studying supply and demand.

A Random Walk Down Wall Street, by Burton G. Malkiel [W.W. Norton & Co., 1999; $29.95, hardcover].
Read this book. It tells you everything you'd get from an MBA course in finance, but in a far more lively style. Malkiel also outlines strategies you can put to work.

Graham and Dodd's Security Analysis, by Sidney Cottle, Roger F. Murray, Frank E. Block, with Martin L. Leibowitz [McGraw-Hill, 1998; $59.95, hardcover].
The "holy book" of investing. I won't promise that you'll enjoy reading it or that you'll be able to get through it quickly, but it will really teach you to invest like a pro.

Small Cap Stocks, edited by Robert A. Klein and Jess Lederman [Probus Publishing Co., 1993; $70.00, hardcover].
This book contains some fantastic research on the small-cap market. It's a must-read for pros, but it would bore most amateurs.

Standard & Poor's SmallCap 600 Guide: 1999 Edition [McGraw-Hill, 1998; $24.95, pap.].
A very good source on small-cap stocks.

Style Investing: Unique Insight into Equity Management, by Richard Bernstein [John Wiley & Sons, 1995; $60.00, hardcover].
If you've read this book and my magazine columns you know I think Bernstein is one of the best strategists on Wall Street. His research is based on facts and rigorous research, and this book will teach you more about the different investing styles than any other.

Value Investing: A Balanced Approach, by Martin J. Whitman [John Wiley & Sons, 1999; $49.95, hardcover].
Marty is one of the great value investors of all time.

Value Investing Made Easy: Benjamin Graham's Classic Investment Strategy Explained for Everyone, by Janet C. Lowe and Irving Kahn [McGraw-Hill, 1997; $14.95, pap.].
A nice little book about Benjamin Graham's life and value investing.

Walker's Manual of Unlisted Stocks, by Harry K. Eisenberg [Walker's Manual Llc., 1999; $85.00, hardcover].
The manual, which you can order by calling 800-932-2922, contains four years of financial data on 500 penny stocks. Read it before you put any money into that market.

What Works on Wall Street, by James P. O'Shaughnessy [McGraw-Hill, 1998; $29.95, hardcover].
A great book that explains which investing strategies beat the market over the long haul.

A Zebra in Lion Country, by Ralph Wanger [Touchstone, 1999; $13.00, pap.].
Wanger is one of the great small-cap investors; I'm sure you'll want to read his book.

NEWSLETTERS AND MAGAZINES

Barron's. Many market professionals consider *Barron's* a must-read for information on all the markets (800-328-6800, ext. 550).

Bloomberg Personal Finance. As an editor, I'm obviously biased toward *Personal*. It contains interviews with and articles by many of the people mentioned in this book. You'll also find stocks that meet some of the investing criteria described here (888-432-5820).

Charles Schwab Mutual Funds Performance Guide. A comprehensive listing of small-cap funds (800-435-4000).

Individual Investor. One of the only magazines that concentrates on small stocks. I like the fact that the editors provide lots of thoroughly researched ideas in each issue. But don't forget that you need to follow up their research with your own (800-383-5901).

Investor's Business Daily. A great source for both stock and fund investors. If you include the paper's special features in your investment analysis and idea generating, your results will improve (800-831-2525).

Kiplinger's Personal Finance Magazine. *Kiplinger's* is a simple, no-nonsense magazine, containing lots of good ideas for managing your finances. Editor Fred Frailey also does great interviews (800-544-0155).

Morningstar Mutual Funds. This loose-leaf binder of 1,600 funds is a great source of mutual fund information. But you pay for what you get. Get your local library to subscribe if it doesn't already. You may be able to get Morningstar reports from your broker or from a fund you are planning to invest in. The company also publishes a monthly newsletter, *Morningstar Investor* (800-876-5005 or 312-696-6000).

Mutual Funds. I started subscribing to this magazine because the subscription rate was really low, about $10. Now I learn something every time I thumb through (800-442-9000).

The No-Load Fund Investor. Sheldon Jacobs, a longtime observer of the mutual fund industry, covers new funds and provides recommendations and suggested portfolios (914-693-7420).

Oberweis Report. Always one of the top-ranked investment newsletters. Its picks have returned more than 28 percent a year since 1976 (630-801-6000 or 800-323-6166).

The Red Chip Review. Marc Robins and his staff really dig to uncover great small companies that nobody else is following. You wouldn't believe how many pros speak highly of this report. It's also good to see that almost everyone on the staff is working to earn the Chartered Financial Analyst designation (503-241-1265, or 800-RedChip/800-838-9248).

SmartMoney. Here's another one to read on your trips to the library. It carries a regular feature on small-cap stocks once a year but doesn't devote much ink to companies with market caps below $500 million. Features on other areas of finance win lots of industry awards, though (800-444-4204).

Value Line Investment Survey. A compendium of one-page company reports published by Value Line, which ranks stocks according to safety and projected performance (800-833-0046).

Vickers Weekly Insider Report (800-645-5043) and **Insiders' Chronicle** (800-243-2324). Two newsletters that give you a window on insider buying and selling.

WEB SITES

THE INTERNET IS SHAPING UP as an extremely valuable source of investment advice. It seems like a new Web page pops up every day. I'll warn you right away, though, that you can't trust everything you read in print and you really can't trust everything you see on the Net. Some sites—like Bloomberg's and those run by our competitors Dow Jones, Standard & Poor's, and Reuters—should provide reliable information. I can vouch for the quality of Bloomberg's data, which is one of the things I really like about the site. There are other so-called information providers, though, that are merely mouthpieces companies pay to tout their stocks. So watch out for deception or just plain inaccuracy.

You should find helpful information at these addresses:

www.aol.com America Online's Personal Finance Channel is a great resource for gathering research on companies and getting market news.

www.bloomberg.com Run by Bloomberg Financial Markets; provides news along with comprehensive stock and bond info.

www.cda.com CDA Investment publishes information on insider buying and selling.

www.dorseywright.com I've been a regular reader of Thomas Dorsey's research for almost ten years. His indicators are a valuable addition to your fundamental analysis, and his reports are full of investing and trading ideas every day.

www.morningstar.com/ Morningstar has a good Web site for coverage of mutual funds. Click on the pull-down menu "Choose a Morningstar product by name."

www.multexinvestor.com This is a site where you can buy analyst reports. If you are planning to make a major investment in a company you should check Multex to see what kind of research is available.

www.nasdaq.com Run by Nasdaq; provides price quotes.

www.pirc.com Run by the Primark Investment Research Center; publishes a list of companies announcing positive earnings surprises.

www.quote.com/info/vickers.html Run by Vickers Insider Trade Report Service; tattles on insider trading.

www.russell.com The Frank Russell Co., which compiles the Russell 2000 index, publishes asset allocation and market performance information on this Web site.

www.sec.gov/edgarhp.htm Edgar (Electronic Data Gathering, Analysis, and Retrieval).

www.stockinfo.standardpoor.com Standard & Poor's Reports-on-Demand service.

www.wsbi.com/spweb Run by Standard & Poor's Investor Center; offers tons of stock info you can download.

www.yahoo.com You should set up your own personalized page on Yahoo!. It is a great place to get custom news and changes in analyst recommendations.

www.zacks.com Run by Zacks Investment Research; will conduct stock searches for $150 a year.

REGIONAL BROKERS

REGIONAL FIRMS CAN BE a good source for ideas. Here are the names of some that were highly ranked in *The Wall Street Journal*'s February 1997 survey of investment houses' stock-picking prowess.

Raymond James and Associates, St. Petersburg, FL: 813-573-3800

A.G. Edwards & Sons, St. Louis, MO: 314-955-3000

Everen Securities, Chicago, IL: 312-574-6000

Edward D. Jones, St. Louis, MO: 314-515-2000

Piper Jaffray, Minneapolis, MN: 612-342-6000

Wheat First, Richmond, VA: 804-649-2311

PERMISSIONS CREDITS

GRATEFUL ACKNOWLEDGMENT IS made to the following publishers and organizations for permission to reproduce copyrighted material. This page constitutes a continuation of the copyright page.

For the data for the graphic in the Introduction, "20-Year Rolling Period Returns," from *Stocks, Bonds, Bills and Inflation*® *1999 Yearbook,* ©1999 Ibbotson Associates, Inc. Based on copyrighted works by Ibbotson and Sinquefield. All rights reserved. Used with permission.

For the graphic reprinted in Chapter 1, "Typical Recommended Asset Allocations": From *A Random Walk Down Wall Street* by Burton G. Malkiel. Copyright ©1990, 1985, 1981, 1975, 1973 by W.W. Norton & Company, Inc. Reprinted by permission of W.W. Norton & Company, Inc.

For the graphic in Chapter 1, "Historical Asset Allocation Portfolios: 1926–96": Calculated by *Fidelity Investments* using information and data presented in Ibbotson Investment Analysis Software, ©1999 Ibbotson Associates, Inc. All rights reserved. Used with permission.

APPENDIX

TICKER	COMPANY NAME	ADDRESS
AIR	AAR Corp	1111 Nicholas Blvd., Elk Grove Village, IL 60007
ABM	ABM Industries Inc	Suite 222, 160 Pacific Ave., San Francisco, CA 94111
ACXM	Acxiom Corp	301 Industrial Blvd., PO Box 2000, Conway, AR 72033-2000
ADAC	Adac Laboratories	540 Alder Dr., Milpitas, CA 95035
ADAP	Adaptive Broadband Corp	555 Twin Dolphin Dr., Redwood City, CA 94065
ATIS	Advanced Tissue Sciences Inc	10933 North Torrey Pines Rd., La Jolla, CA 92037
AD	ADVO Inc	One Univac Lane, PO Box 755, Windsor, CT 06095-0755
AEIC	Air Express Int'l Corp	120 Tokeneke Rd., Darien, CT 06820
ALN	Allen Telecom Inc	25101 Chagrin Blvd., Suite 350, Beachwood, OH 44122-5619
ALLP	Alliance Pharma- ceutical Corp	3040 Science Park Rd., San Diego, CA 92121
ATK	Alliant Techsystems Inc	600 Second St. N.E., Hopkins, MN 55343-8384
AHAA	Alpha Inds	20 Sylvan Rd., PO Box 1044, Woburn, MA 01801
ALO	Alpharma Inc	One Executive Dr., Fort Lee, NJ 07024
AIZ	Amcast Indl Corp	7887 Washington Village Dr., Dayton, OH 45459
ACO	Amcol Int'l Corp	1500 West Shure Dr., Suite 500, Arlington Heights, IL 60004-7803
ABI	American Bankers Insurance Group	11222 Quail Roost Dr., Miami, FL 33157-6596
AFWY	American Freightways Corp	2200 Forward Dr., Harrison, AR 72601
AMSY	American Manage- ment Systems	4050 Legato Rd., Fairfax, VA 22033

COMPANIES THAT WERE members of the S&P 600 Small-Cap Index as of 5/6/99.

PHONE	WEB SITE AS OF 5/6/99	INDUSTRY SUBGROUP
847-439-3939	www.aarcorp.com	Aerospace/Defense Equip
415-733-4000	www.abm.com	Building-Maint & Service
501-336-1000	www.acxiom.com	Data Processing/Mgmt
408-321-9100	www.adaclabs.com	Medical-Imaging Systems
415-596-9000	www.adaptivebroadband.com	Satellite Telecom
619-450-5730	www.advancedtissue.com	Medical-Biomedical/Gene
860-285-6100	www.advo.com	Direct Marketing
203-655-7900	www.aeilogistics.com	Transport-Air Freight
216-765-5800	www.allentele.com	Wireless Equipment
619-558-4300	www.allp.com	Medical-Drugs
612-931-6000	www.atk.com	Aerospace/Defense-Equip
617-935-5150	www.alphaind.com	Electronic Compo-Semicon
201-947-7774	www.alpharma.com	Medical-Generic Drugs
937-291-7000	www.amcast.com	Metal Processors&Fabrica
847-394-8730	www.amcol.com	Diversified Minerals
305-253-2244	www.abig.com	Multi-line Insurance
501-741-9000	www.arfw.com	Transport-Truck
703-267-8000	www.amsinc.com	Data Processing/Mgmt

TICKER	COMPANY NAME	ADDRESS
AORI	American Oncology Resources	16825 Northchase Dr., Suite 1300, Houston, TX 77060
AWR	American States Water Co	630 East Foothill Blvd., San Dimas, CA 91773
ACF	Americredit Corp	200 Bailey Ave., Fort Worth, TX 76107
AMES	Ames Dept Stores Inc	2418 Main St., Rocky Hill, CT 06067
AMMB	Amresco Inc	700 No. Pearl St., Suite 2400, LB 342, Dallas, TX 75201-7424
ALOG	Analogic Corp	8 Centennial Dr., Peabody, MA 01960
ANLY	Analysts Int'l Corp	7615 Metro Blvd., Mpls., MN 55439-3050
ABCW	Anchor Bancorp Wisconsin Inc	25 West Main St., Madison, WI 53703
SLOT	Anchor Gaming	815 Pilot Rd., Suite G, Las Vegas, NV 89119
AGL	Angelica Corp	424 South Woods Mill Rd., Chesterfield, MO 63017-3406
AXE	Anixter Int'l Inc	Two No. Riverside Plz., Ste. 1950, Chicago, IL 60606
ANN	AnnTaylor Stores Corp	142 West 57th St., New York, NY 10019
APOG	Apogee Enterprises Inc	7900 Xerxes Ave. South, Suite 1800, Mpls., MN 55431
APPB	Applebees Int'l Inc	4551 W. 107th St., Suite 100, Overland Park, KS 66207
APZ	Applied Industrial Technology Inc	3600 Euclid Ave., PO Box 6925, Cleveland, OH 44115
APM	Applied Magnetics Corp	75 Robin Hill Rd., Goleta, CA 93117
APW	Applied Power Inc	13000 West Silver Spring Dr., Butler, WI 53007
ATR	Aptargroup Inc	475 West Terra Cotta Ave., Suite E, Crystal Lake, IL 60014
WTR	Aquarion Co	835 Main St., Bridgeport, CT 06604
ACAT	Arctic Cat Inc	600 Brooks Ave. So., Thief River Falls, MN 56701
ABFS	Arkansas Best Corp	3801 Old Greenwood Rd., Fort Smith, AR 72903
ASHW	Ashworth Inc	2791 Loker Ave. West, Carlsbad, CA 92008
ASPT	Aspect Telecommunications	1730 Fox Dr., San Jose, CA 95131-2312
AZPN	Aspen Technology Inc	10 Canal Park, Cambridge, MA 02141

PHONE	WEB SITE AS OF 5/6/99	INDUSTRY SUBGROUP
713-873-2674	www.aori.com	Health Care Cost Contain
909-394-3600	www.aswater.com	Water
817-332-7000	www.americredit.com	Finance-Auto Loans
860-257-2000	www.amesstores.com	Retail-Discount
214-953-7700	www.amresco.com	Finance-Mtge Loan/Banker
508-977-3000	www.analogic.com	Electronic Measur Instr
612-835-5900	www.analysts.com	Computer Services
608-252-8700	www.anchorbank.com	S&L/Thrifts-Central US
702-896-7568		Casino Services
314-854-3800	www.angelica-corp.com	Linen Supply&Rel Items
312-902-1515	www.anixter.com	Networking Products
212-541-3300		Retail-Apparel/Shoe
612-835-1874		Bldg Prod-Doors&Windows
913-967-4000	www.applebees.com	Retail-Restaurants
216-881-8900	www.appliedindustrial.com	Machinery-General Indust
805-683-5353	www.appmag.com	Computers-Memory Devices
414-781-6600	www.apw-enclosures.com	Mach Tools & Rel Products
815-477-0424	www.aptargroup.com	Miscellaneous Manufactur
203-335-2333	www.aquarion.com	Water
218-681-8558	www.arctic-cat.com	Recreational Vehicles
501-785-6000	www.arkbest.com	Transport-Truck
619-438-6610	www.ashworthinc.com	Apparel Manufacturers
408-325-2200	www.aspect.com	Telecommunication Equip
617-577-0100	www.aspentech.com	Computer Software

TICKER	COMPANY NAME	ADDRESS
ASTE	Astec Industries Inc	4101 Jerome Ave., PO Box 72787, Chattanooga, TN 37407
ATO	Atmos Energy Corp	5430 LBJ Freeway, Suite 160, Dallas, TX 75240
ABPCA	Au Bon Pain Co Inc	19 Fid Kennedy Ave., Boston, MA 02210
ASPX	Auspex Systems Inc	5200 Great America Pkwy., Santa Clara, CA 95054
ASM	Authentic Fitness Corp	6040 Bandini Blvd., Commerce, CA 90040
AVS	Aviation Sales Co	6905 Northwest 25th St., Miami, FL 33122
AVID	Avid Technology Inc	Metropolitan Technology Park, One Park West, Tewksbury, MA 01876
AZR	Aztar Corp	2390 East Camelback Rd., Suite 400, Phoenix, AZ 85016-3452
JBAK	Baker (J.) Inc	555 Turnpike St., Canton, MA 02021
BEZ	Baldor Electric	5711 RS Boreham JR St., Fort Smith, AR 72908
BMP	Ballard Medical Products	12050 Lone Peak Pkwy., Draper, UT 84020
BTC	BancTec Inc	4435 Spring Valley Rd., Dallas, TX 75244
BGR	Bangor Hydro-Electric Co	33 State St., Bangor, ME 04401
BKNG	Banknorth Group Inc	300 Financial Plz., PO Box 5420, Burlington, VT 05401
B	Barnes Group Inc	123 Main St., Bristol, CT 06011-0489
BRL	Barr Laboratories Inc	Two Quaker Rd., PO Box 2900, Pomona, NY 10970-0159
BRR	Barrett Resources Corp	1515 Arapahoe St., Tower 3, Suite 1000, Denver, CO 80202
BSET	Bassett Furniture Inds	3525 Fairystone Park Highway, Bassett, VA 24055
BEAV	BE Aerospace Inc	1400 Corporate Center Way, Wellington, FL 33414
BWC	Belden Inc	7701 Forsyth Blvd., Suite 800, St. Louis, MO 63105
BI	Bell Industries Inc	11812 San Vicente Blvd., Los Angeles, CA 90049-5069
BHE	Benchmark Electronics Inc	3000 Technology Dr., Angleton, TX 77515
BNO	Benton Oil & Gas Co	1145 Eugenia Plc., Suite 200, Carpinteria, CA 93013
BILL	Billing Concepts Corp	9311 San Pedro, Suite 400, San Antonio, TX 78216
BDY	Bindley Western Inds	4212 West 71st St., Indianapolis, IN 46268

PHONE	WEB SITE AS OF 5/6/99	INDUSTRY SUBGROUP
423-867-4210	www.astecindustries.com	Machinery-Constr&Mining
972-934-9227	atmosenergy.com	Gas-Distribution
617-423-2100	www.boston.com/aubonpain	Retail-Restaurants
408-986-2000	www.auspex.com	Networking Products
323-726-1262		Apparel Manufacturers
305-592-4055	www.avsales.com	Distribution/Wholesale
508-640-6789	www.avid.com	Communications Software
602-381-4100		Casino Hotels
781-828-9300		Retail-Apparel/Shoe
501-646-4711	www.baldor.com	Machinery-Electrical
801-572-6800	www.bmed.com	Medical Products
972-450-7700	www.banctec.com	Computers-Integrated Sys
207-945-5621	www.bhe.com	Electric-Integrated
802-658-9959	www.banknorth.com	Commer Banks-Eastern US
860-583-7070	www.barnesgroupinc.com	Diversified Manufact Op
914-362-1100	www.barrlabs.com	Medical-Generic Drugs
303-572-3900	www.brr.com	Oil Comp-Explor&Prodtn
540-629-6000	www.bassettfurniture.com	Home Furnishings
561-791-5000	www.beav.com	Aerospace/Defense Equip
314-854-8000	www.belden.com	Wire&Cable Products
310-826-2355	www.bellind.com	Diversified Manufact Op
409-849-6550	www.bench.com	Electronic Compo-Misc
805-566-5600	www.bentonoil.com	Oil Comp-Explor&Prodtn
210-321-6900	www.billingconcepts.com	Commercial Serv-Finance
317-704-4000	www.bindley.com	Medical-Whsle Drug Dist

TICKER	COMPANY NAME	ADDRESS
BTGC	Bio-Technology General Corp	70 Wood Ave. South, Iselin, NJ 08830
BXM	Biomatrix Inc	65 Railroad Ave., Ridgefield, NJ 07657
BIR	Birmingham Steel Corp	1000 Urban Center Pkwy., Suite 300, Birmingham, AL 35242-2516
BSYS	BISYS Group Inc	150 Clove Rd., Little Falls, NJ 07424
BLT/A	Blount International Inc	4520 Executive Park Dr., Montgomery, AL 36116-1602
BMC	BMC Industries Inc-Minn	One Meridian Crossing, Suite 850, Mpls., MN 55423
BBA	The Bombay Co Inc	550 Bailey Ave., Fort Worth, TX 76107
BAMM	Books-A-Million Inc	402 Industrial Lane, Birmingham, AL 35211
BNE	Bowne & Co Inc	345 Hudson St., New York, NY 10014
BRCOA	Brady Corporation	727 W. Glendale Ave., PO Box 571, Milwaukee, WI 53201
BDT	Breed Technologies Inc	5300 Old Tampa Hwy., Lakeland, FL 33811
CELL	Brightpoint Inc	6402 Corporate Dr., Indianapolis, IN 46278
BG	Brown Group Inc	8300 Maryland Ave., St. Louis, MO 63105
BW	Brush Wellman Inc	17876 St. Clair Ave., Cleveland, OH 44110
BKI	Buckeye Technologies Inc	1001 Tillman St., Memphis, TN 38108
BMHC	Building Material Holding Corp	1475 Tyrell Lane, Boise, ID 83706
BBRC	Burr-Brown Corp	6730 So. Tucson Blvd., Tucson, AZ 85706
BBR	Butler MFG Co	BMA Tower, 31st Southwest Trafficway, Kansas City, MO 64108
CHP	C&D Technologies Inc	1400 Union Meeting Rd., PO Box 3053, Blue Bell, PA 19422-0858
CCBL	C-Cor Electronics	60 Decibel Rd., State College, PA 16801
CUBE	C-Cube Microsystems Inc	1778 McCarthy Blvd., Milpitas, CA 95035
CDT	Cable Design Technologies Corp	Foster Plaza 7, 661 Andersen Dr., Pittsburgh, PA 15220
COG	Cabot Oil & Gas Corp	15375 Memorial Dr., Houston, TX 77079
CBM	Cambrex Corp	One Meadowlands Plz., 15th Fl., East Rutherford, NJ 07073

PHONE	WEB SITE AS OF 5/6/99	INDUSTRY SUBGROUP
732-632-8800		Medical-Biomedical/Gene
201-945-9550	www.biomatrix.com	Therapeutics
205-970-1200	www.birsteel.com	Steel-Producers
201-812-8600	www.bisys.com	Computer Services
334-244-4000	www.blount.com	Diversified Manufact Op
612-851-6000	www.bmcind.com	Electronic Compo-Misc
817-347-8200	www.bombayco.com	Retail-Home Furnishings
205-942-3737	www.booksamillion.com	Retail-Bookstore
212-924-5500	www.bowne.com	Printing-Commercial
414-358-6600	www.whbrady.com	Office Supplies&Forms
813-284-6000	www.breedtech.com	Auto/Trk Prts&Equip-Orig
317-297-6100	www.brightpoint.com	Distribution/Wholesale
314-854-4000	www.browngroup.com	Retail-Apparel/Shoe
216-486-4200	www.brushwellman.com	Other-Non-ferrous
901-320-8100	www.bkitech.com	Paper&Related Products
208-331-4410	www.bmcwest.com	Retail-Building Products
520-746-1111	www.burr-brown.com	Electronic Compo-Semicon
816-968-3000	www.butlermfg.com	Bldg&Construct Prod- Misc
215-619-2700		Batteries/Battery Sys
814-238-2461	www.c-cor.com	Electronic Compo-Misc
408-944-6300	www.c-cube.com	Electric Products-Misc
412-937-2300	www.cdtc.com	Wire&Cable Products
281-589-4600	www.cabotog.com	Oil Comp-Explor&Prodtn
201-804-3000	www.cambrex.com	Chemicals-Diversified

TICKER	COMPANY NAME	ADDRESS
CBRNA	Canandaigua Brands Inc	116 Buffalo St., Canandaigua, NY 14424
KRE	Capital Re Corp	1325 Ave. of the Americas, 18th Fl., New York, NY 10019
CSAR	Caraustar Industries Inc	3100 Washington St., Austell, GA 30001
CKE	Carmike Cinemas Inc	1301 First Ave., Columbus, GA 31901
CAFC	Carolina First Corp	102 South Main St., Greenville, SC 29601
CGC	Cascade Natural Gas Corp	222 Fairview Ave. North, Seattle, WA 98109
CASY	Casey's General Stores Inc	One Convenience Blvd., Ankeny, IA 50021
PWN	Cash America Investments Inc	1600 West 7th St., Fort Worth, TX 76102-2599
CAS	Castle (A.M.) & Co	3400 North Wolf Rd., Franklin Park, IL 60131
POS	Catalina Marketing Corp	11300 9th St. North, St. Petersburg, FL 33716
CACOA	Cato Corp	8100 Denmark Rd., Charlotte, NC 28273-5975
CDI	CDI Corp	1717 Arch St., 35th Floor, Philadelphia, PA 19103-2768
CEC	CEC Entertainment Inc	4441 West Airport Freeway, PO Box 152077, Irving, TX 75015
CGRM	Centigram Commun.	91 East Tasman Dr., San Jose, CA 95134
CNH	Central Hudson Gas & Electric	284 South Ave., Poughkeepsie, NY 12601-4879
CPC	Central Parking Corp	2401 21st Ave. So., Ste. 200, Nashville, TN 37212
CV	Central Vermont Public Service	77 Grove St., Rutland, VT 05701
CBC	Centura Banks Inc	134 No. Church St., PO Box 1220, Rocky Mount, NC 27804
CEPH	Cephalon Inc	145 Brandywine Pkwy, West Chester, PA 19380
CERN	Cerner Corp	2800 Rockcreek Pkwy, Suite 601, Kansas City, MO 64117-2551
CHB	Champion Enterprises Inc	2701 University Dr., Suite 320, Auburn Hills, MI 48326
CKP	Checkpoint Sys. Inc	101 Wolf Dr., PO Box 188, Thorofare, NJ 08086

PHONE	WEB SITE AS OF 5/6/99	INDUSTRY SUBGROUP
716-394-7900	www.cwine.com	Beverages-Wine/Spirits
212-974-0100	www.capitalrecorp.com	Financial Guarantee Ins
770-948-3101	www.caraustar.com	Paper&Related Products
706-576-3400	www.carmike.com	Theaters
864-255-7900	www.carolinafirst.com	Commer Banks-Southern US
206-624-3900		Gas-Distribution
515-965-6100	www.caseys.com	Retail-Convenience Store
817-335-1100		Retail-Pawn Shops
847-455-7111	www.amcastle.com	Metal Products-Distrib
813-579-5000	www.catalinamktg.com	Direct Marketing
704-554-8510		Retail-Apparel/Shoe
215-569-2200	www.cdicorp.com	Human Resources
972-258-8507	www.chuckecheese.com	Retail-Restaurants
408-944-0250	www.centigram.com	Telecommunication Equip
914-452-2000	www.cenhud.com	Electric-Integrated
615-297-4255		Commercial Services
802-773-2711	www.cvps.com	Electric-Integrated
919-977-4400	www.centura.com	Commer BanksSouth US
610-344-0200	www.cephalon.com	Medical-Drugs
816-221-1024	www.cerner.com	Medical Information Sys
248-340-9090	www.champent.com	Bldg-Mobil Home/Mfd Hous
609-848-1800	www.checkpointsystems.com	Electronic Security Devices

TICKER	COMPANY NAME	ADDRESS
CAKE	The Cheesecake Factory	26950 Agoura Rd., Calabasas Hills, CA 91301
CHE	Chemed Corp	2600 Chemed Center, 255 East 5th St., Cincinnati, OH 45202-4726
CEM	Chemfirst Inc	700 North St., PO Box 1249, Jackson, MS 39215-1249
CQB	Chiquita Brands Int'l.	250 East Fifth St., Cincinnati, OH 45202
CBR	Ciber Inc	5251 DTC Pkwy, Suite 1400, Englewood, CO 80111
CER	Cilcorp Inc	300 Hamilton Blvd., Suite 300, Peoria, IL 61602
CKR	CKE Restaurant Inc	1200 N. Harbor Blvd., Anaheim, CA 92801
CLC	Clarcor Inc	2323 South Sixth St., Rockford, IL 61104
CMT	CMAC Investment Corp	1601 Market St., 12th Floor, Philadelphia, PA 19103
COA	Coachmen Industries Inc	601 East Beardsley Ave., Elkhart, IN 46514
COKE	Coca-Cola Bottling Co Consolidated	1900 Rexford Rd., Charlotte, NC 28211
CDE	Coeur D'Alene Mines Corp	505 Front Ave., PO Box I, Coeur d'Alene, ID 83816-0316
CGNX	Cognex Corp	One Vision Dr., Natick, MA 01760
COHR	Coherent Inc	5100 Patrick Henry Dr., Santa Clara, CA 95054
CBH	Commerce Bancorp Inc NJ	1701 Route 70 East, Commerce Atrium, Cherry Hill, NJ 08034-5400
CFB	Commercial Federal Corp	2120 South 72nd St., Omaha, NE 68101
CMC	Commer. Metals Co	7800 Stemmons Freeway, Dallas, TX 75247
CES	Commonwealth Energy System	One Main St., Cambridge, MA 02142-9150
CMIN	Commonwealth Industries Inc	500 West Jefferson St., Citizens Plaza, 19th Fl., Louisville, KY 40202-2823
CTV	Commscope Inc	1375 Lenoir-Rhyne Blvd., Box 339, Hickory, NC 28603-0339
CPDN	Compdent Corp	100 Mansell Court East., Suite 400, Roswell, GA 30076
TSK	Computer Task Group Inc	800 Delaware Ave., Buffalo, NY 14209

PHONE	WEB SITE AS OF 5/6/99	INDUSTRY SUBGROUP
818-880-9323	www.thecheesecakefactory.com	Retail-Restaurants
513-762-6900	www.chemed.com	Divers Oper/Commer Serv
601-948-7550	www.chemfirst.com	Chemicals-Diversified
513-784-8000	www.chiquita.com	Food-Misc/Diversified
303-220-0100	www.ciber.com	Computer Services
309-675-8850	www.cilco.com	Electric-Integrated
714-774-5796	www.carlsjr.com	Retail-Restaurants
815-962-8867	www.clarcor.com	Diversified Manufact Op
215-564-6600	www.cmacmi.com	Financial Guarantee Ins
219-262-0123	www.coachmen.com	Bldg-Mobil Home/Mfd Hous
704-551-4400	www.cocacola.com	Beverages-Nonalcoholic
208-667-3511	www.coeur.com	Precious Metals
508-650-3000	www.cognex.com	Indust. Automat/Robot
408-764-4000	www.cohr.com	Lasers-Syst/Components
609-751-9000		Commer Banks-Eastern US
402-554-9200	www.comfedbank.com	S&L/Thrifts-Central US
214-689-4300	www.commercialmetals.com	Metal Processors & Fabrica
617-225-4000	www.comenergy.com	Electric-Integrated
502-589-8100	www.cacky.com	Metal-Aluminum
704-324-2200	www.commscope.com	Telecommunication Equip
770-998-8936	www.compdent.com	Life/Health Insurance
716-882-8000	www.ctg.com	Computer Services

TICKER	COMPANY NAME	ADDRESS
COE	Cone Mills Corp	3101 North Elm St., Greensboro, NC 27408
CNE	Conn. Energy Corp	855 Main St., Bridgeport, CT 06604
CGX	Consolidated Graphics Inc	2210 West Dallas St., Houston, TX 77019
COP	Consolidated Products Inc	500 Century Building, 36 South Pennsylvania St., Indianapolis, IN 46204
COO	Cooper Companies Inc	6140 Stoneridge Mall Rd., Suite 590, Pleasanton, CA 94588
CORR	COR Therapeutics Inc	256 East Grand Ave., South San Francisco, CA 94080
CPO	Corn Products International Inc	6500 South Archer Rd., Bedford Park, IL 60501-1933
CVTY	Coventry Health Care Inc	53 Century Blvd., Suite 250, Nashville, TN 37214
CPY	CPI Corp	1706 Washington Ave., St. Louis, MO 63103-1709
ATX	Cross (A.T.) Co	One Albion Rd., Lincoln, RI 02865
XTO	Cross Timbers Oil Co	810 Houston St., Suite 2000, Fort Worth, TX 76102-6298
CTS	CTS Corp	905 West Blvd. North, Elkhart, IN 46514
CFR	Cullen/Frost Bankers Inc	100 West Houston St., San Antonio, TX 78205
CURE	Curative Health Services Inc	14 Research Way, Box 9052, East Setauket, NY 11733-9052
CUST	CustomTracks Corp	One Galleria Tower, 13355 Noel Rd., Suite 1555, Dallas, TX 75240
CYGN	Cygnus Inc	400 Penobscot Dr., Redwood City, CA 94063
CYRK	Cyrk Inc	3 Pond Rd., Gloucester, MA 01930
DRC	Dain Rauscher Corp	Dain Bosworth Plaza, 60 South 6th St., Mpls., MN 55402-4422
DS	Dallas Semi-conductor Corp	4401 Beltwood Pkwy. So., Dallas, TX 75244-3292
DMRK	Damark International Inc	7101 Winnetka Ave. No., Mpls., MN 55428
DM	Dames & Moore Group	911 Wilshire Blvd., Suite 700, Los Angeles, CA 90017
DAN	Daniel Industries	9753 Pine Lake Dr., Houston, TX 77055

PHONE	WEB SITE AS OF 5/6/99	INDUSTRY SUBGROUP
910-379-6220	www.cone.com	Textile-Apparel
203-579-1732	www.connenergy.com	Gas-Distribution
713-529-4200		Printing-Commercial
317-633-4100		Retail-Restaurants
510-460-3600	www.coopercos.com	Medical Products
415-244-6800	www.corr.com	Therapeutics
708-563-2400		Food-Misc/Diversified
615-391-2440	www.cvty.com	Medical-HMO
314-231-1575	www.cpicorp.com	Photo Equip&Supplies
401-333-1200	www.cross.com	Miscellaneous Manuf.
817-870-2800	www.crosstimbers.com	Oil Comp-Explor&Prodtn
219-293-7511	www.ctscorp.com	Electronic Compo-Misc
210-220-4011	www.frostbank.com	Commer Banks-Central US
516-689-7000	www.curative.com	Medical-Hospitals
972-702-7055	www.customtracks.com	Internet Content
415-369-4300		Drug Delivery Systems
508-283-5800		Advertising Services
612-371-7750		Finance-Invest Bnkr/Brkr
972-371-4000	www.dalsemi.com	Electronic Compo-Semicon
612-531-0066	www.damark.com	Retail-Mail Order
213-996-2200	www.dames.com	Engineering/R&D Services
713-467-6000	www.danielind.com	Oil Field Mach&Equip

TICKER	COMPANY NAME	ADDRESS
DSCP	Datascope Corp	14 Philips Pkwy., Montvale, NJ 07645
DBT	DBT Online Inc	250 Cotorro Court, Las Cruces, NM 88005
DFG	Delphi Financial Group	1105 North Market St., Suite 1230, Wilmington, DE 19899
DLP	Delta & Pineland Co	One Cotton Row, Scott, MS 38772
DLW	Delta Woodside Inds Inc	233 N. Main St., Hammond Square, Suite 200, Greenville, SC 29601
DRTE	Dendrite International Inc	1200 Mount Kemble Ave., Morristown, NJ 07960
DVN	Devon Energy Corp	20 North Broadway, Suite 1500, Oklahoma City, OK 73102-8260
DV	Devry Inc	One Tower Lane, Oakbrook Terrace, IL 60181-4624
DP	Diagnostic Products Corp	5700 W. 96th St., Los Angeles, CA 90045
DLGC	Dialogic Corp	1515 Route 10, Parsippany, NJ 07054
DGII	Digi Int'l Inc	11001 Bren Rd. East, Minnetonka, MN 55343
DMIC	Digital Microwave Corp	170 Rose Orchard Way, San Jose, CA 95134
DMN	Dimon Inc	512 Bridge St., PO Box 681, Danville, VA 24543-0681
DNEX	Dionex Corp	1228 Titan Way, Sunnyvale, CA 94086
DAP	Discount Auto Parts	4900 Frontage Rd. So., Lakeland, FL 33815
DXYN	Dixie Group Inc	1100 South Watkins St., Chattanooga, TN 37404
DSL	Downey Financial Corp	3501 Jamboree Rd., Newport Beach, CA 92660
DHI	DR Horton Inc	1901 Ascension Blvd., Suite 100, Arlington, TX 76006
DBRN	Dress Barn Inc	30 Dunnigan Dr., Suffern, NY 10901
DSP	DSP Communications Inc	20300 Stevens Creek Blvd., Cupertino, CA 95014
DURA	Dura Pharmaceuticals Inc	5880 Pacific Center Blvd., San Diego, CA 92121-4204
DY	Dycom Indust. Inc	4440 PGA Blvd., Palm Beach Gardens, FL 33410-6542
EGR	Earthgrains Co	8400 Maryland Ave., St. Louis, MO 63105

PHONE	WEB SITE AS OF 5/6/99	INDUSTRY SUBGROUP
201-391-8100		Medical Instruments
505-524-4050	www.dbtonline.com	Commercial Services
302-478-5142		Life/Health Insurance
601-742-4500		Agricultural Operations
864-232-8301		Textile-Apparel
201-425-1200	www.drte.com	Medical Information Sys
405-235-3611	www.devonenergy.com	Oil Comp-Explor&Prodtn
630-571-7700	www.devry.com	Schools
213-776-0180	www.dpcweb.com	Diagnostic Kits
201-993-3000	www.dialogic.com	Commun. Software
612-912-3444	www.dgii.com	Commun. Software
408-943-0777	www.dmcwave.com	Wireless Equipment
804-792-7511	www.dimon.com	Tobacco
408-737-0700	www.dionex.com	Instruments-Scientific
941-687-9226	www.discountautoparts.net	Retail-Auto Parts
423-698-2501		Textile-Products
714-854-0300	www.downeysavings.com	S&L/Thrifts-Western US
817-856-8200	www.drhorton.com	Bldg-Residential/Commer
914-369-4500		Retail-Apparel/Shoe
408-777-2700	www.dspc.com	Wireless Equipment
619-457-2553	www.durapharm.com	Medical-Drugs
561-627-7171	www.dycomind.com	Building&Construct-Misc
314-259-7000		Food-Baking

TICKER	COMPANY NAME	ADDRESS
EUA	Eastern Utilities Associates	One Liberty Square, Boston, MA 02109
EV	Eaton Vance Corp	24 Federal St., Boston, MA 02110
ELK	Elcor Corp	14643 Dallas Pkwy., Suite 1000, Wellington Center, Dallas, TX 75240-8871
ESIO	Electro Scientific Inds Inc	13900 North West Science Park Dr., Portland, OR 97229-5497
EGLS	Electroglas Inc	2901 Coronado Dr., Santa Clara, CA 95054
EGN	Energen Corp	2101 6th Ave. No., Birmingham, AL 35203
EFS	Enhance Financial Svcs Group	335 Madison Ave., New York, NY 10017
ENZ	Enzo Biochem Inc	60 Executive Blvd., Farmingdale, NY 11735
EPIC	Epicor Software Corp	195 Technology Dr., Irvine, CA 92618-2402
ESL	Esterline Technologies Corp	10800 North East 8th St., Suite 600, Bellevue, WA 98004
ETEC	Etec Systems Inc	26460 Corporate Ave., Hayward, CA 94545
ETH	Ethan Allen Interiors Inc	Ethan Allen Dr., Danbury, CT 06811
EXBT	Exabyte Corp	1685 38th St., Boulder, CO 80301
ER	Executive Risk Inc	82 Hopmeadow St., PO Box 2002, Simsbury, CT 06070
EXPD	Expeditors Int'l Washington	1015 3rd Ave., 12th Floor, Seattle, WA 98104
ESRX	Express Scripts Inc	14000 Riverport Dr., Maryland Heights, MO 63043
FDS	Factset Research Systems Inc	One Greenwich Plz., Greenwich, CT 06830
FIC	Fair Isaac & Co Inc	120 N. Redwood Dr., San Rafael, CA 94903
FGCI	Family Golf Centers Inc	225 Broadhollow Rd., Melville, NY 11747
FJC	Fedders Corp	505 Martinsville Rd., Liberty Corner, NJ 07938
FNF	Fidelity National Finl Inc	17911 Von Karman Ave., Irvine, CA 92614
FAF	First American Financial Corp	114 East Fifth St., Santa Ana, CA 92701-4642
FILE	Filenet Corp	3565 Harbor Blvd., Costa Mesa, CA 92626

PHONE	WEB SITE AS OF 5/6/99	INDUSTRY SUBGROUP
617-357-9590	www.eua.com	Electric-Integrated
617-482-8260	www.eatonvance.com	Invest Mgmnt/Advis Serv
972-851-0500	www.elcor.com	Bldg&Construct Prod-Misc
503-641-4141	www.esi.com	Lasers-Syst/Components
408-727-6500	www.electroglas.com	Electronic Compo-Semicon
205-326-2700	www.energen.com	Gas-Distribution
212-983-3100		Financial Guarantee Ins
516-755-5500		Medical-Biomedical/Gene
714-453-4000	www.platsoft.com	Applications Software
206-453-9400		Industrial Automat/Robot
510-783-9210	www.etec.com	Electro Compo-Semicon
203-743-8000	www.ethanallen.com	Home Furnishings
303-442-4333	www.exabyte.com	Computers-Memory Devices
860-408-2000	www.execrisk.com	Property/Casualty Ins
206-674-3400	www.expd.com	Transport-Services
314-770-1666	www.express-scripts.com	Pharmacy Services
203-863-1500	www.factset.com	Computer Services
415-472-2211	www.fairisaac.com	Data Processing/Mgmt
516-694-1666	www.familygolf.com	Golf
908-604-8686	www.fedders.com	Appliances
714-622-5000	www.fnf.com	Property/Casualty Ins
714-558-3211	www.firstam.com	Property/Casualty Ins
714-966-3400	www.filenet.com	Computer Software

TICKER	COMPANY NAME	ADDRESS
FBP	First BanCorp/ Puerto Rico	1519 Ponce De Leon Ave., Santurce, PR 00908
FMBI	First Midwest Bancorp Inc/Il	300 Park Blvd., Suite 405, PO Box 459, Itasca, IL 60143-9768
FMER	Firstmerit Corporation III	Cascade Plaza, Akron, OH 44308
FLM	Fleming Companies Inc	6301 Waterford Blvd., PO Box 26647, Oklahoma City, OK 73126-0647
FRK	Florida Rock Inds	155 East 21st St., Jacksonville, FL 32206
FLOW	Flow Int'l Corp	23500-64th Ave. South, Kent, WA 98032
FM	Foodmaker Inc	9330 Balboa Ave., San Diego, CA 92123
FTS	Footstar Inc	933 MacArthur Blvd., Mahwah, NJ 07430
FC	Franklin Covey Co	2200 West Pkwy. Blvd., Salt Lake City, UT 84119-2331
FMT	Fremont General Corp	2020 Santa Monica Blvd., Suite 600, Santa Monica, CA 90404
FRTZ	Fritz Companies Inc	706 Mission St., Suite 900,San Francisco, CA 94103
FTR	Frontier Insurance Group Inc	195 Lake Louise Marie Rd., Rock Hill, NY 12775-8000
FFEX	Frozen Food Express Inds	1145 Empire Central Pl., Dallas, TX 75247
GKSRA	G & K Services Inc	5995 Opus Pkwy., Suite 500, Minnetonka, MN 55343
GNL	Galey & Lord Inc	980 Ave. of the Americas, NY, NY 10018
AJG	Gallagher, Arthur J. & Co	Two Pierce Place, Itasca, IL 60143-3141
GDI	Gardner Denver Machinery Inc	1800 Gardner Expressway, Quincy, IL 62301
GCX	GC Companies Inc	27 Boylston St., Chestnut Hill, MA 02167
GNCMA	General Communication	2550 Denali St., Suite 1000, Anchorage, AK 99503
SEM	General Semi- conductor Inc	8770 West Bryn Mawr Ave., Chicago, IL 60631
GHV	Genesis Health Ventures	148 West State St., Kennett Square, PA 19348

PHONE	WEB SITE AS OF 5/6/99	INDUSTRY SUBGROUP
787-729-8200	www.1bankpr.com	Commer Banks-Southern US
630-875-7450		Commer Banks-Central US
330-996-6300	www.firstmerit.com	Commer Banks-Central US
405-840-7200	www.fleming.com	Food-Wholesale/Distrib
904-355-1781		Bldg Prod-Cement/Aggreg
206-850-3500	www.flowcorp.com	Mach Tools&Rel Prod.
619-571-2121	www.foodmaker.com	Retail-Restaurants
201-934-2000	www.footstar.com	Retail-Apparel/Shoe
801-975-1776	www.franklincovey.com	Consulting Services
310-315-5500		Property/Casualty Ins
415-904-8360	www.fritz.com	Transport-Services
914-796-2100	www.frontierins.com	Property/Casualty Ins
214-630-8090		Transport-Truck
612-912-5500	www.gkcares.com	Linen Supply&Rel Items
212-465-3000		Textile-Apparel
630-773-3800	www.ajg.com	Insurance Brokers
217-222-5400	www.gardnerdenver.com	Machinery-General Indust
617-278-5600		Theaters
907-265-5600		Telecom Services
516-847-3000	www.gensemi.com	Electronic Com Semicon
610-444-6350	www.ghv.com	Medical-Nursing Homes

TICKER	COMPANY NAME	ADDRESS
GNTX	Gentex Corp	600 N. Centennial St., Zeeland, MI 49464
GON	Geon Company	One Geon Center, Avon Lake, OH 44012-0122
GRB	Gerber Scientific Inc	83 Gerber Rd. West, S. Windsor, CT 06074
GGO	Getchell Gold Corp	5460 S. Quebec St., Suite 240, Englewood, CO 80111
GIBG	Gibson Greetings Inc	2100 Section Rd., Cincinnati, OH 45237
GIX	Global Industrial Technologies Inc	2121 San Jacinto St., Suite 2500, Dallas, TX 75201
GDYS	Goody's Family Clothing Inc	400 Goody's Lane, Knoxville, TN 37933-2000
GOT	Gottschalks Inc	7 River Park Place East, Fresno, CA 93720
GGG	Graco Inc	4050 Olson Memorial Highway, Golden Valley, MN 55422-5332
GMP	Green Mountain Power Corp	PO Box 850, 25 Green Mountain Dr., South Burlington, VT 05402
GFF	Griffon Corporation	100 Jericho Quadrangle, Jericho, NY 11753
GFD	Guilford Mills Inc	4925 W. Market St., Greensboro, NC 27407
GYMB	Gymboree Corp	700 Airport Blvd., Suite 200, Burlingame, CA 94010
HMK	Ha-Lo Industries Inc	5980 West Touhy St., Niles, IL 60714
HDCO	Hadco Corp	12A Manor Pkwy., Salem, NH 03079
HGGR	Haggar Corp	6113 Lemmon Ave., Dallas, TX 75209
HLX	Halter Marine Group Inc	13085 Seaway Rd., Gulfport, MS 39503
HKF	Hancock Fabrics Inc	3406 West Main St., Tupelo, MS 38801
HRBC	Harbinger Corp	1055 Lenox Park Blvd., Atlanta, GA 30319
JH	Harland (John H.) Co	PO Box 105250, Decatur, GA 30348
HAR	Harman Int'l	1101 Pennsylvania Ave., N.W., Suite 1010, Washington, DC 20004
HRMN	Harmon Ind. Inc	1300 Jefferson Ct., Blue Springs, MO 64015
HMX	Hartmarx Corp	101 North Wacker Dr., Chicago, IL 60606
HTLD	Heartland Express Inc	2777 Heartland Dr., Coralville, IA 52241
HL	Hecla Mining Co	6500 Mineral Dr., Coeur d'Alene, ID 83814-8788
HELX	Helix Technology Corp	Mansfield Corporate Center, 9 Hampshire St., Mansfield, MA 02048

PHONE	WEB SITE AS OF 5/6/99	INDUSTRY SUBGROUP
616-772-1800	www.gentex.com	Electronic Compo-Misc
440-930-1000	www.geon.com	Chemicals-Plastics
860-644-1551	www.gerberscientific.com	Industrial Automat/Robot
303-771-9000		Gold Mining
513-841-6600	www.gibsongreetings.com	Consumer Products-Misc
214-953-4500		Machinery-Constr&Mining
423-966-2000		Retail-Apparel/Shoe
209-434-8000	www.gottschalks.com	Retail-Regnl Dept Store
612-623-6000	www.graco.com	Machinery-Pumps
802-864-5731	www.gmpvt.com	Electric-Integrated
516-938-5544		Diversified Manufact Op
910-316-4000	www.guilfordmills.com	Textile-Products
415-579-0600		Retail-Apparel/Shoe
847-647-4800	www.ha-lo.com	Advertising Services
603-898-8000	www.hadco.com	Circuits
214-352-8481	www.haggar.com	Apparel Manufacturers
228-896-0029	www.haltermarine.com	Shipbuilding
601-842-2834	www.hancockfabrics.com	Retail-Fabric Store
404-841-4334	www.harbinger.com	Computer Software
770-981-9460	www.harland.net	Office Supplies&Forms
202-393-1101	www.harman.com	Audio/Video Products
816-229-3345	www.harmonind.com	Electronic Compo-Misc
312-372-6300		Apparel Manufacturers
319-645-2728	www.heartlandexpress.com	Transport-Truck
208-769-4100	www.hecla-mining.com	Metal-Diversified
508-337-5111	www.ctihelix.com	Machinery-Pumps

TICKER	COMPANY NAME	ADDRESS
JKHY	Henry (Jack) & Associates	663 West Hwy. 60, Monett, MO 65708
HRH	Hilb, Rogal & Hamilton Co	4235 Innslake Dr., Glen Allen, VA 23060-1220
HNCS	HNC Software	5930 Cornerstone Court West, San Diego, CA 92121
HPK	Hollywood Park Inc	1050 South Prairie Ave., Inglewood, CA 90301
HOLX	Hologic Inc	590 Lincoln St., Waltham, MA 02154
HSE	HS Resources Inc	One Maritime Plaza, 15th Fl., San Francisco, CA 94111
HU	Hudson United Bancorp	1000 MacArthur Blvd., Mahwah, NJ 07430
HUF	Huffy Corp	225 Byers Rd., Miamisburg, OH 45342
HUG	Hughes Supply Inc	20 North Orange Ave., Suite 200, Orlando, FL 32801
HTCH	Hutchinson Technology	40 West Highland Park, Hutchinson, MN 55350
HYSL	Hyperion Solutions Corp	1325 Chesapeake Terrace, Sunnyvale, CA 94089
IDPH	Idec Pharma-ceuticals Corp	11011 Torreyana Rd., San Diego, CA 92121
IDXX	IDEXX Laboratories Inc	One IDEXX Dr., Westbrook, ME 04092
IHOP	IHOP Corp	525 N. Brand Blvd., Glendale, CA 91203-1903
IMR	IMCO Recycling Inc	5215 No. O'Connor Blvd., Suite 940, Irving, TX 75039
IMNR	Immune Response Corp/Del	5935 Darwin Court, Carlsbad, CA 92008
ICO	Inacom Corp	10810 Farnam Dr., Omaha, NE 68154
INCY	Incyte Pharma-ceuticals Inc	3174 Porter Dr., Palo Alto, CA 94304
INVX	Innovex Inc	1313 S. Fifth St., Hopkins, MN 55343-9904
IO	Input/Output Inc	11104 West Airport Blvd., Stafford, TX 77477
NSIT	Insight Enterprises Inc	6820 South Harl Ave., Tempe, AZ 85283

PHONE	WEB SITE AS OF 5/6/99	INDUSTRY SUBGROUP
417-235-6652	www.jackhenry.com	Computers-Integrated Sys
804-747-6500	www.hrh.com	Insurance Brokers
619-546-8877	www.hncs.com	Applications Software
310-419-1500	www.hollywoodpark.com	Gambling (Non-Hotel)
617-890-2300	www.holigic.com	X-Ray Equipment
415-433-5795	www.hsresources.com	Oil Comp-Explor&Prodtn
201-236-2600		Commer Banks-Eastern US
513-866-6251	www.huffy.com	Bicycle Manufacturing
407-841-4755	www.hughessupply.com	Retail-Building Products
320-587-3797	www.htch.com	Computers-Memory Devices
408-727-5800	www.hyperion.com	Applications Software
619-550-8500		Medical Biomedical/Gene
207-856-0300	www.idexx.com	Diagnostic Kits
818-240-6055	www.ihop.com	Retail-Restaurants
972-401-7200	www.imcorecycling.com	Recycling
619-431-7080	www.imnr.com	Medical-Drugs
402-392-3900	www.inacom.com	Computer Services
415-855-0555	www.incyte.com	Medical-Biomedical/Gene
612-938-4155	www.innovexinc.com	Electronic Compo-Misc
281-933-3339	www.i-o.com	Oil Field Mach&Equip
602-902-1001	www.insight.com	Distribution/Wholesale

TICKER	COMPANY NAME	ADDRESS
INSUA	Insituform Technologies Inc	702 Spirit 40 Park Dr., Chesterfield, MO 63005
III	Insteel Industries	1373 Boggs Dr., Mount Airy, NC 27030
IAAI	Insurance Auto Auctions Inc	1270 West Northwest Hwy., Palatine, IL 60067
ICST	Integrated Circuit Systems	2435 Blvd. of the Generals, Valley Forge, PA 19482
IHS	Integrated Health Services	10065 Red Run Blvd., Owings Mills, MD 21117
INTL	Inter-Tel Inc	120 North 44th St., Phoenix, AZ 85034-1822
IFSIA	Interface Inc	2859 Paces Ferry Rd., Suite 2000, Atlanta, GA 30339
IS	Interim Services Inc	2050 Spectrum Blvd.,Fort Lauderdale, FL 33309
IMG	Intermagnetics General Corp	450 Old Niskayuna Rd., PO Box 461, Latham, NY 12110-0461
INMT	Intermet Corp	5445 Corporate Dr., Suite 200, Troy, MI 48098
IRF	International Rectifier Corp	233 Kansas St., El Segundo, CA 90245
INTV	Intervoice Inc	17811 Waterview Pkwy, Dallas, TX 75252
IVCR	Invacare Corp	899 Cleveland St., PO Box 4028, Elyria, OH 44035
ION	Ionics Inc	65 Grove St., Watertown, MA 02172
ITRI	Itron Inc	2818 N. Sullivan Rd, Spokane, WA 99216-1897
JJSF	J & J Snack Foods Corp	6000 Central Highway, Pennsauken, NJ 08109
JBM	JAN Bell Marketing Inc	13801 N.W. 14th St., Sunrise, FL 33323
JEF	Jefferies Group Inc	11100 Santa Monica Blvd., Los Angeles, CA 90025
JLG	JLG Industries Inc	1 JLG Dr, McConnellsburg, PA 17233-9533
JAS/A	Jo-Ann Stores Inc	5555 Darrow Rd., Hudson, OH 44236
JMED	Jones Pharma Inc	1945 Craig Rd., St. Louis, MO 63146
JSB	JSB Financial Inc	303 Merrick Rd., Lynbrook, NY 11563
JUNO	Juno Lighting Inc	1300 South Wolf Rd., PO Box 5065, Des Plaines, IL 60017-5065

PHONE	WEB SITE AS OF 5/6/99	INDUSTRY SUBGROUP
314-530-8000	www.insituform.com	Building&Construct-Misc
910-786-2141		Wire&Cable Products
847-705-9550	www.iaai.com	Commercial Services
610-630-5300	www.icst.com	Circuits
410-998-8400	www.ihs-inc.com	Medical-Hospitals
602-302-8900	www.inter-tel.com	Commun. Software
770-437-6800	www.ifsia.com	Office Furnishings-Orig
954-938-7600	www.interim.com	Human Resources
518-782-1122	www.igc.com	Superconductor Prod & Sys
810-952-2500	www.intermet.com	Metal Process.&Fabrica
310-726-8000	www.irf.com	Electronic Compo-Semicon
972-454-8000	www.intervoice.com	Computers Voice Recogn
216-329-6000	www.invacare.com	Hospital Beds/Equip.
617-926-2500	www.ionics.com	Water Treatment Syst.
509-924-9900	www.itron.com	Electronic Measur Instr
609-665-9533	www.jjsnack.com	Food-Misc/Diversified
954-846-2705		Retail-Jewelry
310-445-1199	www.jefco.com	Finance-Invest Bnkr/Brk
717-485-5161	www.jlg.com	Machinery- Constr&Mining
330-656-2600	www.joann.com	Retail-Fabric Store
314-576-6100		Medical-Drugs
516-887-7000	www.jsbf.com	S&L/Thrifts-Eastern US
847-827-9880		Bldg Prod-Light Fixtures

TICKER	COMPANY NAME	ADDRESS
FEET	Just For Feet Inc	153 Cahaba Valley Pkwy North, Birmingham, AL 35124
JSTN	Justin Industries	2821 West Seventh St., Fort Worth, TX 76101
KSWS	K-Swiss Inc	20664 Bahama St, Chatsworth, CA 91311
KTO	K2 Inc	4900 South Eastern Ave., Suite200, Los Angeles, CA 90040-2962
KAMNA	Kaman Corp	1332 Blue Hills Ave., Bloomfield, CT 06002
KWD	Kellwood Co	600 Kellwood Pkwy, Chesterfield, MO 63017-5897
KMET	KEMET Corp	2835 Kemet Way, Simpsonville, SC 29681
KNT	Kent Electronics Corp	7433 Harwin Dr., Houston, TX 77036-2015
KEX	Kirby Corp	1775 St. James Place, Suite 300, Houston, TX 77056
KMAG	Komag Inc	275 South Hillview Dr., Milpitas, CA 95035
KROG	Kroll-O'Gara Co	9113 LeSaint Dr., Fairfield, OH 45014
KRON	Kronos Inc	400 Fifth Ave., Waltham, MA 02154
KLIC	Kulicke & Soffa Industries	2101 Blair Mill Rd., Willow Grove, PA 19090
LZB	La-Z-Boy Inc	1284 N. Telegraph Rd, Monroe, MI 48162-3390
LDRY	Landry's Seafood Restaurant	1400 Post Oak Blvd., Suite 1010, Houston, TX 77056
LSTR	Landstar System Inc	First Shelton Place, 1000 Bridgeport Ave., Shelton, CT 06484
LSON	Lason Inc	1305 Stephenson Hwy, Troy, MI 48083
LSCC	Lattice Semiconductor Corp	5555 North East Moore Court, Hillsboro, OR 97124-6421
LAWS	Lawson Products	1666 East Touhy Ave, Des Plaines, IL 60018
LM	Legg Mason Inc	100 Light St., Baltimore, MD 21202
LBY	Libbey Inc	300 Madison Ave., PO Box 10060, Toledo, OH 43699-0060
LVC	Lillian Vernon Corp	543 Main St., New Rochelle, NY 10801
LI	Lilly Industries Inc	733 South West St., Indianapolis, IN 46225
LNN	Lindsay Manufacturing Co	East Highway 91, Lindsay, NE 68644
LIN	Linens 'N Things Inc	6 Brighton Rd., Clifton, NJ 07015
LIPO	Liposome Co Inc	One Research Way, Princeton Forrestal Center Princeton, NJ 08540

PHONE	WEB SITE AS OF 5/6/99	INDUSTRY SUBGROUP
205-403-8000	www.feet.com	Retail-Apparel/Shoe
817-336-5125	www.justinind.com	Diversified Manufact Op
818-998-3388	www.kswiss.com	Athletic Footwear
213-724-2800	www.k2sports.com	Leisure&Rec Products
860-243-7100	www.kaman.com	Aerospace/Defense-Eq.
314-576-3100	www.kwdco.com	Apparel Manufacturers
864-963-6300	www.kemet.com	Capacitors
713-780-7770	www.kentelectronics.com	Electronic Parts Distrib
713-629-9370	www.kmtc.com	Transport-Marine
408-946-2300	www.komag.com	Computers-Memory Devices
513-874-2112		Security Services
617-890-3232	www.kronos.com	Computers-Integrated Sys
215-784-6000	www.kns.com	Machinery-General Ind.
313-241-4414	www.lazyboy.com	Home Furnishings
713-850-1010	www.landrysseafood.com	Retail-Restaurants
203-925-2900	www.landstar.com	Transport-Truck
810-597-5800	www.lason.com	Commercial Services
503-681-0118	www.lscc.com	Electronic Compo-Semi
847-827-9666	www.lawsonprod.com	Metal Products-Distrib
410-539-0000	www.leggmason.com	Finance-Invest Bnkr/Brk
419-325-2100	www.libbey.com	Housewares
914-576-6400	www.lillianvernon.com	Retail-Catalog Shopping
317-687-6700	www.lillyindustries.com	Paint&Related Products
402-428-2131	www.zimmatic.com	Machinery-Farm
201-778-1300	www.linensnthings.com	Retail-Bedding
609-452-7060	www.lipo.com	Medical-Biomedical/Gene

TICKER	COMPANY NAME	ADDRESS
LCE	Lone Star Industries	300 First Stamford Place, PO Box 120014, Stamford, CT 06912-0014
LUB	Luby's Inc	2211 Northeast Loop 410, San Antonio, TX 78265-3039
LDL	Lydall Inc	One Colonial Rd, Manchester, CT 06040
MRD	Macdermid Inc	245 Freight St., Waterbury, CT 06702-0671
MACR	Macromedia Inc	600 Townsend St., San Fransico, CA 94103
MAFB	MAF Bancorp Inc	55th St. & Holmes Ave., Clarendon Hills, IL 60514-1596
MGL	Magellan Health Services	3414 Peachtree Rd., N.E., Suite 1400, Atlanta, GA 30326
MTW	Manitowoc Co	500 South 16th St., PO Box 66, Manitowoc, WI 54221-0066
MCS	Marcus Corp	250 East Wisconsin Ave., Suite 1700, Milwaukee, WI 53202-4200
MPN	Mariner Post Acute Network	One Ravinia Dr., Suite 1500, Atlanta, GA 30346
MI	Marshall Industries	9320 Telstar Ave, El Monte, CA 91731-2895
MSX	Mascotech Inc	21001 Van Born Rd., Taylor, MI 48180
MSC	Material Sciences Corp	2300 East Pratt Blvd., Elk Grove Village, IL 60007
MAM	Maxxim Medical Inc	104 Industrial Blvd., Sugar Land, TX 77478
MWT	McWhorter Technologies Inc	400 East Cottage Place,Carpentersville, IL 60110
MDC	MDC Holdings Inc	3600 South Yosemite St., Suite 900, Denver, CO 80237
MEDQ	Medquist Inc	Five Greentree Centre, Suite 311, Marlton, NJ 08053
SUIT	Men's Wearhouse Inc	5803 Glenmont Dr., Houston, TX 77081-1701
MNTR	Mentor Corp	5425 Hollister Ave., Santa Barbara, CA 93111
MERQ	Mercury Interactive Corp	470 Potrero Ave., Sunnyvale, CA 94086
MRLL	Merrill Corporation	One Merrill Circle, St. Paul, MN 55108
MESA	Mesa Air Group Inc	2325 East 30th St., Farmington, NM 87401
METHA	Methode Electronics	7444 West Wilson Ave., Chicago, IL 60656

PHONE	WEB SITE AS OF 5/6/99	INDUSTRY SUBGROUP
203-969-8600	www.lonestarind.com	Bldg Prod-Cement/Aggreg
210-654-9000	www.lubys.com	Retail-Restaurants
860-646-1233	www.lydall.com	Diversified Manufac Op
203-575-5700	www.macdermid.com	Chemicals-Specialty
415-252-2000	www.macromedia.com	Computer Software
630-325-7300	www.mafbancorp.com	S&L/Thrifts-Central US
404-841-9200	www.magellanhealth.com	Medical-Hospitals
920-684-4410	www.manitowoc.com	Machinery Constr&Mining
414-272-6020	www.marcuscorp.com	Hotels&Motels
770-393-0199	www.marinerhealth.com	Medical-Hospitals
818-307-6000	www.marshall.com	Electronic Compo-Semicon
313-274-7405	www.mascotech.com	Diversified Manufact Op
847-439-8270	www.matsci.com	Steel-Specialty
281-240-5588	www.maxximmedical.com	Disposable Medical Prod
847-428-2657		Chemicals-Specialty
303-773-1100	www.richmondamerican.com	Bldg-Residential/Commer
609-596-8877	www.medquist.com	Health Care Cost Contain
713-592-7200	www.menswearhouse.com	Retail-Apparel/Shoes
805-681-6000	www.mentorcorp.com	Medical Products
408-523-9900	www.merc-int.com	Computer Software
612-646-4501	www.merrillcorp.com	Printing-Commercial
505-326-4410	www.mesa-air.com	Airlines
708-867-9600	www.methode.com	Electronic Compo-Misc

TICKER	COMPANY NAME	ADDRESS
MTNT	Metro Networks Inc	2800 Post Oak Rd. Blvd., Suite 4000, Houston, TX 77056
MIKL	Michael Foods Inc	324 Park National Bank Building, 5353 Wayzata Blvd, Minneapolis, MN 55416
MIKE	Michaels Stores Inc	8000 Bent Branch Dr., Irving, TX 75063
MCRL	Micrel Inc	1849 Fortune Dr., San Jose, CA 95131
MICA	Microage Inc	2400 South MicroAge Way, Tempe, AZ 85282-1896
MCRS	Micros Systems Inc	12000 Baltimore Ave., Beltsville, MD 20705-1291
MWY	Midway Games Inc	3401 N.California Ave., Chicago, IL 60618
GRO	Mississippi Chemical Corp	PO Box 388, Yazoo City, MS 39194
MB	Molecular Biosystems Inc	10030 Barnes Canyon Rd., San Diego, CA 92121
MK	Morris Knudsen	Morris Knudsen Plz., Boise,ID, 83729
MLI	Mueller Industries Inc	8285 Tournament Drive, Suite 150, Memphis, TN 38125
MSCA	MS Carriers Inc	3171 Directors Row, Memphis, TN 38131
MM	Mutual Risk Management Ltd. Inc	44 Church St., Hamilton HM 12, Bermuda
MYE	Myers Indust. Inc	1293 South Main St., Akron, OH 44301
NRC	NAC RE Corp	One Greenwich Plaza, PO Box 2568, Greenwich, CT 06836-2568
NAFC	Nash Finch Co	7600 France Ave. South, Suite 200, Edina, MN 55435
NSH	Nashua Corp	44 Franklin St., PO Box 2002, Nashua, NH 03061-2002
NLCS	National Computer SYS Inc	11000 Prairie Lakes Dr., Eden Prairie, MN 55344
NDC	National Data Corp	National Data Plaza, Atlanta, GA 30329-2010
NATI	National Instruments Corp	6504 Bridge Point Pkwy., Austin, TX 78730
NPK	National Presto Inds Inc	3925 North Hastings Way, Eau Claire, WI 54703
NATR	Natures Sunshine Prods Inc	75 East 1700 South, Provo, UT 84606

PHONE	WEB SITE AS OF 5/6/99	INDUSTRY SUBGROUP
713-407-6000	www.metronetworks.com	Broadcast Serv/Program
612-546-1500	www.michaelfoods.com	Food-Misc/Diversified
972-409-1300	www.michaels.com	Retail-Arts&Crafts
408-944-0800	www.micrel.com	Circuits
602-804-2000	www.microage.com	Computer Services
301-210-6000	www.micros.com	Computers-Integrated Sys
773-961-2222	www.midway.com	Entertainment Software
601-746-4131	www.misschem.com	Fertilizers
619-452-0681	www.mobi.com	Ultra Sound Imaging Sys
208-386-5000	www.mk.com	Building-Heavy Constr.
901-753-3200		Metal Processors&Fabrica
901-332-2500	www.mscarriers.com	Transport-Truck
441-295-5688	www.mrm.com	Property/Casualty Ins
330-253-5592	www.myersind.com	Diversified Manufac Op
203-622-5200	www.nacre.com	Property/Casualty Ins
612-832-0534	www.nashfinch.com	Food-Wholesale/Distrib
603-880-2323	www.nashua.com	Office Supplies&Forms
612-829-3000	www.ncs.com	Computers-Integrated Systems
404-728-2000	www.ndcorp.com	Data Processing/Mgmt
512-794-0100	www.natinst.com	Applications Software
715-839-2121	www.presto-net.com	Housewares
801-342-4300	www.natr.com	Vitamins&Nutrition Prod

TICKER	COMPANY NAME	ADDRESS
NAUT	Nautica Enterprises Inc	40 West 57th St., New York, NY 10019
NBTY	NBTY Inc	90 Orville Dr., Bohemia, NY 11716
NCSS	NCS Healthcare Inc	3201 Enterprise Pkwy., Suite 220, Beechwood, OH 44122
NWK	Network Equipment Technologies Inc	800 Saginaw Dr., Redwood City, CA 94063
NEB	New England Business SVC Inc	500 Main St., Groton, MA 01471
NJR	New Jersey Resources	1415 Wyckoff Rd., Wall, NJ 07719
NFX	Newfield Exploration Co	363 North Sam Houston Pkwy. East, Suite 2020, Houston, TX 77060
NFO	NFO Worldwide Inc	2 Pickwick Plaza, Greenwich, CT 06830
NRL	Norrell Corp	3535 Piedmont Rd., N.E., Atlanta, GA 30305
NVX	North American Vaccine Inc	12103 Indian Creek Crt, Beltsville, MD 20705
NWNG	Northwest Natural Gas Co	220 Northwest Second Ave.,Portland, OR 97209
NVLS	Novellus Syst. Inc	3970 North First St., San Jose, CA 95134
NOVN	Noven Pharma-ceuticals Inc	11960 Southwest 144th St., Miami, FL 33186
ORLY	O'Reilly Automotive Inc	233 South Patterson Ave., Springfield, MO 65802
OSL	O'Sullivan Corp	1944 Valley Ave., Winchester, VA 22601
OAK	Oak Industries Inc	1000 Winter St., Waltham, MA 02154
OH	Oakwood Homes	7800 McCloud Rd., Greensboro, NC 27409-9634
OII	Oceaneering International Inc	16001 Park Ten Place, Suite 600, Houston, TX 77084
OLOG	Offshore Logistics	224 Rue de Jean, Lafayette, LA 70508
OMP	OM Group Inc	50 Public Square, 3800 Terminal Tower, Cleveland, OH 44113-2204
ORU	Orange & Rockland Utilities	One Blue Hill Plaza, Pearl River, NY 10965
ORB	Orbital Sciences Corp	21700 Atlantic Blvd., Dulles, VA 20166
ORG	Organogenesis Inc	150 Dan Rd., Canton, MA 02021
OC	Orion Capital Corp	600 Fifth Ave., New York, NY 10020-2302

PHONE	WEB SITE AS OF 5/6/99	INDUSTRY SUBGROUP
212-541-5990	www.nautica.com	Apparel Manufacturers
516-567-9500	www.puritanspride.com	Vitamins&Nutrition Pro
216-514-3350	www.ncshealth.com	Pharmacy Services
415-366-4400	www.net.com	Telecommunication Equip
508-448-6111	www.nebs.com	Office Supplies&Forms
908-938-1480	www.njresources.com	Gas-Distribution
281-847-6000	www.newfld.com	Oil Comp-Explor&Prodtn
203-629-8888	www.nfow.com	Commercial Services
404-240-3000	www.norrell.com	Human Resources
301-470-6100	www.nava.com	Medical-Drugs
503-226-4211	www.nwnatural.com	Gas-Distribution
408-943-9700	www.novellus.com	Electronic Compo-Semicon
305-253-5099	www.noven.com	Drug Delivery Systems
417-862-3333	www.oreillyauto.com	Retail-Auto Parts
540-667-6666	www.osul.com	Rubber&Plastics
781-890-0400	www.oakind.com	Electronic Compo-Misc
910-664-2400	www.oakwooodhomes.com	Bldg-Mobil Home/Mfd-Hous
281-578-8868	www.oceaneering.com	Oil-Field Services
318-233-1221		Transport-Services
216-781-0083	www.omgi.com	Chemicals-Specialty
914-352-6000	www.oru.com	Electric-Integrated
703-406-5000	www.orbital.com	Aerospace/Defense-Equip
617-575-0775	www.organogenesis.com	Medical-Biomedical/Gene
212-332-8080	www.orioncapital.com	Property/Casualty Ins

TICKER	COMPANY NAME	ADDRESS
OCA	Orthodontic Centers of America	13000 Sawgrass Village Circle, Suite 41, Ponte Vedra Beach, FL 32082
GOSHA	OshKosh B'Gosh Inc	112 Otter Ave., Oshkosh, WI 54901
OMI	Owens & Minor Inc Hldg Co	4800 Cox Rd., Glen Allen, VA 23060
OXM	Oxford Indust. Inc	222 Piedmont Ave., N.E., Atlanta, GA 30308
PCMS	P-Com Inc	3175 S. Winchester Blvd., Campbell, CA 95008
PSUN	Pacific Sunwear of California	5037 E. Hunter Ave., Anaheim, CA 92807
PRXL	Parexel International Corp	195 West St., Waltham, MA 02154
PKE	Park Electro-chemical Corp	5 Dakota Dr., Lake Success, NY 11042
PDCO	Patterson Dental Co	1031 Mendota Hghts Rd, St. Paul, MN 55120
PXR	Paxar Corp	105 Corporate Park Dr.,White Plains, NY 10604-3814
PDX	Pediatrix Medical Group Inc	1455 Northpark Dr., Fort Lauderdale, FL 33326
PENX	Penford Corp	777-108th Ave. NE, Suite 2390, Bellevue, WA 98004-5193
PNT	Penn Enterprises Inc	Wilkes-Barre Center, 39 Public Square, Wilkes-Barre, PA 18711-0601
PPDI	Pharmaceutical Product Devel	3151 South 17th St., Wilmington, NC 28412
PSC	Philadelphia Suburban Corp	762 Lancaster Ave., Bryn Mawr, PA 19010-3489
PVH	Phillips-Van Heusen	200 Madison Ave., New York, NY 10016
PLAB	Photronics Inc	1061 E. Indiantown Rd., Jupiter, FL 33477
PHYC	PhyCor Inc	30 Burton Hills Blvd., Suite 400, Nashville, TN 37215
PCTL	PictureTel Corp	100 Minuteman Rd., Andover, MA 01810
PNY	Piedmont Natural Gas Co	1915 Rexford Rd., Charlotte, NC 28211
PIR	Pier 1 Imports Inc	301 Commerce St., Suite 600, Fort Worth, TX 76102
PTX	Pillowtex Corp	4111 Mint Way, Dallas, TX 75237

PHONE	WEB SITE AS OF 5/6/99	INDUSTRY SUBGROUP
904-273-0004	www.ocai.com	Health Care Cost Contain
414-231-8800	www.oshkoshbgosh.com	Apparel Manufacturers
804-747-9794	www.owens-minor.com	Distribution/Wholesale
404-659-2424		Apparel Manufacturers
408-866-3666	www.p-com.com	Wireless Equipment
714-693-8066	www.pacificsunwear.com	Retail-Apparel/Shoe
617-487-9900	www.parexel.com	Research&Development
516-354-4100	www.parkelectro.com	Circuit Boards
651-686-1600	www.pattersondental.com	Dental Supplies&Equip
914-697-6800	www.paxar.com	Identification Sys/Dev
954-384-0175	www.pediatrix.com	Health Care Cost Contai
206-462-6000	www.penw.com	Chemicals-Specialty
717-829-8843	www.pnt.com	Gas-Distribution
910-251-0081	www.ppdi.com	Research&Developmen
610-527-8000	www.suburbanwater.com	Water
212-381-3500	www.pvh.com	Apparel Manufacturers
561-745-1222	www.photronics.com	Electronic Compo-Semicon
615-665-9066	www.phycor.com	Health Care Cost Contain
508-292-5000	www.picturetel.com	Telecommunication Eq
704-364-3120	www.piedmontng.com	Gas-Distribution
817-878-8000	www.pier1.com	Retail-Home Furnishings
214-333-3225	www.pillowtex.com	Textile-Home Furnishings

TICKER	COMPANY NAME	ADDRESS
PIOG	Pioneer Group Inc	60 State St., Boston, MA 02109
PIOS	Pioneer Standard Electronics	4800 East 131st St., Cleveland, OH 44105
PZX	Pittston Bax Group	1000 Virginia Center Pkwy., PO Box 4229, Glen Allen, VA 23058-4229
PLX	Plains Resources Inc	500 Dallas St., Houston, TX 77002
PLT	Plantronics Inc	337 Encinal St., PO Box 1802, Santa Cruz, CA 95061-1802
PLAY	Players Int'l. Inc	Suite 800, 1300 Atlantic Ave., Atlantic City, NJ 08401
PLXS	Plexus Corp	55 Jewelers Park Dr., PO Box 156, Neenah, WI 54957-0156
PPP	Pogo Producing Co	5 Greenway Plaza, Suite 2700,Houston, TX 77046-0504
PII	Polaris Indust. Inc	1225 Highway 169 North, Mpls., MN 55441
PESC	Pool Energy Services Co	10375 Richmond Ave., Houston, TX 77042
POP	Pope & Talbot Inc	1500 S.W. First Ave., Portland, OR 97201
PWAV	Powerwave Technologies Inc	2026 McGaw Ave., Irvine, CA 92614
PMB	Premier Bancshares Inc	2180 Atlanta Plaza, 950 East Paces Ferry Rd., Atlanta, GA 30326
PPD	Prepaid Legal Services Inc	321 East Main, Ada, OK 74820
PDE	Pride Internat. Inc	1500 City West Blvd., Suite 400,Houston, TX 77042
PMK	Primark Corp	1000 Winter St., Suite 4300N, Waltham, MA 02154-1248
PDQ	Prime Hospitality Co	700 Route 46 East, Fairfield, NJ 07004
PHCC	Priority Healthcare Corp	285 West Central Pkwy., Altamonte Springs, FL 32714
PRGX	Profit Recovery Group International	2300 Windy Ridge Pkwy., Suite 100 North, Atlanta, GA 30339-8426
PRGS	Progress Software Corp	14 Oak Park, Bedford, MA 01730

PHONE	WEB SITE AS OF 5/6/99	INDUSTRY SUBGROUP
617-742-7825	www.pioneerfunds.com	Invest Mgmnt/Advis Serv
216-587-3600	www.pios.com	Electronic Compo-Semi
804-553-3600	www.pittston.com	Transport-Air Freight
713-654-1414		Oil Comp-Explor&Prodt
408-426-6060	www.plantronics.com	Telecommunication Eq
609-449-7777		Gambling (Non-Hotel)
414-722-3451	www.plexus.com	Commercial Services
713-297-5000		Oil Comp-Explor&Prodtn
612-542-0500	www.polarisindustries.com	Recreational Vehicles
713-954-3000		Oil Field Services
503-228-9161	www.poptal.com	Paper&Related Products
949-757-0530	www.powerwave.com	Wireless Equipment
404-814-3090	www.premierbancshares.com	Commer Banks-Southern US
580-436-1234	www.pplsi.com	Commercial Services
713-789-1400	www.prde.com	Oil&Gas Drilling
617-466-6611	www.primark.com	Commercial Services
973-882-1010		Hotels&Motels
407-869-7001	www.priorityhealthcare.com	Medical-Whsle Drug Dist
770-779-3900	www.prgx.com	Commercial Serv-Finance
617-280-4000	www.progress.com	Applications Software

TICKER	COMPANY NAME	ADDRESS
PDLI	Protein Design Labs Inc	2375 Garcia Ave., Mountain View, CA 94043
PBKS	Provident Bankshares Corp	114 East Lexington St., Baltimore, MD 21202
PGS	Public Service Co of NC	400 Cox Rd., Gastonia, NC 28054
KWR	Quaker Chemical Corp	Elm and Lee St., Conshohocken, PA 19428
NX	Quanex Corp	1900 West Loop South, Suite 1500, Houston, TX 77027
QCSB	Queens County Bancorp Inc	38-25 Main St., Flushing, NY 11354
ZQK	Quiksilver Inc	1740 Monrovia Ave., Costa Mesa, CA 92627
RTEX	Railtex Inc	4040 Broadway, Suite 200, San Antonio, TX 78209
RAH	Ralcorp Holdings Inc	800 Market St., Suite 2900, St. Louis, MO 63101
RJF	Raymond James Financial Corp	880 Carillon Pkwy., St. Petersburg, FL 33716
RDRT	Read-Rite Corp	345 Los Coches St., Milpitas, CA 95035
RBC	Regal Beloit	200 State St., Beloit, WI 53511-6254
REGN	Regeneron Pharmaceutical	777 Old Saw Mill River Rd., Tarrytown, NY 10591-6707
RGIS	Regis Corp	7201 Metro Blvd., Minneapolis, MN 55439
RS	Reliance Steel & Aluminum	2550 East 25th St., Los Angeles, CA 90058
ROIL	Remington Oil & Gas Corp	8201 Preston Rd., Suite 600, Dallas, TX 75225-6211
RCGI	Renal Care Group Inc	2100 West End Ave., Suite 800, Nashville, TN 37203
RGC	Republic Group Inc	811 East 30th Ave., Hutchinson, KS 67502-4341
RSND	Resound Corp	220 Saginaw Dr., Seaport Centre, Redwood City, CA 94063
RESP	Respironics Inc	1001 Murry Ridge Dr., Murrysville, PA 15668-8550
RFH	Richfood Holdings Inc	8258 Richfood Rd., Mechanicsville, VA 23116

PHONE	WEB SITE AS OF 5/6/99	INDUSTRY SUBGROUP
415-903-3700	www.pdl.com	Medical-Biomedical/Gene
410-281-7000	www.providentbankmd.com	Commer Banks-Eastern US
704-864-6731	www.psnc.com	Gas-Distribution
610-832-4000	www.quakerchem.com	Chemicals-Specialty
713-961-4600	www.quanex.com	Metal Processors&Fabrica
718-359-6400	www.qcsb.com	S&L/Thrifts-Eastern US
714-645-1395	www.quiksilver.com	Apparel Manufacturers
210-841-7600	www.railtex.com	Transport-Rail
314-877-7000	www.ralcorp.com	Food-Misc/Diversified
813-573-3800	www.raymondjames.com	Finance-Invest Bnkr/Brkr
408-262-6700	www.readrite.com	Computers-Memory Devices
608-364-8800		Mach Tools&Rel Products
914-347-7000	www.regeneron.com	Medical-Biomedical/Gene
612-947-7777	www.regiscorp.com	Retail-Hair Salons
213-582-2272	www.rsac.com	Steel-Producers
214-210-2650		Oil Comp-Explor&Prodtn
615-321-2333	www.renalcaregroup.com	Dialysis Centers
316-727-2700	www.republic-group.com	Bldg&Construct Prod-Misc
415-780-7800	www.resound.com	Medical Products
412-733-0200	www.respironics.com	Respiratory Products
804-746-6000	www.richfood.com	Food-Wholesale/Distrib

TICKER	COMPANY NAME	ADDRESS
RIGS	Riggs Nat'l Corp Washington, DC	1503 Pennsylvania Ave., NW, Washington, DC 20005
RBN	Robbins & Myers Inc	1400 Kettering Tower, Dayton, OH 45423
RPC	Roberts Pharmaceutical Corp	Meridian Center II, 4 Industrial Way West, Eatontown, NJ 07724
RLC	Rollins Truck Leasing Corp	One Rollins Plaza, Wilmington, DE 19803
ROP	Roper Industries Inc	160 Ben Burton Rd., Bogart, GA 30622
RAM	Royal Appliance Manufacturing	650 Alpha Dr., Cleveland, OH 44143
RTI	RTI International Metals Inc	1000 Warren Ave., Niles, OH 44446-0269
RI	Ruby Tuesday Inc	150 W. Church Ave., Maryville, TN 37801
RURL	Rural/Metro Corp	8401 E. Indian School Rd,Scottsdale, AZ 85251
RUS	Russ Berrie & Co Inc	111 Bauer Dr., Oakland, NJ 07436
RYAN	Ryan's Family Steak Houses Inc	405 Lancaster Ave., Greer, SC 29652
RYL	Ryland Group Inc	11000 Broken Land Pkwy., Columbia, MD 21044
SIII	S3 Inc	2801 Mission College Blvd., Santa Clara, CA 95052-8058
SFSK	Safeskin Corp	12671 High Bluff Dr., San Diego, CA 92130
SWM	Schweitzer-Mauduit International Inc	100 North Point Center East, Suite 600 Alpharetta, GA 30022-8246
SCTT	Scott Technologies Inc	5875 Landerbrook Dr., Suite 250, Mayfield, OH 44124
SMG	The Scotts Company	14111 Scottslawn Rd., Marysville, OH 43041
CKH	Seacor Smit Inc	11200 Westheimer Rd., Suite 850, Houston, TX 77042
SDTI	Security Dynamics Technologies Inc	1 Alewife Center, Cambridge, MA 02140
SEIC	SEI Investments Co	1 Freedom Valley Dr., Oaks, PA 19456
SEI	Seitel Inc	50 Briar Hollow Lane, West Building, 7th Fl., Houston, TX 77027
SIGI	Selective Insurance Group	40 Wantage Ave., Branchville, NJ 07826
SVE	Service Experts Inc	1134 Murfreesboro Rd., Nash., TN 37217

PHONE	WEB SITE AS OF 5/6/99	INDUSTRY SUBGROUP
202-835-4309	www.riggsbank.com	Commer Banks-East US
937-222-2610	www.robn.com	Machinery-General Indust
908-389-1182	www.robertspharm.com	Therapeutics
302-426-2700	www.rlc-corp.com	Trucking&Leasing
706-369-7170	www.roperind.com	Diversified Manufact Op
216-449-6150	www.dirtdevil.com	Appliances
330-544-7622	www.rmititanium.com	Other-Non-ferrous
423-379-5700		Retail-Restaurants
602-994-3886	www.ruralmetro.com	Protection-Safety
201-337-9000	www.russberrie.com	Consumer Products-Misc
864-879-1000		Retail-Restaurants
410-715-7000	www.ryland.com	Bldg-Residential/Commer
408-588-8000	www.s3.com	Computers-Peripher Equip
619-794-8111	www.safeskin.com	Disposable Medical Pro
770-569-4200		Paper&Related Products
440-446-1333		Filtration/Separat Prod
937-644-0011	www.scottscompany.com	Consumer Products-Mis
713-782-5990		Oil-Field Services
617-547-7820	www.securitydynamics.com	Computer Data Security
610-676-1000	www.seic.com	Data Processing/Mgmt
713-881-8900	www.seitel_inc.com	Seismic Data Collection
201-948-3000	www.selectiveinsurance.com	Property/Casualty Ins
615-391-4600	www.serx.com	Building-Maint&Service

TICKER	COMPANY NAME	ADDRESS
SKO	Shopko Stores Inc	700 Pilgrim Way, Green Bay, WI 54304
SWD	Shorewood Packaging Corp	277 Park Ave., New York, NY 10172
SIE	Sierra Health Servi.	2724 N. Tenaya Way, Las Vegas, NV 89128
SRP	Sierra Pacific Resor.	6100 Neil Rd., Reno, NV 89511
SIVB	Silicon Valley Bancshares	3003 Tasman Dr., Santa Clara, CA 95054-1191
SVGI	Silicon Valley Group Inc	101 Metro Dr., Suite 400, San Jose, CA 95110
SMPS	Simpson Industries	47603 Halyard Dr., Plymouth, MI 48170-2429
SSD	Simpson Manu- facturing Co Inc	4637 Chabot Dr., Suite 200, Pleasanton, CA 94588
SKY	Skyline Corp	2520 By-Pass Rd., Elkhart, IN 46514
SKYW	Skywest Inc	444 South River Rd., St. George, UT 84790
AOS	Smith (A.O.) Corp	11270 West Park Place, PO Box 23972, Milwaukee, WI 53223-0972
SFDS	Smithfield Foods Inc	900 Dominion Tower, 999 Waterside Dr., Norfolk, VA 23510
SOL	Sola International Inc	2420 Sand Hill Rd., Suite 200, Menlo Park, CA 94025
SONC	Sonic Corp	101 Park Ave., Oklahoma City, OK 73102
SEHI	Southern Energy Homes Inc	Highway 41 North, Addison, AL 35540
SWX	Southwest Gas Corp	5241 Spring Mountain Rd., PO Box 98510, Las Vegas, NV 89193-8510
SWN	Southwestern Energy Company	1083 Sain St., PO Box 1408, Fayetteville, AR 72702-1408
SLMD	Spacelabs Medical Inc	15220 N.E. 40th St., Redmond, WA 98052
SPAR	Spartan Motors Inc	1000 Reynolds Rd., Charlotte, MI 48813
SFAM	SpeedFam-IPEC Inc	305 North 54th St., Chandler, AZ 85226
TSA	Sports Authority Inc	3383 North State Rd. 7, Fort Lauderdale, FL 33319
ST	SPS Technologies Inc	101 Greenwood Ave., Suite 470, Jenkintown, PA 19046
SJK	St. John Knits Inc	17422 Derian Ave., Irvine, CA 92614

PHONE	WEB SITE AS OF 5/6/99	INDUSTRY SUBGROUP
414-497-2211	www.shopko.com	Retail-Discount
212-371-1500	www.shorepak.com	Containers-Paper/Plastic
702-242-7000	www.sierrahealth.com	Medical-HMO
702-689-3600	www.sierrapacific.com	Electric-Integrated
408-654-7282	www.svb.com	Commer Banks-Western US
408-434-0500	www.svg.com	Electronic Compo-Semicon
734-207-6200		Auto/Trk Prts&Equip
925-460-9912	www.strongtie.com	Bldg&Construct Prod-Misc
219-294-6521	www.skylinecorp.com	Bldg-Mobil Home/Mfd-Hous
801-634-3000	www.skywest.com	Airlines
414-359-4000	www.aosmith.com	Miscellaneous Manufactur
757-365-3000	www.smithfield-companies.com	Food-Meat Products
415-324-6868	www.sola.com	Optical Supplies
405-280-7654	www.sonicdrin.com	Retail-Restaurants
256-747-8589		Bldg-Mobil Home/ Mfd Hous
702-876-7237	www.swgas.com	Gas-Distribution
501-521-1141	www.swn.com	Gas-Distribution
206-882-3700	www.spacelabs.com	Patient Monitoring Equip
517-543-6400	www.spartanmotors.com	Auto/Trk Prts&Equip-Orig
602-705-2100	www.speedfam.com	Machinery-General Ind.ust
954-735-1701	www.sportsauthority.com	Retail-Sporting Goods
215-517-2000	www.spstech.com	Diversified Manufact Op
949-863-1171		Apparel Manufacturers

TICKER	COMPANY NAME	ADDRESS
MARY	St. Mary Land & Exploration	1776 Lincoln St., Suite 1100, Denver, CO 80203
SPBC	St. Paul Bancorp Inc	6700 West N. Ave, Chicago, IL 60707-3937
SMSC	Standard Microsystems Corp	80 Arkay Dr., Hauppauge, NY 11788
SMP	Standard Motor Prods	37-18 Northern Blvd., Long Island City, NY 11101
SPD	Standard Products Co	2401 South Gulley Rd., Dearborn, MI 48124
SPF	Standard-Pacific Corp	1565 West MacArthur Blvd., Costa Mesa, CA 92626
SXI	Standex International Corp	6 Manor Pkwy., Salem, NH 03079
STTX	Steel Technologies Inc	15415 Shelbyville Rd., Louisville, KY 40245
SMRT	Stein Mart Inc	1200 Riverplace Blvd., Jacksonville, FL 32207
SWC	Stillwater Mining Co	1200 Seventeenth St., Suite 900, Denver, CO 80202
SGY	Stone Energy Corp	625 East Kaliste Saloom Rd., Lafayette, LA 70508
SW	Stone & Webster Inc	245 Summer St., Boston, MA 02210
SRR	Stride Rite Corp	191 Spring St., PO Box 9191, Lexington, MA 02420-9191
RGR	Sturm Ruger & Co	1 Lacey Place, Southport, CT 06490
BEAM	Summit Technology Inc	21 Hickory Dr., Waltham, MA 02154
SMD	Sunrise Medical Inc	2382 Faraday Ave., Suite 200, Carlsbad, CA 92008
SUPR	Superior Services Inc	125 South 84th St., Suite 200, Milwaukee, WI 53214
SUSQ	Susquehanna Bancshares Inc	26 North Cedar St., PO Box 1000, Lititz, PA 17543-7000
SABI	Swiss Army Brands Inc	One Research Dr., Shelton, CT 06484
SYMM	Symmetricom Inc	85 West Tasman Dr., San Jose, CA 95134-1703
SCOR	Syncor Int'l Corp-Del	20001 Prairie St., Chatsworth, CA 91311

PHONE	WEB SITE AS OF 5/6/99	INDUSTRY SUBGROUP
303-861-8140	www.stmaryland.com	Oil Comp-Explor&Prodtn
773-622-5000	www.stpaulbank.com	S&L/Thrifts-Central US
516-435-6000	www.smsc.com	Circuits
718-392-0200		Auto/Trk Prts&Equip-Repl
313-561-1100	www.standardproducts.com	Auto/Trk Prts&Equip-Orig
714-668-4300		Bldg-Residential/Commer
603-893-9701	www.standex.com	Diversified Manufact Op
502-245-2110		Steel-Producers
904-346-1500	www.steinmart.com	Retail-Apparel/Shoe
303-352-2060		Precious Metals
318-237-0410		Oil Comp-Explor&Prodtn
617-589-5111	www.stoneweb.com	Building-Heavy Construct
617-824-6000	www.striderite.com	Footwear&Related Apparel
203-259-7843	www.ruger-firearms.com	Firearms&Ammunition
617-890-1234	www.sum-tech.com	Medical Laser Systems
619-930-1500	www.sunrisemedical.com	Hospital Beds/Equipment
414-479-7800		Non-hazardous Waste Disp
717-626-4721	www.susqbanc.com	Commer Banks-Eastern US
203-929-6391	www.swissarmy.com	Consumer Products-Misc
408-943-9403	www.symmetricom.com	Telecommunication Equip
818-886-7400	www.syncor.com	Med.-Whsle Drug Dist

TICKER	COMPANY NAME	ADDRESS
SSAX	System Software Associates Inc	500 West Madison St., 32nd Floor, Chicago, IL 60661
TACO	Taco Cabana	8918 Tesoro Dr., Suite 200, San Antonio, TX 78217
TALK	Talk.com Inc	6805 Route 202, New Hope, PA 18938
TBCC	TBC Corp	4770 Hickory Hill Rd., PO Box 18342, Memphis, TN 38181-0342
TBY	TCBY Enterprises Inc	425 West Capitol Ave., Suite 1200, Little Rock, AR 72201
TCSI	TCSI Corporation	1080 Marina Village Pkwy, Alameda, CA 94501
TNL	Technitrol Inc	1210 Northbrook Dr., Suite 385, Trevose, PA 19053
TSCC	Technology Solutions Co	205 North Michigan Ave., Suite 1500, Chicago, IL 60601
TLXN	Telxon Corp	3330 West Market St., Akron, OH 44333
WATR	Tetra Tech Inc	670 N. Rosemead Blvd., Pasadena, CA 91107
TTI	Tetra Tech. Inc	25025 I-45 N., The Woodlands, TX 77380
TXI	Texas Industries Inc	1341 West Mockingbird Lane, Suite 700W, Dallas, TX 75247-6913
TII	Thomas Industries Inc	4360 Brownsboro Rd., PO Box 35120, Suite 300, Louisville, KY 40232
TNM	Thomas Nelson Inc	501 Nelson Pl., Nashville, TN 37214-1000
THO	Thor Industries Inc	419 W. Pike St., Jackson Center, OH 45334
TFS	Three-Five Systems Inc	1600 North Desert Dr., Tempe, AZ 85281
TBL	Timberland Co	200 Domain Dr., Stratham, NH 03885
TWI	Titan Inter. Inc	2701 Spruce St., Quincy, IL 62301
TJCO	TJ International Inc	200 E. Mallard Dr., Boise, ID 83706
TNP	TNP Enterprises Inc	4100 International Plaza, Fort Worth, TX 76109
TOL	Toll Brothers Inc	3103 Philmont Ave., Huntington Valley, PA 19006-4298
TTC	Toro Co	8111 Lyndale Ave. South, Bloomington, MN 55420-1196
TWR	Tower Automotive Inc	4508 IDS Center, Minneapolis, MN 55402

PHONE	WEB SITE AS OF 5/6/99	INDUSTRY SUBGROUP
312-258-6000	www.ssax.com	Applications Software
210-804-0990		Retail-Restaurants
215-862-1500	www.talk.com	Telecom Services
901-363-8030		Retail-Auto Parts
501-688-8229	www.tcby.com	Retail-Restaurants
510-749-8500	www.tcsi.com	Commun.Software
215-355-2900	www.technitrol.com	Electronic Compo-Misc
312-228-4500	www.techsol.com	Computer Services
330-664-1000	www.telxon.com	Computers
818-351-4664	www.tetratech.com	Environ Consulting&Eng
281-367-1983	www.tetratec.com	Chemicals-Specialty
972-647-6700	www.txi.com	Bldg Prod-Cement/Aggreg
502-893-4600	www.thomasind.com	Machinery-Pumps
615-889-9000	www.thomasnelson.com	Publishing-Books
937-596-6849	www.thorindustries.com	Bldg-Mobil Home/Mfd Houses
602-389-8600	www.threefive.com	Electronic Compo-Semicon
603-772-9500	www.timberland.com	Footwear&Related Apparel
217-228-6011	www.titan-intl.com	Auto/Trk Prts&Equip-Orig
208-364-3300	www.tjco.com	Bldg Prod-Wood
817-731-0099	www.tnpe.com	Electric-Integrated
215-938-8000	www.tollbrothers.com	Bldg-Residential/Comm
612-888-8801	www.toro.com	Garden Products
612-342-2310	www.towerautomotive.com	Auto/Trk Prts&Equip-Orig

TICKER	COMPANY NAME	ADDRESS
TG	Tredegar Indust. Inc	1100 Boulders Pkwy, Richmond, VA 23225
TREN	Trenwick Group Inc	Metro Center, One Station Place, Stamford, CT 06902
TRY	Triarc Companies	280 Park Ave., New York, NY 10017
TRMB	Trimble Navigation Ltd.	645 North Mary Ave., Sunnyvale, CA 94088
TNO	True North Communications	FCB Center, 101 East Erie St., Chicago, IL 60611-2897
TRST	Trustco Bank Corp NY	320 State St., Schenectady, NY 12305
TBI	Tuboscope Inc	2835 Holmes Rd., Houston, TX 77051
UH	U S Home Corp	1800 West Loop South, Houston, TX 77027
UTEK	Ultratech Stepper Inc	3050 Zanker Rd., San Jose, CA 95134
UBSI	United Bankshares Inc	514 Market St., Parkersburg, WV 26101
UIL	United Illuminating Co	157 Church St., New Haven, CT 06506
UWR	United Water Resources Inc	200 Old Hook Rd., Harrington Park, NJ 07640
UTR	Unitrode Corp	7 Continental Blvd., Merrimack, NH 03054
UFPI	Universal Forest Products	2801 East Beltline, N.E., Grand Rapids, MI 49525
UHS	Universal Health Services	367 South Gulph Rd., King of Prussia, PA 19406
UBS	US Bioscience Inc	One Tower Bridge, 100 Front St., Suite 24, West Conshohocken, PA 19428
UTC	US Trust Corp	114 West 47th St., New York, NY 10036
USAD	USA Detergents Inc	1735 Jersey Ave., North Brunswick, NJ 08902
USFC	USFreightways Corp	9700 Higgins Rd., Suite 570, Rosemont, IL 60018
USTB	UST Corp	40 Court St., Boston, MA 02108
VCI	Valassis Communications Inc	19975 Victor Pkwy., Livonia, MI 48152
VLNC	Valence Technology Inc	301 Conestoga Way, Henderson, NV 89015
VALM	Valmont Industries	PO Box 358, Valley, NE 68064
VNTV	Vantive Corp	2455 Augustine Dr., Santa Clara, CA 95054

PHONE	WEB SITE AS OF 5/6/99	INDUSTRY SUBGROUP
804-330-1000	www.tredegar.com	Diversified Manufact Op
203-353-5500		Property/Casualty Ins
212-451-3000		Diversified Operations
408-481-8000	www.trimble.com	Instruments-Controls
312-425-6500		Advertising Agencies
518-377-3311		Commer Banks-Eastern US
713-799-5100	www.tuboscope.com.	Oil-Field Services
713-877-1211	www.ushome.com	Bldg-Residential/Commer
408-321-8835		Electronic Compo-Semicon
304-424-8800	www.patriotpnb.com	Commer Banks-Southern US
203-499-2000	www.uinet.com	Electric-Integrated
201-784-9434	www.unitedwater.com	Water
603-424-2410	www.unitrode.com	Electronic Compo-Semicon
616-364-6161	www.ufpinc.com	Bldg Prod-Wood
610-768-3300	www.uhsinc.com	Medical-Hospitals
610-832-0570	www.usbio.com	Therapeutics
212-852-1000	www.ustrust.com	Commer Banks-Eastern US
732-828-1800		Soap&Cleaning Prepar
847-696-0200	www.usfreightways.com	Transport-Truck
617-726-7000	www.ustcorp.com	Commer Banks-Eastern US
734-591-3000	www.valassis.com	Printing-Commercial
702-558-1000	www.valence-tech.com	Batteries/Battery Sys
402-359-2201	www.valmont.com	Steel Pipe&Tube
408-982-5700	www.vantive.com	Applications Software

TICKER	COMPANY NAME	ADDRESS
VAR	Varian Medical Systems Inc	3050 Hansen Way, Palo Alto, CA 94304
VRTX	Vertex Pharmaceuticals Inc	130 Waverly St., Cambridge, MA 02139
VICR	Vicor Corp	23 Frontage Rd., Andover, MA 01810
VPI	Vintage Petroleum Inc	4200 One Williams Center, Tulsa, OK 74172
VISX	VISX Inc	3400 Central Expressway, Santa Clara, CA 95051
VITL	Vital Signs Inc	20 Campus Rd., Totawa, NJ 07512
VLSI	VLSI Technology Inc	1109 McKay Dr., San Jose, CA 95131
VOL	Volt Information Sciences Inc	1221 Ave. of the Americas, New York, NY 10020-1579
WNC	Wabash National Corp	1000 Sagamore Pkwy. South, Lafayette, IN 47905
WALB	Walbro Corp	6242 Garfield St., Cass City, MI 48726-1325
WALL	Wall Data Inc	11332 N.E. 122nd Way, Kirkland, WA 98034
WJ	Watkins-Johnson Co	3333 Hillview Ave., Palo Alto, CA 94304
WSO	Watsco Inc	2665 South Bayshore Dr., Suite 901, Coconut Grove, FL 33133
WDFC	WD-40 Co	1061 Cudahy Place, San Diego, CA 92110
WERN	Werner Enterprises Inc	14507 Frontier Rd., PO Box 45308, Omaha, NE 68145-0308
WON	Westwood One Inc	9540 Washington Blvd., Culver City, CA 90232
WTNY	Whitney Holding Corp	228 St. Charles Ave., PO Box 61260,New Orleans, LA 70161-1260
WKR	Whittaker Corp	1955 North Surveyor Ave.,Simi Valley, CA 93063-3386
WHIT	Whittman-Hart c In	311 South Wacker Dr.,Suite 3500, Chicago, IL 60606
WFMI	Whole Foods Market Inc	601 North Lamar, Suite 300, Austin, TX 78703
WHX	WHX Corporation	110 East 59th St., New York, NY 10022
WIC	Wicor Inc	626 E. Wisconsin Ave., Milwaukee, WI 53202
WSM	Williams-Sonoma Inc	3250 Van Ness Ave., San Francisco, CA 94109
WGO	Winnebago Inds.	605 West Crystal Lake Rd., Forest City, IA 50436

PHONE	WEB SITE AS OF 5/6/99	INDUSTRY SUBGROUP
415-493-4000	www.varian.com/vms	Medical Products
617-577-6000	www.vpharm.com	Medical-Drugs
978-470-2900	www.vicr.com	Power Conv/Supply Eq
918-592-0101		Oil Comp-Explor&Prodtn
408-733-2020	www.visx.com	Medical Laser Systems
201-790-1330	www.vital-signs.com	Medical Products
408-434-3000	www.vlsi.com	Electronic Compo-Semicon
212-704-2400	www.volt.com	Divers Oper/Commer Serv
765-448-1591	www.wncwabash.com/wabash	Auto-Truck Trailers
517-872-2131	www.walbro.com	Auto/Trk Prts&Equip-Orig
206-814-9255	www.walldata.com	Network Software
415-493-4141	www.wj.com	Electronic Compo-Semicon
305-858-0828	www.watsco.com	Distribution/Wholesale
619-275-1400	www.wd-40.com	Oil Refining&Marketing
402-895-6640	www.werner.com	Transport-Truck
310-204-5000	www.westwoodone.com	Radio
504-586-7272		Commer Banks-Southern US
805-526-5700	www.wkr.com	Instruments-Controls
312-922-9200	www.whittman-hart.com	Computer Services
512-477-4455	www.wholefoods.com	Food-Retail
212-355-5200	www.wpsc.com	Steel-Producers
414-291-7026	www.wicor.com	Gas-Distribution
415-421-7900	www.williams-sonoma.com	Retail-Mail Order
515-582-3535	www.winnebagoind.com	Bldg-Mobil Home/Mfd Hous

TICKER	COMPANY NAME	ADDRESS
WLV	Wolverine Tube Inc	1525 Perimeter Pkwy., Suite 210, Huntsville, AL 35806
WWW	Wolverine World Wide	9341 Courtland Dr., Rockford, MI 49351
WRC	World Color Press Inc	340 Pemberwick Rd., Greenwich, CT 06831
WN	Wynn's International Inc	500 North State College Blvd., Suite 700, Orange, CA 92868
XRIT	X-Rite Inc	3100 44th St. S.W., Grandville, MI 49418
XIRC	Xircom Inc	2300 Corporate Center Dr., Thousand Oaks, CA 91320-1420
YELL	Yellow Corporation	10990 Roe Ave., Overland Park, KS 66211
ZLC	Zale Corp	901 West Walnut Hill Lane, Irving, TX 75038-1003
ZBRA	Zebra Technologies Corp	333 Corporate Woods Pkwy., Vernon Hills, IL 60061
ZNT	Zenith National Insurance Corp	21255 Califa St., Woodland Hills, CA 91367-5021

PHONE	WEB SITE AS OF 5/6/99	INDUSTRY SUBGROUP
256-353-1310	www.wlv.com	Metal Processors&Fabrica
616-866-5500	www.wolverineworldwide.com	Footwear&Related Apparel
203-532-4200		Printing-Commercial
714-938-3700	www.wynns.com	Auto/Trk Prts&Equip-Repl
616-534-7663	www.x-rite.com	Instruments-Controls
805-376-9300	www.xircom.com	Networking Products
913-696-6100	www.yellowfreight.com	Transport-Truck
972-580-4000	www.zalecorp.com	Retail-Jewelry
847-634-6700	www.zebra.com	Machinery-Print Trade
818-713-1000	www.zenithnational.com	Property/Casualty Ins

SMALL-CAPS
State by State

HERE IS A STATE BY STATE directory to the companies in the first part of this Appendix.

ALABAMA

Birmingham Steel Corp.
Blount International Inc.
Books-A-Million Inc.
Energen Corp.
Just For Feet Inc.
Southern Energy Homes Inc.
Wolverine Tube Inc.

ALASKA

General Communication

ARIZONA

Aztar Corp.
Burr-Brown Corp.
Insight Enterprises Inc.
Inter-Tel Inc.
Microage Inc.
Rural/Metro Corp.
SpeedFam-IPEC Inc.
Three-Five Systems Inc.

ARKANSAS

Acxiom Corp.
American Freightways Corp.
Arkansas Best Corp.
Baldor Electric
Southwestern Energy Co.
TCBY Enterprises Inc.

BERMUDA

Mutual Risk Management Ltd.

CALIFORNIA

ABM Industries Inc.
Adac Laboratories
Adaptive Broadband Corp.
Advanced Tissue Sciences Inc.
Alliance Pharmaceutical Corp
American States Water Co
Applied Magnetics Corp.
Ashworth Inc.
Aspect Telecommunications
Auspex Systems Inc.
Authentic Fitness Corp.
Bell Industries Inc.
Benton Oil & Gas Co.
C-Cube Microsystems Inc.
Centigram Communications
Cheesecake Factory (The)

CKE Restaurant Inc.

Coherent Inc.

Cooper Companies Inc.

COR Therapeutics Inc.

Cygnus Inc.

Dames & Moore Group

Diagnostic Products Corp.

Digital Microwave Corp.

Dionex Corp.

Downey Financial Corp.

DSP Communications Inc.

Dura Pharmaceuticals Inc.

Electroglas Inc.

Epicor Software Corp.

Etec Systems Inc.

Fair Issac & Company Inc.

Fidelity National Finl Inc.

Filenet Corp.

First American Financial Corp.

Foodmaker Inc.

Fremont General Corp.

Fritz Companies Inc.

Gottschalks Inc.

Gymboree Corp.

HNC Software

Hollywood Park Inc.

HS Resources Inc.

Hyperion Solutions Corp.

Idec Pharmaceuticals Corp.

IHOP Corp.

Immune Response Corp/Del

Incyte Pharmaceuticals Inc.

International Rectifier Corp.

Jefferies Group Inc.

K-Swiss Inc.

K2 Inc.

Komag Inc.

Macromedia Inc.

Marshall Industries

Mentor Corp.

Mercury Interactive Corp.

Micrel Inc.

Molecular Biosystems Inc.

Network Equipment Tech Inc.

Novellus Systems Inc.

P-Com Inc.

Pacific Sunwear of California

Plantronics Inc.

Powerwave Technologies Inc.

Protein Design Labs Inc.

Quiksilver Inc.

Read-Rite Corp.

Reliance Steel & Aluminum

Resound Corp.

S3 Inc.

Safeskin Corp.

Silicon Valley Bancshares

Silicon Valley Group Inc.

Simpson Manufacturing Co. Inc.

Sola International Inc.

St. John Knits Inc.

Standard-Pacific Corp.

Sunrise Medical Inc.

Symmetricom Inc.

Syncor International Corp-Del

TCSI Corporation

Tetra Tech Inc.

Trimble Navigation Ltd.

Ultratech Stepper Inc.

Vantive Corp.

Varian Medical Systems Inc.

VISX Inc.

VLSI Technology Inc.

CALIFORNIA (continued)

Watkins-Johnson Company
WD-40 Co.
Westwood One Inc.
Whittaker Corp.
Williams-Sonoma Inc.
Wynn's International Inc.
Xircom Inc.
Zenith National Insurance Corp

COLORADO

Barrett Resources Corp.
Ciber Inc.
Exabyte Corp.
Getchell Gold Corp.
MDC Holdings Inc.
St. Mary Land & Exploration
Stillwater Mining Company

CONNECTICUT

ADVO Inc.
Air Express International Corp
Ames Dept Stores Inc.
Aquarion Co.
Barnes Group Inc.
Connecticut Energy Corp.
Ethan Allen Interiors Inc.
Executive Risk Inc.
Factset Research Systems Inc.
Gerber Scientific Inc.
Kaman Corp.
Landstar System Inc.
Lone Star Industries
Lydall Inc.
Macdermid Inc.
NAC RE Corp.
NFO Worldwide Inc.

Sturm Ruger & Co. Inc.
Swiss Army Brands Inc.
Trenwick Group Inc.
United Illuminating Co.
World Color Press Inc.

DELAWARE

Delphi Financial Group
Rollins Truck Leasing Corp.

DISTRICT OF COLUMBIA

Harman International
Riggs Natl Corp. Wash D C

FLORIDA

American Bankers Insur Group
Aviation Sales Company
BE Aerospace Inc.
Breed Technologies Inc.
Catalina Marketing Corp.
Discount Auto Parts
Dycom Industries Inc.
Florida Rock Inds
Hughes Supply Inc.
Interim Services Inc.
JAN Bell Marketing Inc.
Noven Pharmaceuticals Inc.
Orthodontic Centers of America
Pediatrix Medical Group Inc.
Photronics Inc.
Priority Healthcare Corp.
Raymond James Financial Corp.
Sports Authority Inc.
Stein Mart Inc.
Watsco Inc.

GEORGIA

Caraustar Industries Inc.
Carmike Cinemas Inc.
Compdent Corporation
Harbinger Corp.
Harland (John H.) Co.
Interface Inc.
Magellan Health Services
Mariner Post-Acute Network
National Data Corp.
Norrell Corp.
Oxford Industries Inc.
Premier Bancshares Inc.
Profit Recovery Group Intl.
Roper Industries Inc.
Schweitzer-Mauduit Intl. Inc.

IDAHO

Building Material Holding Corp.
Coeur D'Alene Mines Corp.
Hecla Mining Co.
Morrison Knudsen Corp.
TJ International Inc.

ILLINOIS

AAR Corp.
Amcol International Corp.
Anixter International Inc.
Aptargroup Inc.
Castle (A.M.) & Co.
Cilcorp Inc.
Clarcor Inc.
Corn Products Intl. Inc.
Devry Inc.
First Midwest Bancorp Inc./II
Gallagher, Arthur J. & Co.
Gardner Denver Machinery Inc.

General Semiconductor Inc.
Ha-Lo Industries Inc.
Hartmarx Corp.
Insurance Auto Auctions Inc.
Juno Lighting Inc.
Lawson Products
MAF Bancorp Inc.
Material Sciences Corp.
McWhorter Technologies Inc.
Methode Electronics
Midway Games Inc.
St. Paul Bancorp Inc.
System Software Associates Inc.
Technology Solutions Co.
Titan International Inc.
True North Communications
USFreightways Corporation
Whittman-Hart Inc.
Zebra Technologies Corp.

INDIANA

Bindley Western Inds
Brightpoint Inc.
Coachmen Industries Inc.
Consolidated Products Inc.
CTS Corp.
Lilly Industries Inc.
Skyline Corp.
Wabash National Corp.

IOWA

Casey's General Stores Inc.
Heartland Express Inc.
Winnebago Industries

KANSAS

Applebees International Inc.

KANSAS (continued)

Republic Group Inc.
Yellow Corporation

KENTUCKY

Commonwealth Industries Inc.
Steel Technologies Inc.
Thomas Industries Inc.

LOUISIANA

Offshore Logistics
Stone Energy Corp.
Whitney Holding Corp.

MAINE

Bangor Hydro-Electric Co.
IDEXX Laboratories Inc.

MARYLAND

Integrated Health Services
Legg Mason Inc.
Micros Systems Inc.
North American Vaccine Inc.
Provident Bankshares Corp.
Ryland Group Inc.

MASSACHUSETTS

Alpha Inds
Analogic Corp.
Aspen Technology Inc.
Au Bon Pain Co. Inc.
Avid Technology Inc.
Baker (J.) Inc.
Cognex Corp.
Commonwealth Energy System
Cyrk Inc.
Eastern Utilities Associates

Eaton Vance Corp.
GC Companies Inc.
Helix Technology Corp.
Hologic Inc.
Ionics Inc.
Kronos Inc.
New England Business SVC Inc.
Oak Industries Inc.
Organogenesis Inc.
Parexel International Corp.
PictureTel Corp.
Pioneer Group Inc.
Primark Corp.
Progress Software Corp.
Security Dynamics Tech. Inc.
Stone & Webster Inc.
Stride Rite Corp.
Summit Technology Inc.
UST Corp.
Vertex Pharmaceuticals Inc.
Vicor Corp.

MICHIGAN

Champion Enterprises Inc.
Gentex Corp.
Intermet Corp.
La-Z-Boy Inc.
Lason Inc.
Mascotech Inc.
Simpson Industries
Spartan Motors Inc.
Standard Products Co.
Universal Forest Products
Valassis Communications Inc.
Walbro Corp.
Wolverine World Wide
X-Rite Inc.

MINNESOTA

Alliant Techsystems Inc.

Analysts International Corp.

Apogee Enterprises Inc.

Arctic Cat Inc.

BMC Industries Inc-Minn

Dain Rauscher Corp.

Damark International Inc.

Digi International Inc.

G & K Services Inc.

Graco Inc.

Hutchinson Technology

Innovex Inc.

Merrill Corporation

Michael Foods Inc.

Nash Finch Co.

National Computer SYS Inc.

Patterson Dental Company

Polaris Industries Inc.

Regis Corp.

Toro Co.

Tower Automotive Inc.

MISSISSIPPI

Chemfirst Inc.

Delta & Pineland Company

Halter Marine Group Inc.

Hancock Fabrics Inc.

Mississippi Chemical Corp.

MONTANA

Angelica Corp.

Belden Inc.

Brown Group Inc.

Butler MFG Co.

Cerner Corp.

CPI Corp.

Earthgrains Company

Express Scripts Inc.

Harmon Industries Inc.

Henry (Jack) & Associates

Insituform Technologies Inc.

Jones Pharma Inc.

Kellwood Co.

O'Reilly Automotive Inc.

Ralcorp Holdings Inc.

NEBRASKA

Commercial Federal Corp.

Inacom Corp.

Lindsay Manufacturing Co.

Valmont Industries

Werner Enterprises Inc.

NEW HAMPSHIRE

Hadco Corp.

Nashua Corp.

Standex International Corp.

Timberland Company

Unitrode Corp.

NEW JERSEY

Alpharma Inc.

Bio-Technology General Corp.

Biomatrix Inc.

BISYS Group Inc.

Cambrex Corp.

Checkpoint Systems Inc.

Commerce Bancorp Inc. NJ

Datascope Corp.

Dendrite International Inc.

Dialogic Corp.

Fedders Corp.

Footstar Inc.

NEW JERSEY (continued)

Hudson United Bancorp
J & J Snack Foods Corp.
Linens 'N Things Inc.
Liposome Company Inc.
Medquist Inc.
New Jersey Resources
Players International Inc.
Prime Hospitality Corp.
Roberts Pharmaceutical Corp.
Russ Berrie & Co. Inc.
Selective Insurance Group
United Water Resources Inc.
USA Detergents Inc.
Vital Signs Inc.

NEW MEXICO

DBT Online Inc.
Mesa Air Group Inc.

NEVADA

Anchor Gaming
Sierra Health Services
Sierra Pacific Resources
Southwest Gas Corp.
Valence Technology Inc.

NEW YORK

AnnTaylor Stores Corp.
Barr Laboratories Inc.
Bowne & Co. Inc.
Canandaigua Brands Inc.
Capital Re Corp.
Central Hudson Gas & Electric
Computer Task Group Inc.
Curative Health Services Inc.
Dress Barn Inc.

Enhance Financial Svcs Group
Enzo Biochem Inc.
Family Golf Centers Inc.
Frontier Insurance Group Inc.
Galey & Lord Inc.
Griffon Corporation
Intermagnetics General Corp.
JSB Financial Inc.
Lillian Vernon Corp.
Nautica Enterprises Inc.
NBTY Inc.
Orange & Rockland Utilities
Orion Capital Corp.
Park Electrochemical Corp.
Paxar Corp.
Phillips-Van Heusen
Queens County Bancorp Inc.
Regeneron Pharmaceutical
Shorewood Packaging Corp.
Standard Microsystems Corp.
Standard Motor Prods
Triarc Companies
Trustco Bank Corp. NY
US Trust Corp.
Volt Information Sciences Inc.
WHX Corporation

NORTH CAROLINA

Cato Corp.
Centura Banks Inc.
Coca-Cola Bottling Co. Consolidated
Commscope Inc.
Cone Mills Corp.
Guilford Mills Inc.
Insteel Industries
Oakwood Homes

Pharmaceutical Product Devel
Piedmont Natural Gas Co.
Public Service Co. of N C

OHIO

Allen Telecom Inc.
Amcast Indl Corp.
Applied Industrial Tech. Inc.
Brush Wellman Inc.
Chemed Corp.
Chiquita Brands International
Firstmerit Corporation
Geon Company
Gibson Greetings Inc.
Huffy Corp.
Invacare Corp.
Jo-Ann Stores Inc.
Kroll-O'Gara Company
Libbey Inc.
Myers Industries Inc.
NCS Healthcare Inc.
OM Group Inc.
Pioneer Standard Electronics
Robbins & Myers Inc.
Royal Appliance Manufacturing
RTI International Metals Inc.
Scott Technologies Inc.
Scotts Company (The)
Telxon Corp.
Thor Industries Inc.

OKLAHOMA

Devon Energy Corporation
Fleming Companies Inc.
Prepaid Legal Services Inc.
Sonic Corp.
Vintage Petroleum Inc.

OREGON

Electro Scientific Inds Inc.
Lattice Semiconductor Corp.
Northwest Natural Gas Co.
Pope & Talbot Inc.

PENNSYLVANIA

C&D Technologies Inc.
C-Cor Electronics
Cable Design Tech. Corp.
CDI Corp.
Cephalon Inc.
CMAC Investment Corp.
Genesis Health Ventures
Integrated Circuit Systems
JLG Industries Inc.
Kulicke & Soffa Industries
Penn Enterprises Inc.
Philadelphia Suburban Corp.
Quaker Chemical Corp.
Respironics Inc.
SEI Investments Co.
SPS Technologies Inc.
Susquehanna Bancshares Inc.
Talk.com Inc.
Technitrol Inc.
Toll Brothers Inc.
Universal Health Services
US Bioscience Inc.

PUERTO RICO

First BanCorp/Puerto Rico

RHODE ISLAND

Cross (A.T.) Company

SOUTH CAROLINA

Carolina First Corp.
Delta Woodside Inds Inc.
KEMET Corp.
Ryan's Family Stk Houses Inc.

TENNESSEE

Astec Industries Inc.
Buckeye Technologies Inc.
Central Parking Corp.
Coventry Health Care Inc.
Dixie Group Inc.
Goody's Family Clothing Inc.
MS Carriers Inc.
Mueller Industries Inc.
PhyCor Inc.
Renal Care Group Inc.
Ruby Tuesday Inc.
Service Experts Inc.
TBC Corp.
Thomas Nelson Inc.

TEXAS

American Oncology Resources
Americredit Corp.
Amresco Inc.
Atmos Energy Corp.
BancTec Inc.
Benchmark Electronics Inc.
Billing Concepts Corp.
Bombay Company Inc. (The)
Cabot Oil & Gas Corp.
Cash America Investments Inc.
CEC Entertainment Inc.
Commercial Metals Co.
Consolidated Graphics Inc.
Cross Timbers Oil Co.

Cullen/Frost Bankers Inc.
CustomTracks Corp.
Dallas Semiconductor Corp.
Daniel Industries
DR Horton Inc.
Elcor Corp.
Frozen Food Express Inds
Global Industries Tech. Inc.
Haggar Corp.
IMCO Recycling Inc.
Input/Output Inc.
Intervoice Inc.
Justin Industries
Kent Electronics Corp.
Kirby Corp.
Landry's Seafood Restaurant
Luby's Inc.
Maxxim Medical Inc.
Men's Wearhouse Inc.
Metro Networks Inc.
Michaels Stores Inc.
National Instruments Corp.
Newfield Exploration Company
Oceaneering International Inc.
Pier 1 Imports Inc.
Pillowtex Corp.
Plains Resources Inc.
Pogo Producing Co.
Pool Energy Services Co.
Pride International Inc.
Quanex Corp.
Railtex Inc.
Remington Oil & Gas Corp.
Seacor Smit Inc.
Seitel Inc.
Taco Cabana
Tetra Technologies Inc.

Texas Industries Inc.
TNP Enterprises Inc.
Tuboscope Inc.
U S Home Corp.
Whole Foods Market Inc.
Zale Corp.

UTAH

Ballard Medical Products
Franklin Covey Co.
Natures Sunshine Prods Inc.
Skywest Inc.

VERMONT

Banknorth Group Inc.
Central Vermont Public Service
Green Mountain Power Corp.

VIRGINIA

American Management Systems
Bassett Furniture Inds
Dimon Inc.
Hilb, Rogal & Hamilton Co.
O'Sullivan Corp.
Orbital Sciences Corp.
Owens & Minor Inc. Hldg Co.
Pittston Bax Group
Richfood Holdings Inc.
Smithfield Foods Inc.
Tredegar Industries Inc.

WASHINGTON

Cascade Natural Gas Corp.
Esterline Technologies Corp.
Expeditors Intl. Washington
Flow International Corp.
Itron Inc.

Penford Corporation
Spacelabs Medical Inc.
Wall Data Inc.

WEST VIRGINIA

United Bankshares Inc.

WISCONSIN

Anchor Bancorp Wisconsin Inc.
Applied Power Inc.
Brady Corporation
Manitowoc Co.
Marcus Corp.
National Presto Inds Inc.
OshKosh B'Gosh Inc.
Plexus Corp.
Regal Beloit
Shopko Stores Inc.
Smith (A.O.) Corp.
Superior Services Inc.
Wicor Inc.

INDEX

ABOUT BLOOMBERG

Bloomberg L.P., founded in 1981, is a global information services, news, and media company. Headquartered in New York, the company has nine sales offices, two data centers, and 80 news bureaus worldwide.

Bloomberg Financial Markets, serving customers in 100 countries around the world, holds a unique position within the financial services industry by providing an unparalleled combination of news, information, and analytic tools in a single package known as the BLOOMBERG® service.

BLOOMBERG NEWS℠, founded in 1990, offers worldwide coverage of economies, companies, industries, governments, financial markets, politics, and sports. The news service is the main content provider for Bloomberg's broadcast media, which include BLOOMBERG TELEVISION®— the 24-hour cable television network available in ten languages worldwide—and BLOOMBERG NEWS RADIO™—an international radio network anchored by flagship station BLOOMBERG NEWS RADIO AM 1130℠ in New York.

The company information in the Appendix of this book was provided by Bloomberg's **Equity Department**, which maintains detailed current data and analytic functions on over 60,000 companies in 80 countries.

In addition to the BLOOMBERG PRESS® line of books, Bloomberg publishes three magazines:

◆ *BLOOMBERG® MAGAZINE*, for market professionals subscribing to the BLOOMBERG® service
◆ *BLOOMBERG WEALTH MANAGER*™, for financial planners and advisers
◆ *BLOOMBERG PERSONAL FINANCE*™, for sophisticated individual investors. It provides information about financial markets and investment strategies with unique insights into the ways of Wall Street. Contact *BLOOMBERG PERSONAL FINANCE*™ by calling 888-432-5820; or online at www.bloomberg.com/personal.

ABOUT THE AUTHORS

Christopher Graja is executive markets editor for *Bloomberg* magazine and *Bloomberg Personal Finance* magazine and senior markets editor for *Bloomberg Wealth Manager.* He holds an MBA from Rutgers University and was the director of training and a senior researcher for Bloomberg L.P.'s research division. An acknowledged authority on small-cap stock investing, he meets frequently with analysts and fund managers in the field.

Mr. Graja welcomes readers' comments and suggestions for future editions of this book. He may be reached by mail in care of Bloomberg Press, P.O. Box 888, Princeton, NJ 08542-0888, or via e-mail at cgraja@bloomberg.net.

Elizabeth Ungar, Ph.D., is senior editor for *Bloomberg Personal Finance* magazine, where she regularly converts highly technical subjects into highly readable prose. She has worked for major magazines such as *Institutional Investor, Business Month,* and *Manhattan, inc.* She has also taught at Trinity College, Dublin, and holds degrees in French and linguistics.